Text
al as-
ult...

The person charging this material is re-

Sexual Assault

Sexual Assault

The Victim and the Rapist

Edited by
Marcia J. Walker
Stanley L. Brodsky
The University of Alabama

Lexington Books
D.C. Heath and Company
Lexington, Massachusetts
Toronto   London

Library of Congress Cataloging in Publication Data

Main entry under title:
    Sexual assault.

    Includes index.
    1. Rape—Addresses, essays, lectures. 2. Rape—Prevention—Addresses,
essays, lectures. I. Walker, Marcia J. II. Brodsky, Stanley L., 1939-
[DNLM: 1. Rape—Congresses. W795 S5183 1975]
HV6558.S49   364.1'53   75-24560
ISBN 0-669-00196-1

Published simultaneously in Canada.

Printed in the United States of America.

International Standard Book Number: 0-669-00196-1

Library of Congress Catalog Card Number: 75-24560

LAW

Contents

	Introduction	vii
Chapter 1	Sexual Assault: Perspectives on Prevention and Assailants *Stanley L. Brodsky*	1
Chapter 2	Forcible Rape and the Criminal Justice System: Surveying Present Practices and Projecting Future Trends *Duncan Chappell*	9
Chapter 3	Rape: Its Effect on Task Performance at Varying Stages in the Life Cycle *Ann Wolbert Burgess* and *Lynda Lytle Holmstrom*	23
Chapter 4	Rape at Work *Carroll M. Brodsky*	35
Chapter 5	Medical Treatment for the Victim: The Development of a Rape Treatment Center *Dorothy J. Hicks* and *Charlotte R. Platt*	53
Chapter 6	Present and Future Measures of Victimization in Forcible Rape *Lynn A. Curtis*	61
Chapter 7	History of Women's Movement in Changing Attitudes, Laws, and Treatment toward Rape Victims *Mary Ann Largen*	69
Chapter 8	Prevention of Rape: Deterrence by the Potential Victim *Stanley L. Brodsky*	75
Chapter 9	The Rapist in Treatment: Professional Myths and Psychological Realities *Asher R. Pacht*	91

Chapter 10   **Psychological Treatment of Rapists**
              Gene G. Abel, Edward B. Blanchard, and
              Judith V. Becker   99

Chapter 11   **Rape, Race, and Culture: Some Speculations in**
              Search of a Theory
              Lynn A. Curtis   117

Chapter 12   **The Social Definition of Rape**
              Susan H. Klemmack and *David L. Klemmack*   135

Chapter 13   **Justice After Rape: Legal Reform in Michigan**
              Jan BenDor   149

Chapter 14   **Changing Perspectives in Sex Crimes Investigations**
              Mary L. Keefe and *Henry T. O'Reilly*   161

Chapter 15   **Rape Reduction: A Citywide Program**
              David I. Sheppard, Thomas Giacinti, and
              Claus Tjaden   169

              Index   177

              List of Contributors   187

              About the Editors   189

Introduction

While filming a movie at the Mansfield Reformatory in Ohio, the actor James Caan spoke of his distress at seeing depressing conditions in prison. He said, "I'm not going to do anything wrong any more, except maybe for an occasional rape" (*Newsweek*, September 15, 1975, p. 48).

A peculiar thing happens when you start writing or become actively engaged in work related to rape. People make jokes; sometimes they make fun of you. If you are a male, they ask whether you have had a chance to rape anyone. If you are a female, they ask whether you have had a chance to be raped. You are flooded with lecherous jokes and cynical, not-so-funny remarks about rape as fun. You develop a high awareness of this joking game.

We have identified this game as the "leering-smirking syndrome," in which people make fun of one's involvement and suggest that there are underlying sexual motives in workers and researchers of rape. The quick cure for this syndrome is calling it to the attention of the jesters. Once it reaches awareness, then the joking and sexually risqué comments fade quickly and disappear altogether.

Some of our colleagues have a "skinned-knee" sensitivity to such remarks and react with bristling anger whenever humor is used in a discussion of rape. Being on the receiving end of such anger is discomforting. One of us was accused and attacked when, as part of a professional talk on self-defense as rape prevention, he noted that "among the porcupines, rape is unknown." The general joking about rape is quite a different matter and is quite remedial.

Our introduction to a discussion of rape begins with this kind of effort to heighten your awareness. Many of the chapters in this book are presented readably and with wit. Still, the effort to heighten awareness is made to emphasize the severity and harm of sexual assault. Indeed it is serious. Our motive for assembling this book is to collect the best professional knowledge, scientific research, and informed observations into a single document. Our audiences are professionals, scientists, and activists working in rape prevention, counseling, and research.

The Rape Research Group at the Psychology Department of the University of Alabama was the parent of this publication effort. The Rape Research Group came into being as a series of collaborative, investigatory efforts among psychologists, students, academicians, and professionals deeply concerned about rape victims, the rape act, and treatment of the rapist. In early 1975 a conference was held on the topic "Rape: Research, Action, Prevention." The conference brought together 250 people primarily interested in rape and rape issues. A long-lost sibling phenomenon was observed at this conference. People who had heard of each other met; people who were engaged in similar activities showed great joy and enthusiasm in discovering one another; and after the papers were presented, a consensus arose that the important materials, ideas, and suggestions should be gathered and published.

Thus this book began with presentations at the conference. The chapters with Pacht, Largen, BenDor, Sheppard, Abel, Burgess, Curtis, Hicks, S. Brodsky, Keefe, and Chappell as senior authors are revisions or expansions of presentations at this meeting. As we began the editing, we became aware of other contemporary work, and so we invited chapters to be written by the Klemmacks, by Carroll Brodsky, and by Lynn Curtis.

This book was prepared at a time when the number of books on rape is expanding almost geometrically. This book is intended to achieve the following goals: (1) to raise the complex issues of causes and prevention of rape and to offer some preliminary answers, (2) to show the range of current developments in dealing with the victim and understanding rape, (3) to offer a book that will be both readable and have scientific soundness.

Most popular books on sexual assault offer advice (including self-defense books) on how to deal with rapists or with having been raped. At the other extreme are books that are like the Sahara Desert in their parched-sand dryness. These books are laden with tables, are moderately inaccessible to most scientific readers, and are totally inaccessible in style to most persons in the field who are concerned about rape.

Our goals were to present readable and interesting chapters, well founded on scientific knowledge and professional experience. For the most part, both of these objectives were accomplished. Occasionally a chapter seated more in popular interest or in scientific methodology has been included because of the substantial contribution or special perspectives offered.

Developments are emerging in the knowledge of sexual assault so rapidly that many documents are outdated before they appear. This is an encouraging professional sign; if the findings of this book are obsolete within a year or two, it will be a high compliment indeed to our state of knowledge about the rape act, the victim, and the assailant.

The material presented here begins with an examination of assumptions about the nature of sexual assault and how they are related to prevention strategies. Then Duncan Chappell notes in Chapter 2 how the criminal justice system defines, perceives, and handles sexual assaults, and he presents a context in which other chapters can be viewed.

A section on victims of rape calls attention to the catastrophic consequences for most rape victims and some innovative approaches to lessening these traumas. In Chapter 3 Burgess and Holmstrom describe long-term interference with normal life events as a result of being a rape victim. Carroll Brodsky reports the nature and consequences of being raped in a work setting (Chapter 4). Burgess and Holmstrom and Brodsky include a number of case histories which graphically and powerfully illustrate the debilitating effects of being a rape victim. Early assistance methods for the victim are presented in Chapter 5 by

Hicks and Platt about the development of a rape treatment center in a large urban hospital.

Lynn Curtis reports in Chapter 6 the incidence of victimization of forcible rape, figures which are often contradictory or uncertain. The question is, who reports and when? A historical perspective is provided in Chapter 7 as Mary Ann Largen observes the role of the women's movement in terms of mobilizing rape victim programs.

Prevention of rape can be conceptualized from a number of perspectives. In Chapter 8 by Stanley Brodsky, what the potential victim can do at the moment she is assaulted or threatened, with special reference to verbal responses, is researched. Two chapters are devoted to changing the rapist. Pacht notes the psychological myths and realities in conceptualizing the rapist himself (Chapter 9). Abel, Blanchard, and Becker review the research on psychological treatment of rapists and describe their own successful program (Chapter 10).

In Chapter 11 by Lynn Curtis, the meaning of rape in black communities is explored. The controversial notion of a violent contraculture within black communities is posited.

The definition of rape depends on one's perspective. The changing laws and community mores influence how one sees rape. Klemmack and Klemmack note in Chapter 12 that a clear rape to one person is not a rape to another, and that this view is related to one's own sexual experience and values. This social definition process is illustrated dramatically by BenDor (Chapter 13) in her report of legal reform to promote justice after the rape act. The conflicting values of the defense lawyers and judges on the one hand and reformers on the other are described in the context of this Michigan legislative reform effort.

In the repeated accusations in rape-related issues, criminal justice agencies have received more than their share of fingers pointed, from victims, from rapists, and from women's movement activists. Criminal justice agencies do respond to such criticism. Chapter 14 by Keefe and O'Reilly and Chapter 15 by Sheppard, Giacinti, and Tjaden indicate how two cities responded constructively and thoughtfully. Keefe and O'Reilly describe the Sex Crimes Investigation Unit in New York City, which received national publicity. It allocated police resources in a crime-specific design to stop the destructive influence of insensitive sex crime investigations. Sheppard, Giacinti, and Tjaden report on a citywide program that includes changes in sex crime investigations and a broader criminal justice effort to reduce the rape incidence in a city with an apparently high rape rate.

These chapters are diverse. They draw on varied knowledge about sexual assaults. If they seem fragmented to the reader, they may accurately reflect the broad scope of rape research and action. Criminal justice functioning is fragmented in following both the victim and offender, and not all efforts are from criminal justice agencies. We are talking about communities, about national values, about prisons, courts, police, and women who dead-bolt themselves in their rooms late at night. These are part of rape prevention and amelioration efforts around the country.

Sexual assault as it appears in the media, as well as in some professional journals, is shown in ways full of nonsense, myths, foolishness, and stereotypes. We sometimes grind our teeth as we watch a television show or read an article in a weekly Sunday supplement that deals with rape. Correction of myths is a tough job, for stereotypes and false beliefs persist despite one's best efforts to correct them. Look at how people continue to defend the deterrent value of capital punishment contrary to the research evidence suggesting that it is ineffective as a crime deterrent. This book is intended to be a modest step in the destruction of myths, stereotypes, and nonsensical beliefs. If we do not have an A-bomb intensity explosion of such myths, at least we may light some firecrackers underneath these stationary societal delusions.

A few acknowledgments are in order. Our typist, colleague, and friend has been Susan H. Maynard. Her humor, incredible patience, and good will have sustained us through moments of impossible demands and late deadlines. She has typed the manuscript repeatedly, corrected chapters, and joined us in copyediting. Her efforts and work are recognized with deep gratitude. Additional thanks are extended to the persons enrolled in the Psychology of Rape seminar at the University of Alabama in the fall of 1975 for their thoughtful and constructive comments. The members of the Rape Research Group at the University of Alabama, and particularly Sue Klemmack and Connie Mahan, are thanked for their assistance. And finally the wonderful and enthusiastic people who attended our rape conference in January inspired us, enthused us, and encouraged us. We thank them.

When we talk at a restaurant or at other places about our work on the book, waitresses or bystanders stop and tell us of their own experiences with sexual assaults. We then get a tiny hint of the great burdens rape victims carry with them. It is with these thoughts and shared burdens in mind that we have prepared this book.

Marcia J. Walker
Stanley L. Brodsky

Tuscaloosa, Alabama
September 1975

Sexual Assault

1   Sexual Assault: Perspectives on Prevention and Assailants

Stanley L. Brodsky

Take small groups of three to five people. Ask each group to design a plan to prevent criminal sexual assaults. Study each of the prevention plans, and an important observation may be made: there are pervasive, consistent assumptions about the causes and nature of rape that underlie all prevention planning. Furthermore, examine a group's scheme for rape prevention, and you can immediately tell its underlying models for attribution of blame. Four blame models may be seen: victim blame, offender blame, societal blame, and situation blame. Each of these models with their accompanying prevention assumptions will be considered.

Victim Blame and Prevention

Ryan (1971) has noted that there is a widespread use of victim-blame models in assault, poverty, and sickness. Victim blame in sexual assault is characterized by statements attributing seductive or sexual behaviors or dress to the victim. The "just-world hypothesis" applies; the victim gets what she deserves. Prevention? Keep potential victims from eliciting attacks. Impose dress codes. Teach them how to say no. Eliminate sexual teasing through education.

Offender Blame and Prevention

Sexual assault is assumed to be the product of individual, deviant assailants, inappropriately driven by overwhelming lust and aggression. Such assailants acquire labels of "criminal sexual psychopath" or "character disorder." Plans to prevent rapists focus on either *before* or *after* solutions. *Before* solutions refer to stopping the assailant before he carries out his antisocial potential. This primary prevention takes place by early identification of the deviant party, followed by intensive therapeutic treatment, and, if necessary, preventive involuntary commitment to mental hospitals. *After*-the-act solutions seek to psychologically repair or physically impair the deviant drive. Psychological approaches include psychotherapy and psychosexual development programs. The physical approaches include imprisonment, castration, hormone maintenance, death, dismemberment, and transportation to isolated locations.

1

Societal Blame and Prevention

The term "sick society" is often used by those accepting a societal-blame model. It is believed that there is something fundamentally wrong with widely held social values and mores if sexual assaults are so present. Specific targets for responsibility are machismo upbringing of males, violence in the media, the double standard, women as an oppressed class, and unresponsive, ineffective criminal justice/social control mechanisms. Comparisons are often made between Western society and some obscure South Seas island tribe in which sexual assault, aggression, and professional football are absent.

Most societal prevention strategies are broad-ranging. Strategies are developed to promote equality in sex-role perceptions and public school socialization. Child-rearing practices and adolescent adjustment patterns are special targets.

Sexual assaults in general, rather than individual assaults, are viewed in this context as the product of deeply seated antagonism toward women and sexual-aggressive confusion.

Situation and Blame and Prevention

Dark alleys, passive women, overcrowded buildings, drunkenness, and misunder-stood messages are some of these situational determinants. The situation is the catalyst, the piece of dust in the supersaturated solution that allows societal, victim, and offender predispositions to come together. Monahan (1975) has identified three strategies for situational prevention: modifying the situation itself, modifying the potential victim's response, and simple prevention of the situation. Situational modification strategies are often called target-hardening, and range from high-intensity mercury vapor street lights to teaching self-defense techniques to women.

These blame and prevention models are not necessarily exclusive of one another. It is possible to consider all these factors operating simultaneously, perhaps together, as the sine qua non of sexual assault. The development of prevention programs should include some self-knowledge of operating assump-tions. The ability to relate assumed causes to presumed effects may be the beginning of innovative prevention thought. And that brings us to innovation.

Unconventional Proposals for Rape Prevention

A repetitive quality is present when one listens to proposals for rape prevention among both citizens and criminal justice professionals. The same few ideas are put forth again and again. Women should learn self-defense and assertiveness and stay out of dangerous areas. Rehabilitation programs should be developed for convicted rapists. Laws should be changed to reflect the realities of rape. Many more versions of these consistent themes were presented earlier in this discussion and will be offered throughout the text. However, there is a great need for development of ideas that depart from the mold. Whorf (1940) and Korzybski (1948) have suggested that we are captives of our language and thought patterns. We think much as a train runs, on fixed tracks, with no opportunity for moving aside—indeed, even little awareness that we are so restricted. Some ideas that seem provocative and off the fixed tracks of thinking are presented here.[1]

Reporting Assaults

While much of the trauma of sexual assault lies in the "assault" part and less in the "sexual" aspect, the difficulties with police investigations come from the sexual aspect. Thus it is proposed that women who have been raped report only the assault and battery aspects of the offense, and not the sexual attacks proper. This is most applicable in any case in which obvious physical harm is received. In this way "secondary rape" by the justice agencies may be avoided. The burden of proof for assault never subjects the victim to probing questions of consent. And much of the sense of embarrassment and guilt on the part of the victim will be alleviated. A preliminary inquiry by this author indicated that while men would feel uncomfortable about reporting assault, women who would have major reservations about reporting a rape would have none about reporting an assault to police.

Undercut Machismo Motives

This proposal is based on the belief that rape and other sexual assaults are seen by some subcultures or groups as affirmations of masculinity. Reports of required rapes for entry into aggressive motorcycle gangs typify this belief that rape demonstrates male self-worth. Furthermore, among lower-class social groups, there appears to be some acceptance of this belief, without the gang rites as a transition to social acceptance. It is proposed that a series of experiments be conducted to undercut these belief systems. Public education—and perhaps even group infiltration—might be undertaken to promote the belief that "Rape Is Impotent" or "Rape Is for Sissies." If support of such beliefs could be developed among the groups most committed to the proving of masculine self-worth, then this proposal would have considerable chance of success.

There is a logical extension of this proposal, which is to reduce widespread attention to penis-vagina contact for sexual desirability. Instead, males might be encouraged to value masturbation, oral sexual relations, and so on. One suggestion has been that a public relations campaign on this theme could appear under the general title, "There's a better way." Such an anti-penis campaign, however, produces future spectres that are more harmful than the disease, if such a ploy were successful. In the Vonnegut story, *Welcome to the Monkey House*, the "ethical" solution to birth control was to numb all citizens from the waist down. The title originated from a pharmacist who was distressed at seeing monkeys openly masturbating and devised a potion to numb their bodies and eliminate their desires. We may be as uncomfortable with sexual assaults as that small town visitor to the monkey house, but the potential for doing as much harm as good should be recognized.

Resocialization

One societal-blame cause is that many men believe that a woman's no may always be a yes. If women are socialized to play yes-no games of ambivalently refusing sexual invitations, then a change in socialization is in order. Girls and women should be taught to say what they mean, openly, directly. In turn males will be taught—and will learn as a result of women's changed behaviors—that they should take refusals seriously. The moral of this campaign could be "A No Is a No Is a No." Such a campaign for interpersonal honesty would also have positive effects on human adjustment in general.

Technological Prevention

There is always some wise-mouth who will ask, "If we can put a man on the moon, why can't we . . . [Insert your favorite social injustice to be cured] ." I'm one such wise-mouth. Why can't we draw on existing technological knowledge, or impending discoveries, and do the following?

. . . Issue portable emergency calling devices to all citizens. These might be buttons that could be pressed in one's hand and telemetrically tracked for location, and aid would be quickly dispatched. They probably could be made tiny, silent, and inexpensive. In temporary lieu of that action, let us encourage fire boxes to be used for all emergency calling purposes.

. . . The impotence ray. Why couldn't women carry a small weapon, ring, pen, or "phaser" that would temporarily and harmlessly render an attacker impotent? This might work chemically, visually, auditorially, or psychologically.

. . . Dentata, or vaginal teeth. There have been reports that such a device is in use in some Asian countries. Dentata refers to an oval-shaped object with sharp, inward directed points that is vaginally worn. Working somewhat on the principle of shark's teeth, it would lacerate penises inserted past it. Its deterrence value might be greater than its actual value in rape situations.

As prevention innovations are considered, it should be noted that society is organized for crime prevention through criminal justice agencies. These agencies have the most prolonged and closest contact with the assailant, in law enforcement, in the courts, and in corrections. Because of the availability and visibility of the assailant, he becomes the target of most change and prevention efforts by justice agencies. Therefore it is especially relevant now to examine prevention and the assailant.

The Assailant

Picture in your mind what it would be like to sit in a room full of convicted rapists. A mental picture is probably evoked of brutal, aggressive, angry, and physically imposing men. In actuality such a group is composed of quite different individuals. If one were not to know the reason for assembling them, one might ask, what possibly does a strange motley, assorted group of men like this have in common? In such a group there are always some who openly admit the malicious nature of their offense, others who are cognizant of what happened but describe it as being accidental or a chance circumstance, some who deny that the assault occurred, and some who cannot remember the act because of alcohol use.

Among these men are highly aggressive individuals and very passive and neurotic individuals. There are brilliant men and retarded men. There are those who are indignant at being punished, those who are puzzled at their punishment, and those who accept punishment with considerable self-blame and personal responsibility. A search for a single psychological type of assailant is futile in view of the diversity of individuals and personal reactions. In addition, it is not known if nonapprehended assailants are like those who make it through the justice system's progressive filtration process. Some offenders are reported; of these only a subgroup are arrested, and so on, through identification, arraignment, and subsequent conviction or plea bargaining. The nonapprehended number is not as great as the number of unreported assaults since there are many multiple-offense assailants. If we accept victimization statistics that only one-third of actual rapes are reported, perhaps half of the sexual offenders are apprehended. What are the implications for social control and punishment of such a diverse group? At least part of the response to that query will come from a personal perspective. *

I find myself terribly moved and emotionally touched as I speak to a very distressed rape victim about her experience. Sometimes I feel equally moved when I speak to a first-offense, convicted sexual assailant in a maximum security penitentiary. The memory burns clearly in my mind of talking to an 18-year-old black man serving a 60-year sentence. This young man looked 13 and had been convicted of assault with intent to ravish. Plaintively he asked me whether he would have to grow up in this oppressive and awful prison. He had learned to fight to protect himself, to carry a knife with him, and he saw himself changing into a kind of person he didn't like. He asked, wasn't there anything I could do? There was little I could do then for him as an individual. With the perspective of time and distance, it seems there are related actions that can be taken both for him and for the prevention of rape.

These are as follows.

(1) The imposition of more variable sentences that fit the severity of the sexual assault. Not all sexual assaults merit long sentences or harsh punishment. The position taken by the National Organization for Women and developed in the Michigan law reform and other legislation described in this book call for variable, offense-related sentencing. Vindictive judges and outraged newspaper editors should not be the major determiners of sentences.

(2) Meaningful treatment programs for those who need it. Psychotherapeutic treatment programs are not appropriate for all offenders. The issue is difficult in a prison setting where treatment is not necessarily voluntary. Pressures are so widespread and subtle that the prisoner cannot volunteer for programs unless its participation is totally independent of decision-making related to his release. Nevertheless, there are powerful ways of psychotherapeutically assisting such sexual assailants who genuinely seek help. These programs should be made available on a widespread basis in hospitals, prison, and community outpatient settings.

(3) Heightened awareness of victim impact. A song in the movie "Cabaret" goes "If only you knew what I know." If the sexual assailants only knew what we know, and what rape crisis workers know, the first-hand knowledge of the suffering, the terrible disruption of victims' lives, it would make a great impact on them. They would be considerably deterred by seeing the life-cycle disruptions described by Burgess and Holmstrom in Chapter 3, by seeing the lasting fear, the paranoia, the trauma. There are many reservations about instituting this effort with the assailant's own victim; however, possibilities for listening to taped case histories and for training in rape crisis center knowledge (and perhaps even work) are steps to make their own sexual assaults salient and personally repugnant to the assailant.

Conclusion

Working with the assailant is only one perspective on preventing future assaults. As we examine rape prevention in general and assailant-blame models, it becomes apparent that there is no simple solution to the complex problems of sexual assault. Some promising paths include awareness of assumptions and moving out of stereotyped myths and beliefs. The radical and unconventional prevention methods suggested here are intended primarily to stimulate such thinking about additional means and strategies. The assailant-blame model has been especially considered here and found to be both lacking and simplistic.

A plea for calm and unemotional consideration of sexual assault issues is often heard from the scientific and professional communities. And many of the chapters in this book satisfy this plea. This chapter has indeed been based on emotion and personal feelings. It is such strong indignation and compassion that has moved social institutions and scientists alike to their many responses and programs. Let us not be irrationally distracted by these emotions, but let us also not lose track of the essence of the human experiences about which we are concerned.

Note

1. The ideas presented here were drawn in part from a workshop on Radical Proposals for Rape Prevention, led by the author and by Mary Ann Owings at the January 1975 University of Alabama Conference on *Rape: Research, Action, Prevention.* The very early suggestions of Wilma Scott Heide for unconventional proposals are also gratefully acknowledged.

References

Korzybski, Alfred. *Science and Sanity: An Introduction to Non-Aristotelean Systems and General Semantics* (3rd Ed.). Lakeville, New York: The Non-Aristotelian Library, 1948.

Monahan, John. The Prediction of Violence. In Duncan Chappell and John Monahan (Eds.), *Violence and Criminal Justice.* Lexington, Mass.: Lexington Books, 1975.

Ryan, William. *Blaming the Victim.* New York: Vintage, 1971.

Vonnegut, Kurt, Jr. *Welcome to the Monkey House.* New York: Dell, 1970.

Whorf, Benjamin Lee. Science and Linguistics. *Technology Review*, 1940, *44*, 229-231, 247-248.

2

Forcible Rape and the Criminal Justice System: Surveying Present Practices and Projecting Future Trends

Duncan Chappell

The Stimulus for Change

Considering the development of the crime of forcible rape and allied offenses against women in his authoritative *History of the Criminal Law of England* (1886), the nineteenth-century jurist Sir James Fitzjames Stephen wrote:

I pass over many sections punishing particular acts of violence . . . in particular the whole series of offenses relating to the abduction of women, rape, and other such crimes. Their history possesses no special interest and does not illustrate either our political or our social history. (pp. 117-118)

Stephen's disdainful dismissal of the importance of these crimes may appear remarkable today, yet his attitude reflects, until very recently, the predominant response of the criminal justice system to this category of criminal behavior. Currently, we are experiencing a marked modification of this response, which is largely the product of compelling political and social forces outside the immediate parameters of the criminal justice system. Of particular importance and influence is the movement to effect change in the status and role of women in our society. In this context the definition and administration of the laws relating to the crime of forcible rape have achieved a special significance, placing forcible rape among the vanguard of those issues affecting women's rights.

Many women regard this area of the criminal law as one motivated to protect male property rights, rather than the integrity of a female's body. In the words of Kate Millet (1971, p. 44), "traditionally rape has been viewed as an offense one male commits upon another—a matter of abusing 'his woman.' " According to this view, a male-dominated system of criminal justice sustains this attitude, refusing to prosecute or convict all but a handful of rapists. Meanwhile the victim of rape is subjected to a host of indignities at the hands of the police and other personnel of the system.

In addition to such issues, questions about the race of rapists and their victims also have impact upon the response of the criminal justice system to the crime of forcible rape. The ideological component of interracial forcible rape was cogently expressed by Eldridge Cleaver in *Soul on Ice* (1968):

Rape was an insurrectionary act. It delighted me that I was defying and trampling upon the white man's law, upon his system of values, and that I was defiling his women—and this point, I believe, was the most satisfying to me because I was very resentful over the historical fact of how the white man had used the black women. I felt I was getting revenge. (p. 14)

For a substantial period of American history the revenge exacted by the white man upon black men who raped white women tended to be death, whether by lynching in earlier times or by officially justified execution in more "civilized" years (Kooninger, 1969; Partington, 1965). It is significant that the landmark 1972 Supreme Court decision of *Furman v. Georgia*, ending, at least for the time being, capital punishment in the United States, involved a black offender sentenced to death for rape. On the other hand, capital punishment for white men raping black women has been virtually unknown in America. Historically, black females were regarded as notably accessible to white men—if not by the choice of the female, then by use of force which involved little, if any, likelihood of subsequent penalty (Wolfgang and Cohen, 1970; Agopian, Chappell, and Geis, 1974).

Quite apart from the influence of the debates about women's rights, race, and the death penalty upon the contemporary response of the criminal justice system to forcible rape, concern about this crime has been further stimulated by the apparent startling increase in the incidence of this type of sexual assault. During the past decade, rates of forcible rape have more than doubled. The pace of increasing rates has become more rapid since 1967 and in the early 1970s reached a speed outstripping all other major categories of violent crime.[1]

Documenting and Evaluating New System Responses

The rapidity with which the crime of forcible rape has become the focus of national concern almost certainly has caught the criminal justice system by surprise. The system, like many federal, state, and local politicians, is now struggling to catch up with the momentum for action and change. Many proposed or effected reforms of the substantive criminal law in this area have been matched by numerous attempts to strengthen the capabilities of criminal justice agencies to deal with forcible rape and related crimes. Across the nation innovative procedures are being developed and implemented to facilitate the apprehension and conviction of rapists and to reduce the incidence of rape.

Central to many of these efforts is the desire to ameliorate the plight of the rape victim and enhance the victim's cooperation with all elements of the criminal justice system. Despite the clear advances made in recent times in the system's handling of forcible rape, a number of major and related dilemmas remain.

The advances made so far have been on an ad hoc basis. Separate agencies in different parts of the country are experimenting with fresh approaches to the crime of forcible rape without necessarily being aware of what is being tried elsewhere and without subjecting their own innovations to rigorous evaluation. The development of and agreement upon possible model procedures for criminal justice agencies in this area have so far been minimal. Information about new approaches which do or do not work has yet to be communicated on any extensive basis. Moreover, no centralized information source currently exists to which criminal justice agencies can refer for assistance in determining an appropriate response to the crime of forcible rape. Even were such a source available, no systematic attempt has yet been made on a national level to identify the nature or dimension of the problems and needs of the criminal justice system in dealing with this crime.

In a major national study of the crime of forcible rape, funded by a grant from the National Institute of Law Enforcement and Criminal Justice, a concerted effort is now being made to resolve the dilemmas which have been mentioned. This author is directing this study, titled "Research and Development of Model Procedures for Criminal Justice Involvement with the Crime of Forcible Rape." Commencing in September 1974, the research program is scheduled to run for a period of two years.

The study is intended to provide a comprehensive documentation of present system practices for the handling of forcible rape as well as indicating fruitful directions for future developments in dealing with this and allied crimes. A brief description follows of the major components of the research project.

National Surveys of Police and Prosecution
Agencies

Comprehensive questionnaires were designed and distributed to samples of police agencies and prosecutor offices around the United States. The samples were selected to be representative of factors such as size, geographic location, and rural and urban characteristics of the two types of agencies. Without describing the sampling procedures in detail, it should be noted that wherever possible, agencies included in the police sample overlapped geographically to some degree with those in the prosecutor sample. All 27 cities with populations in excess of 500,000 were selected in the police sample, and the 22 counties with a population over 1 million were included in the prosecutor sample.

The content of the questionnaires covered a wide range of topics intended: to provide baseline data on rape and existing criminal justice procedures in this crime area; to identify problems associated with the investigation, apprehension, and prosecution of offenders; to obtain information about perceived personnel and training needs; to secure copies of forms, manuals, and other documents used within agencies; to identify innovative programs and procedures within agencies; and to obtain information and suggestions about legislative reforms.

In the police segment of the study, a structured random sample was taken of the 30,000 or more law enforcement agencies in the United States responsible for investigating rape. Some 234 agencies were incorporated in the final sample, including all those serving populations over a half million, and representative samples of those serving populations between 100,000 and 500,000, 50,000 and 100,000, and 25,000 and 50,000. A number of county police agencies and university police departments were also contacted in the sample. Of the 234 agencies contacted, over 90 percent ultimately agreed to participate in the study and returned a completed questionnaire.

It is clear from the excellent survey response rate, as well as from the comments of agency personnel contacted by phone as part of the survey, that there is widespread concern about the crime of rape. There is also keen desire among law enforcement agencies to obtain information about the most appropriate methods for handling this crime. Preliminary analysis of the survey data indicated that a wide range of agencies are now experimenting with new techniques to deal with rape cases. However, there is a divergence of opinion concerning the effectiveness and appropriateness of these techniques. The importance attached to the subject of rape by police agencies was indicated in the response to a survey question asking whether an agency believed there had been a recent increase in the crime. An increase was reported by about two-thirds of all agencies within all size categories. Major reasons given for the increase were as follows.

	Percent of agencies giving this reason
General increase in violence	70
More reporting—change in public attitudes	66
Sexual permissiveness	34
More reporting—increased criminal justice system sensitivity	29
Women's liberation	23
Change in legislation	17
Influence of pornography	10
More reporting—increased convictions	2
Racial tensions	1

Police agencies were asked about the extent of local community resources available to rape victims in order to assess the degree of community involvement, concern, and cooperation in dealing with the crime of forcible rape. In over three-fourths of the agencies surveyed there were special medical services, and also counseling services, available for rape victims. An encouraging feature of these community-based facilities was that the relationship between them and police departments was said to be most cooperative in an overwhelming proportion of cases.

Police departments were also asked if their agencies provided any special handout materials for rape victims to explain the procedure for handling rape complaints. This question was considered important since once of the primary complaints of victims in the past has been the lack of information from the criminal justice system concerning the processing of a rape case. Only 18 percent of the surveyed departments indicated that they had such materials. Of the departments 81 percent felt materials of this type would be helpful, if available. It is the intent of the research program to design such victim assistance materials as part of the model procedure package.

Another issue examined in the police survey was the availability within agencies of written guidelines for the interviewing of rape victims. Only 19 percent of agencies indicated that they had such guidelines. However, a major proportion of the survey sample thought such guidelines would be useful if developed. Substantial concern was expressed by agencies about the lack of private interview facilities within police buildings for the questioning of rape victims.

Another important issue to police and to prosecutors is the level of specialized resource allocation required to investigate and prosecute rape cases. As might be expected, the larger jurisdictions in the sample specialized more frequently in rape investigations than the smaller jurisdictions. The nature of the investigative units varied widely. The model ranged from units exclusively handling rape and being staffed primarily by women to units handling all types of violent crime with no female members. The effectiveness of different types of investigative units, as well as the specific techniques adopted by such units, remains an open question which is currently being explored as part of the research program.

On the subject of training, the police survey sought information about levels of training throughout departments related to the handling of rape cases. In only 75 percent of the agencies surveyed did the officers have preservice basic training of any type. In-service training covering problems of forcible rape existed in about 60 percent of the jurisdictions surveyed.

Another survey question asked police agencies what were the three most important needed improvements in dealing with the problem of forcible rape. These improvements were listed as follows:

Public education	69 percent
Victim services	45 percent
Sentencing	44 percent
Prosecution policies	31 percent
Revision of law	30 percent
Police investigative techniques	26 percent

Police training	24 percent
Treatment and rehabilitation of offenders	16 percent
Plea bargaining system	12 percent

It is interesting that police agencies tended to identify as most important those changes outside the justice system, i.e., public education and victim services.

The prosecutor survey also comprised a sample which takes account of the size and geographic location of these agencies across the United States.[2] The response rate to the survey has been most encouraging, exceeding 75 percent. Analysis of the survey results has yet to be completed. Since many of the topics covered in the police survey have also been included in the prosecutor questionnaires, the resource needs of these two agencies will be compared.

Pilot City Study

Successful in-depth completion of this analysis of special problem areas requires the cooperation and assistance of criminal justice agencies; extensive access to official records and allied data concerning the crime of forcible rape is necessary. A preliminary step to any second-year commitment of research resources to this extensive field examination is a pilot study. The feasibility of both the analysis and the research methodology was tested in Seattle, Washington, which already had in place an innovative rape program. This pilot study included conducting structured interviews with:

1. All members of the police agency with special responsibilities for investigating rape
2. A general sample of police officers from the agency about the attitudes and problems encountered by police in cases of rape
3. All members of the prosecutor's office working with rape prosecutions
4. Judges responsible for hearing of rape cases
5. A sample of defense attorneys dealing with rape cases to test their attitudes and opinions concerning the procedures currently adopted by police and prosecutors in the area of rape

In addition to these interviews, field observations of the operational application of police and prosecution procedures also have been carried out at the pilot site.

Obtaining access to victims was one criterion for the selection of locations for the second-year research effort. As part of the pilot city study, the problems likely to be encountered in gaining such access were explored, and the research instruments to be used when conducting interviews with victims were developed and tested.

Interviews with 100 victims of forcible rape were completed in Seattle. Primary access to victims was obtained through a close collaborative relationship with the Seattle Rape Reduction Project, the Sexual Assault Center established at a major urban hospital, and Rape Relief, a rape crisis center which provides third-party reporting facilities, counseling, and advocacy services for victims in the Seattle-King County area. Interviewers were drawn from women working with victims in the centers.

Among the 100 interviews conducted, about one-third were with nonreporting victims who contacted the rape crisis center but did not wish to become involved in an official complaint to the authorities. Interviews with victims ranged over such topics as the circumstances and reactions to the offense; treatment by medical facilities, police, prosecutors, and courts; methods of resistance used, if any; and outcome. The latter subject is viewed as one of substantial importance in the design of potential preventive strategies for rape.

Legislative Digest

To provide an assessment of legislative developments related to forcible rape, a digest of rape statutes around the country has been prepared by the National Legal Data Center. This digest will be updated on a continuing basis during the life of the project and should provide a valuable resource on the rapidly changing legislative situation in this area.

Conclusions

The eventual major products of this comprehensive research effort over a two-year time span should be of direct utility to criminal justice agencies at all levels of government and to victims, researchers, community organizations, and all others confronting the problem of rape prevention and control. These products will include model guidelines for the handling of forcible rape cases by police at the patrol and investigative levels, as well as by prosecutors.

The results of the various state-of-the-art surveys described above are not yet available. This fact makes it difficult to project future trends within the criminal justice system relating to forcible rape. However, the balance of this chapter will speculate about a number of these practices and trends which appear particularly significant from the perspective of an observer in the midst of a constantly shifting scene.

Defining the Crime of Forcible Rape

A core issue in the entire contemporary debate about forcible rape is that of reaching some consensus on the appropriate definition of the crime. From a strict legal perspective this definition has been almost totally ossified for centuries in common law and statute law. In the ungainly and archaic language of the common law, rape is unlawful carnal knowledge of a woman by force and without her consent (Clark and Marshall, 1967). A more typical statutory definition, adopted in many American states, is that rape is the act of sexual intercourse with a woman other than the wife of the offender committed without her lawful consent. Emission is not necessary, and any sexual penetration, however slight, is sufficient to complete the crime. Excluded from this definition, at common law and by statutes in most jurisdictions, are anal or oral acts of intercourse, as well as homosexual assaults.

Recent criticisms of these omissions have resulted in substantive law reforms in some settings which would encompass a broader description of the crime of forcible rape.[3] Such reforms are certainly long overdue, bringing this area of the criminal law into accord with contemporary sexual behavior and mores. However, in the longer term, it is not the legal definition of the crime of forcible rape which is in need of reform so much as the interpretation given this definition by those responsible for administering the law and by society at large.

The official application of the present legal definition of forcible rape to the facts of a particular situation commonly results in widely varying interpretations of the scope of rape. As Svalastoga (1962) has aptly stated:

Rape is commonly defined as enforced coitus. But this very definition suggests that there is more to the offense than the use of force alone. This must be so, since no society has equipped itself with the means for measuring the amount of force applied in an act of coitus. Hence rape, like any other kind of crime, carries a heavy social component. The act itself is not a sufficient criteria. The act must be interpreted as rape by the female actee, and her interpretation must be similarly evaluated by a number of officials and agencies before the official designation of "rape" can be legitimately applied. (p. 48)

Much of the current controversy in the United States and other countries swirls around the official designation ultimately given to rape. According to many women, what on the surface is a crime encompassing a wide range of sexual assaults has in practice been applied to only a handful of particularly gross and violent incidents.[4]

There are those, at least in the past, who would argue that this is an appropriate application, if not interpretation, of the law relating to forcible rape. Ploscowe (1951), for instance, has remarked that:

the extensiveness of the legal concept of rape ... causes a waste in human resources through the excessive penalization of what may be nominal behavior in a man's cultural, social, or racial milieu. A revision of the term "rape" so that it more nearly corresponds with traditional concepts is a compelling necessity for the legal reformer. (p. 166)

By "traditional concepts" Ploscowe had in mind situations where "a man by means of force and violence imposes his will and has sexual intercourse with a woman who desperately repels his advances."

It is this "traditional concept" which is now under sustained attack by women, and there is no doubt that this attack is beginning to produce results. Already the unique evidentiary burdens cast upon the prosecution to bolster the "traditional concept" of forcible rape are being pushed aside. Very few jurisdictions now retain special corroboration requirements for forcible rape,[5] and increasingly the permissible scope of defense questioning about the prior sexual behavior of a victim of forcible rape is being circumscribed. Social and political pressures are now forcing the criminal justice system to reappraise its approach to this crime. The present official definition, as well as the legal definition, of forcible rape seems to be undergoing real modification. However, the extensiveness and uniformity of this modification process has yet to be documented.

Recording and Reporting Cases of Forcible Rape

The eventual outcome of the definitional trends discussed above may well be a more evenly, broadly, and uniformly applied forcible rape law with a wider base of acceptance across society and the criminal justice system. However, achievement of this outcome is likely to be an arduous and frustrating task, particularly within the highly fragmented and diversified segments of this country's criminal justice system.

Formerly there was a dearth of comparative research into the administration of most areas of the criminal law, including that concerned with forcible rape. One recent comparative examination of police records of forcible rape in Los Angeles and Boston, conducted by the present writer and several colleagues, suggests that very wide variations exist between law enforcement agencies in the conduct they record and report to the FBI as forcible rape (Chappell, Geis, Schafer, and Siegel, 1972). It became very obvious from our examination of the forcible rape records in Boston and Los Angeles that a far more embracing definition of what constituted forcible rape prevailed in Los Angeles as contrasted to Boston. It appears likely that it is this definitional quirk which has for many years placed Los Angeles above the remainder of the nation's cities in its reported rate of forcible rape. Indeed, in Los Angeles virtually any instance in which a person appeared to be seeking "sexual gratification," a term favored by that city's detectives, was apt to be classified as a forcible rape. For instance, one case we studied involved a man who sidled up to two young girls on a busy suburban street, and then pinched one of them on the bottom. A police officer happened to witness this heinous assault and immediately arrested the man. In a subsequent statement the offender admitted he frequently engaged in this type of activity, gaining his main satisfaction from frightening the girls. The case was classified by the Los Angeles Police Department as an attempt at forcible rape. Unfortunately, no record of the ultimate disposition of the case was included in the report!

In contrast, Boston police comply with the FBI's guidelines that an offense should be classified as forcible or attempted forcible rape if it involved actual or attempted sexual intercourse with a female forcibly against her will. Boston police classify as forcible rape statistics only victims who seemingly suffer a "fate worse than death." This definition excluded specifically cases of statutory rape, in which no force was employed and the victim was under the legal age of consent or otherwise was legally incapacitated from agreeing to participate in the act. Sodomy and incest offenses were also eliminated by definition from the forcible rape category. The classification rules seem reasonably clear. It is another matter, however, to apply the rules carefully and uniformly around the 40,000 or more police forces in the United States.

These comparative observations about police records of forcible rape in two American cities illustrate the dilemmas of drawing any firm conclusions about trends in this category of crime from official statistics. This is particularly the case at a time when the legal and official definitions of forcible rape are in such a state of flux across the nation. It is clear that the adoption of a broadened official definition of the crime of forcible rape by major urban police departments could have a dramatic impact upon the reported incidence of this offense.[6] Coupled with an increasing willingness on the part of victims of forcible rape to notify the police of the commission of a crime, this development could account for the bulk of the present escalation in rape rates.[7]

Further comparative and longitudinal studies are now required in a large number of cities located in different parts of the country to plot changing patterns in criminal justice agency recording and reporting practices with respect to forcible rape. These studies should, among other things, lead to the adoption of more meaningful typologies of forcible rape for use in reporting official statistics of the crime.[8]

The System and the Changing Status of Victims and Women

An increasing willingness of rape victims to make an official report of their victimization experience and to cooperate with criminal justice agencies in the task of apprehending and prosecuting rapists is largely the product of changing attitudes and procedures within these agencies. The nature of these changes varies greatly between agencies, but all seem to reflect widespread recognition of the inappropriate and inadequate response frequently encountered in the past by women who had been raped and who had reported this fact to the authorities.

From the nationwide surge of criminal justice activity in the field, a number of important developments appear to be taking place which ultimately transcend the crime of forcible rape. First, an immediate focus upon the plight of victims of forcible rape within the criminal justice system is now broadening into concern about the treatment of victims of other forms of sexual assault, and crime victims at large. Second, and related to the first point, the system is beginning to place greater emphasis upon the notion of providing service to the victims of crime as well as pursuing traditional enforcement and prosecution goals. Third, the emerging professional role of women within the criminal justice system is being assisted and advanced by their increasing involvement in the investigation and prosecution of forcible rape.

It is apparent that many of the criticisms made of the criminal justice system's handling of forcible rape victims can be applied also to its general involvement with other sexual assault victims. Although probably less so than in the case of forcible rape, sympathetic and proficient responses have not been the hallmark of the system's concern with victims of crimes like sodomy, child abuse, and incest. Now many of the innovations designed to remedy past defects in the handling of forcible rape can also be used to advantage with these crimes. Take, for example, the increased emphasis in police departments upon the role of women as detectives in sex crime units investigating rape and upon more sophisticated and extensive training for such units. While it presently remains a matter for conjecture what proportion of a unit of this type should be staffed by women and what training is best suited to the unit's needs, it seems logical to extend this enhanced staffing and training capability to other crimes normally dealt with by these units.

Two factors suggesting the need for a broadening of investigative and allied concerns affecting victims beyond the crime of forcible rape per se are cost and general equitable considerations. Critical though it may be to revamp the system's response to the victims of forcible rape, they do represent only a proportion, albeit growing, of the total sexual assault victim population. Present social and political forces probably dictate a disparate allocation of a limited pool of professional personnel in police and prosecutor agencies to handle rape cases. In the future, however, these forces may diminish somewhat, and a fresh balance of investigative and prosecutive priorities and resources may be reached in sex crime units.

It appears likely that cost considerations, as well as some reassessment of reapportionment of priorities, will also result in extending present services for victims of forcible rape to other categories of crime victims. Thus the improved facilities and examinations being provided for victims of forcible rape in several hospital emergency rooms may well be made available to other crime victims requiring emergency medical aid and subsequent follow-up care. Similarly, rape crisis centers, staffed mostly by community volunteers, could readily extend their services to the victims of other crimes producing the trauma and reporting dilemmas now associated only with forcible rape.

The new service emphasis on the part of the criminal justice system toward crime victims, which seems to stem in large part from criticism of its handling of rape victims, is evidenced by a number of recent developments. Among the more significant of these is the establishment by the National District Attorneys Association of a Commission for Victim Witness Assistance. As part of this commission's work, a number of demonstration projects are being established in prosecutors' offices to provide special advice and assistance to victims and witnesses involved with the ongoing prosecution of crimes. Too often in the past victims and witnesses in all categories of crime—particularly forcible rape—have been largely ignored in the prosecution process. Court scheduling, witness interviewing and briefing, plea bargaining, and allied matters have been conducted without reference to those most intimately involved and concerned with the outcome of the case—the crime victims.

Experience already gained in a number of prosecutors' offices around the country in providing supportive assistance and advice to rape victims should prove valuable in setting up this broader victim/witness assistance program. In the case of rape, there is increasing use in several prosecutors' offices of female attorneys to handle this crime. An evaluation of the results of this change in practice has yet to be presented However, this expanded role of women in the prosecutive process matches a similar development already noted in police agencies. Through the immediate opportunities afforded them in the area of rape, it appears many women will in the future be assigned vastly expanded responsibilities within the criminal justice system at large.

Conclusions

In this chapter a fairly optimistic account has been presented of what is happening within this country's criminal justice system to cope with a problem of intense public concern. The principal stimulus for change has been described, as has a research project intended to provide both documentation of the current practices of the criminal justice system relating to forcible rape and projection of future trends. A number of significant issues of broad import for the criminal justice system which stem from existing developments about rape have also been discussed.

Within the criminal justice system, the predominant climate is encouraging for the acceptance of change. However, it should be recalled that the attitudes and traditions upon which the system has been functioning when dealing with the crime of forcible rape are not unique to police, prosecutors, or judges. Experience with jurors suggest that many of these same attitudes and traditions are shared by society at large. Even if the police and prosecution are able to construct a strong case, convincing a jury that a woman has been raped is an exceptionally difficult task. As one experienced prosecutor has commented:

Unless her head is bashed in or she's 95 years old or it's some other kind of extreme case, jurors just can't believe a woman was raped. There's a suspicion that it was her fault, that she led the guy on, or consented—consent is the hardest thing to disprove. It's just his word against hers. (Stumbo, 1972, p. 9)

Changing ingrained community beliefs in this or any other field is no easy endeavor, although the women's movement, in particular, has achieved quite remarkable success in overturning massively entrenched beliefs and practices related to rape in a very short time. The presence of many more women on juries, together with the comprehensive mass media attention to the crime of forcible rape, possibly may produce rapid change even in the jury room and society.

Whatever the outcome of this and other issues addressed in this chapter, future historians, unlike Sir James Fitzjames Stephen, will certainly review with substantial interest present political and social events associated with "offenses relating to the abduction of women, rape and other such crimes."

Notes

1. Nationally, for the decade 1960-1970, the number of rapes per 100,000 "eligible females" (excluding those under 5 and those 75 and over) rose from 21.9 in 1960 to 41.3 in 1970.

2. The prosecutor segments of the research, together with a review of the legislation relating to forcible rape, are being performed by the National Legal Data Center located in Los Angeles.

3. The Model Penal Code broadened the definition of rape to cover so-called "deviate" sexual intercourse enforced upon a woman, recognizing that nonconsensual forceful intercourse of any kind is a grave crime.

4. Research-based data are not readily available to support this contention although there is every indication from the low conviction rate for rapists that only cases of this type ultimately proceed through the system.

5. Special corroboration requirements are believed to now be required in only six states, and in the District of Columbia. With regard to victim character testimony, California has recently led a trend toward prohibiting such testimony except in very restricted circumstances.

6. Apart from a general broadening of the official definition of rape, changing practices in relation to unfounded offenses and in classifying a crime as attempted rape may also increase current rape statistics.

7. Victimization studies have established that the rate of commission of

forcible rape in the community far outstrips the reported rate. Estimates of the gap between the two rates vary: the National Victimization Study conducted in 1967 for the President's Crime Commission suggested a ratio of between 3 and 4 actual rapes for each one reported. A more recent Law Enforcement Assistance Administration Pilot Survey in two American cities suggested a 2-to-1 ratio, possibly indicating a change in victim reporting behavior since 1967. Clearly, a comparatively minor change in this behavior could produce quite a major impact upon the statistics of forcible rape.

8. New classifications of major offenses have been developed extensively in the United Kingdom for adoption in that country's crime statistics. The classifications are based, in the main, upon the social rather than the legal circumstances of an offense, unmasking a great deal of valuable data formerly concealed by criminal law definition.

References

Agopian, M., Chappell, D., and Geis, G. Interracial forcible rape in a North American city: An analysis of 63 cases. In I. Drapkin and E. Viano (Eds.), *Victimology*. Lexington, Mass.: Lexington Books, 1974, pp. 93-102.

Chappell, D., Geis, G., Schafer, S., and Siegel, L. Forcible rape: A comparative study of offenses known to the police in Boston and Los Angeles. In L. Curtis, Criminal Violence: Inquiries into National Patterns and Behavior. Ph.D. Dissertation, 1972, University of Pennsylvania.

Clark, W., and Marshall, W. *A Treatise on the Law of Crimes* (7th ed.). Mundelein, Ill.: Callaghan & Co., 1967, pp. 752-762.

Cleaver, E. *Soul on Ice*. New York: McGraw-Hill, 1968.

Federal Bureau of Investigation. *Uniform Crime Reporting Handbook*. Washington, D.C.: United States Government Printing Office, 1966.

Furman v. Georgia, 408 U.S. 238 (1972).

Kooninger, R. Capital punishment in Texas. *Crime and Delinquency*, 1969, 15: 132-141.

Millett, K. *Sexual Politics*. New York: Avon Books, Equinox Ed., 1971.

Partington, D. The incidence of the death penalty for rape in Virginia. *Washington and Lee Law Review*, 1965, 22: 43-75.

Ploscowe, M. *Sex and the Law*. New York: Prentice-Hall, 1951. © 1951 by Prentice-Hall, Inc.

Stephen, J. *History of the Criminal Law of England*. London: Butterworths, 1886.

Stumbo, B. Rape: Does justice turn its head? *Los Angeles Times*, 12 March, 1972, p. 1.

Svalastoga, K. Rape and social structure. *Pacific Sociological Review*, 1962, 5: 48-53. Reprinted by permission of the Publisher, Sage Publications, Inc.

Wolfgang, M., and Cohen, B. *Crime and Race*. New York: Institute of Human Relations, American Jewish Committee, 1970.

3

Rape: Its Effect on Task Performance at Varying Stages in the Life Cycle

Ann Wolbert Burgess
and Lynda Lytle Holmstrom

Rape has an enormous impact not only on the socioemotional aspects of the victim's life, but on task performance as well. The present chapter documents this latter disruption. This aspect of rape, so far, has received much less attention than the emotional upset, yet our data clearly show its importance. Our findings are that rape and its aftermath seriously affect the victims' ability to continue to perform the normal duties expected of them. For grade school and adolescent victims, task disruption at this point in the life cycle occurs in school attendance and performance. For adult victims, task disruption occurs in three areas: housewifery and parenting, employment, and schooling.

Method

Victim Counseling Program

As a response to the problem of rape in the greater Boston area, the Victim Counseling Program was organized and initiated on July 20, 1972 as a voluntary collaborative effort between Boston College School of Nursing and the Boston City Hospital Emergency Services Department. The program was staffed for the first year of the project by a psychiatric nurse and a sociologist (coauthors of this chapter) to provide 24-hour-a-day crisis intervention for rape victims.

Originally, services were provided to adult victims. However, in December 1972 the Pediatric Walk-in Clinic of the Boston City Hospital requested the staff's services. Thus the victim population was expanded to include not only adult victims, but also child victims of rape, attempted rape, sexual assault, or molestation. Referrals were also received from the police, the district attorney's office, and several hospitals in the greater Boston area.

Objectives of the Program

The first-year objectives of the program were these: (1) studying the problems the victim experiences as a result of being in the hospital, in the community, and in court; (2) developing a counseling program to help the victim that was preventive of serious emotional problems, cost-effective, and applicable in other areas of the country; and (3) making policy recommendations for those institutional systems that deal with rape.

The second year of the program had these objectives: (1) training victim counselors to continue the program at Boston City Hospital; (2) studying the problems of training victim counselors; and (3) providing consultation to other victim counseling programs.

Sample and Data Collection

The data for this chapter include the rape victims from the first year of the program, that is, 92 adult women, 21 preadult females, and 2 preadult males. We were telephoned when a victim was admitted to the emergency floor; we immediately went to the hospital. This method of crisis counseling and research provided the opportunity for interviewing the victim at the impact period of the crisis, as well as for observing and talking with the police and hospital staff. Follow-up service with the victim was conducted by use of telephone counseling or home visit.

Diagnostic Categories of Sexual Trauma

We analyzed all cases of sexual assault admitted to Boston City Hospital—146 total—and devised three diagnostic categories: rape trauma, accessory to sex, and sex-stress situation. This category system focuses on the issue of consent.

Rape Trauma. Rape is forced, violent sexual penetration against the victim's will and without the victim's consent. Most victims of attempted rape as well as completed forcible rape developed a pattern of symptoms we call rape trauma syndrome (Burgess and Holmstrom, 1974a). The trauma syndrome is a crisis reaction to a life-threatening situation and includes an acute phase of disorganization to the victim's life-style. From the first year, 79 percent of victims were diagnosed as rape trauma.

Accessory to Sex. A second group of sexual assault victims—most of whom are children and young adolescents—we call accessory-to-sex victims (Burgess and Holmstrom, 1975). In this type of sexual assault, victims are pressured into sexual activity by a person who, through age, authority, or some other way, is in a power position over them. The victims are unable to make an informed decision of consent because of their stage of personality or cognitive development. Of the first-year victims 5 percent were diagnosed in this category.

Sex-stress Situation. Sex-stress situation is an anxiety reaction that occurs as a result of the circumstances of a sexual situation in which both parties initially consent (Burgess and Holmstrom, 1974b). The person for whom the sexual situation produces the most anxiety usually brings the situation to the attention of the professional staff, such as police or hospital personnel. Of the victims from the first year 16 percent were diagnosed in this category.

Findings

Task Disruption in Child and Adolescent Victims

Task Expectation. A developmental task of the school-age person is interaction with social systems outside the home, that is, with the formal organizations of a community, such as school and church, and the informal organizations, such as neighborhood and peer group. School thus becomes the main task-oriented duty in a young person's life and is, therefore, one area of his/her life-style in which it would be important to investigate whether there is a posttrauma reaction.

For the young person, school presents many structural demands. He or she must travel to and from home, interact with peers and authority figures, and is expected to concentrate on the lessons. It is reasonable to expect that rape trauma will interrupt these three areas. Therefore, it is anticipated that school difficulties or a school phobia may appear in the child.

In our victim sample of preadults, the following list shows the school attendance of rape victims, age 5 through 16, at the time of the rape.

Attending school	17
Grammar school	4
Junior high	10
Senior high	3
Not in school	6
Summer	2
Not enrolled	4

Disruption in School Attendance. All school-enrolled victims experienced disruption in their school life; 41 percent either stopped school abruptly or changed schools. The following list illustrates the problems of young rape victims in attempting to cope with the normal task of basic education.

Stopped school	2
Changed school within two months	5
Tried to change school	2

Truancy problem	2
Academic or phobia problem	6
Not in school at time of rape	6

Returning to school is a difficult action for the school-aged victim. Most victims report missing an average of 2 to 5 days immediately after the rape. They may give such reasons as the need to keep medical or legal appointments or physical discomfort from the accompanying bruises of the rape.

When the absence from school continues for longer than one week, the symptoms of an acute phobic reaction are observed. Children give various reasons for not going back to school, such as worrying that "everyone will know what happened." This worry contributes to disruption in the interaction with informal groups in community, neighborhood, and school groups. One adolescent victim said:

I can't play with my old friends because they all know. It's embarrassing that they know. I can't trust anyone and I liked them. I'd have to make new friends.

Some children simply refuse to go to school. Some parents make the decision for the child so that she or he does not have to return. Other victims are truant from school, and the parents do not know until the school officials notify them. As the mother of one 13-year-old said:

She is up and down and she has been playing hooky from school. . . . The school called me up. I didn't realize it and told them to let me know when she isn't at school.

Academic difficulties after the rape are almost universal in the sample of victims. As one 14-year-old said:

School is terrible. I'm flunking everything. I keep missing so many classes, and I'm not in the course I wanted to be in. I missed the whole week following the rape, and all the dozen times I had to be in court I missed.

In this case, the family did not wish to tell the school authorities why she was absent. However, with the girl's declining academic record after the rape and the time required to be in court, specifically during the final examination week, they decided to tell. The father finally made an agreement with the principal of the school that no one else be told the reason for his daughter's absence.

Task Disruption in the Adult Victim

Task Expectations. In the developmental phase of adulthood, women in our society have three major tasks expected of them: to be a homemaker and parent, to be employed, and/or to be in school. In our adult victim sample, a majority of the rape victims—60 percent—were in some type of working situation at the time of the rape. The following chart illustrates their main task activity.

High school student	6
Employee	45
Employee and college student	11
Welfare recipient	15
Unemployment funds recipient	4
Homemaker	8
Institutional client	3
Total	92

Disruption in Homemaking and Parenting. There are many domestic-oriented tasks that are usually performed by the adult woman. Such tasks include marketing, cooking meals, washing dishes, doing laundry, ironing, vacuuming. And there are other home-related tasks, such as assuming primary responsibility for entertaining in the home, transporting children to their various activities, representing the family at school meetings or for health care, and fulfilling civic responsibilities (Holmstrom, 1972).

Rape trauma dramatically disrupts all these tasks normally performed by the adult woman. The rape victims from our study were unable to initially cope with household tasks or child care and required assistance from their husbands or other family members such as mother, sister, or aunt.

For some women, their physical condition after the rape disrupted their functioning. A 35-year-old mother of teen-aged sons said:

I've been in bed ever since I came home. So sore . . . from the beating . . . and my leg is swollen. And the shots too. I've been trying to get all the sleep I can. . . . My face is so swollen and my mouth . . .

Some women found they could not cook because of nausea. One said, "My stomach is just too upset." Another woman said, "Bothers me to eat. I think he loosened my teeth in the struggle."

Most women regain their coping skills within the first week and gradually begin to resume their usual work style within the home. As one 40-year-old mother of ten children said:

I just could not do anything yesterday. I couldn't even get out of my room. I was able to sleep a bit last night. Today I am trying to do something like housework but I still . . . just seem to be totally immobilized.

The emotional reactions from rape trauma contribute to their inability to cope. As this same woman said:

Have no interest in things . . . can't move . . . usually am go, go, go all the time . . . now just hanging around the house.

Resuming outside activities can be difficult due to the development of the phobic symptoms. One woman said:

I went to the store with my daughter . . . felt tired, not physically but headachy . . . not too enthused about going and I love to shop. But didn't buy anything . . . Had to park the car away from the store . . . never worried about that before . . . gave me a funny feeling . . .

One of the striking features is that women are aware of their crisis behavior. They realize it is not usual for them, and they neither like it nor want it to continue. This motivation is important in the therapeutic process. Women would keep this thought uppermost in their mind as they confronted each task. As one woman said, "I keep thinking I have to do what I always do, even if I don't feel like it."

Women who have child care responsibilities relied on assistance from family members to cope with the immediate disruption. For example, husbands would take their children to activities such as the movies in order that the wife could rest. Victims would often move to a family member's home for a few days or a week so that others could assist in task performance.

Disruption in a life-style task may become so troublesome that it is the reason for seeking help. One of our referral cases was directed to us specifically for this reason. The victim's opening statement was:

I beat my four-year-old son . . . I have never done that. He was just being naughty, and for no reason I took a strap and beat him.

This 32-year-old victim later went on to say that she had been crying for two days (following the rape) and then said, ". . . my sister is taking my son for the weekend and I'm going to my mother's." Counseling was needed for this woman, first to cope with the crisis of rape and second to resume child care responsibilities.

Disruption in Employment. Disruption in employment occurs when there is interference in the task that one must perform in order to be paid a wage or salary. A majority of the adult victims were employed at the time of the rape. The range of occupation types included school teachers, researcher, assembly-line worker, waitress, business manager, shop manager, secretaries, health workers, models, dancers, store clerks, and counselor.

The degree of disruption that the rape created in the occupational life-style is seen when looking at the number of victims who either quit or changed jobs within a short time period following the rape. Such changes by those women whose main activity was employment areas follows.

Changed or quit job within 2 to 3 weeks	10
Changed or quit job within 4 to 6 weeks	9
Quit or changed jobs within 6 months	3
No explicit disruption in job	21
No data	2
Total	45

Stopping Work. There may be many reasons why a victim decides to quit her job. Very often, the need to move and to change residence becomes part of the decision. Several victims who quit work abruptly moved back to their families in other states. Victims become fearful that the assailant will retaliate. One victim who was frightened of the assailant (who was the uncle of her boyfriend) stated:

I have found out he has raped two other girls in the neighborhood. . . . They are all so scared . . . my boyfriend talked to him, and he denied it and made some terrible accusations about me. . . . He could kill me. He has a record . . . I am going home to another state.

Some victims find it difficult to explain what has happened to fellow employees and employers. Sometimes the victim will talk about this during the hospital interview or on follow-up. One victim who quit her job because of this factor said:

I had those big bandages on my knees from the bruises I got from being pushed on the ground and it really hurt to walk. Well, I had to make up stories about those bandages for work, and it got to be such a hassle that is one reason I quit the job.

Some victims quit work because the distressing symptoms they develop as an aftermath interfere with their ability to tolerate work conditions. Such was the case with a 25-year-old victim who worked as a stripper. She said several months after the rape:

I was a stripper at the time of the rape. Afterwards I got very paranoid. I tried staying home from work; but the feeling would get worse, and when I was at work it was bad. . . . I found I couldn't take stripping . . . couldn't stand all those men making remarks and such. Taking off my clothes was too much.

This victim, new to this occupation, had been a go-go dancer prior to this job. She found herself very critical of her work following the rape and remarked that "stripping had a different clientele . . . the mentality of the men . . . really got to me."

Women can be quite ambivalent about their work following a rape. In one case, a victim used her part-time sales clerk job as a way to have time and money for herself, since she had major homemaking and parenting responsibilities in the home. She said:

I have been thinking of leaving [my job] ... Now this has happened I think I will ... I just have the feeling that everyone knows what happened. I know they really don't, but I still have the feeling when I think of seeing people. I have an unclean feeling. Those are the thoughts that come to me.

This victim was able to resume her job after being absent for about 2½ weeks.

No Disruption in Job. Slightly under half of the victims were able to maintain their jobs despite the rape. We found there were many economic realities which caused the victim to maintain her present employment. As one woman said, "I can't change jobs ... even though I would want to ... I need this one so I have to stay here."

One coping strategy of victims was not to tell anyone at their place of employment. These victims believed this silence aided their ability to maintain their performance level.

Disruption in School. Some of the adult victims were students or were students employed part time. Often people face conflict over what they feel versus reality factors, such as the need to make money and obtain a school degree. The following is an example of a woman who planned to finish high school, but the emotional aftermath of the rape was too great. She dropped out of school and took a job as a clerk in an insurance company with the plan to finish high school by taking an equivalency exam. This victim said:

Everyone at school knows, and I'm furious. The girls said I wanted it. I told two school officials, but they offered no help.

This rape involved seven males, and the news of the rape did become public knowledge at the school. In such cases where there is no social network support either from peers or from authority figures, the victim has to cope with the crisis alone. It is not surprising to see the coping strategy of "flight" or avoidance when the person receives no support.

Adult victims tend to be more able to speak up for themselves if they are having school difficulties rather than remaining silent as seen in younger victims. For example, one college student was having difficulty concentrating on completing a term paper. She was able to go to her professor and request an extension.

Implications for Counseling

An important question becomes how to help victims cope with the crisis of rape trauma as it affects task performance during different points in the life cycle.

One technique we used in telephone counseling was the pursuit of reality details. That is, we would inquire specifically into those functions and duties of task performance in order to assess the coping abilities of the victim. For example, we would ask the victim what she was able to do each day and help her to see any progress she was making in completing task expectations. The following is an example from one of our follow-up calls.

I'm doing OK . . . in fact, just doing a wash so I am trying to do things. I know it is going to take a while to feel myself. I feel different now [from last week] and can only hope I will feel better in time.

While the daily reality details of the life cycle task performance are sometimes relegated to a minor role in psychotherapy, they become of major significance in crisis counseling. The goal in counseling is for the victim to resume her precrisis state, including resuming the usual task performance expected at the particular point in the life cycle. This would be school attendance and performance in the preadult. For the adult victim, one would have to inquire, if applicable, as to homemaking and child care performance, employment, and/or school.

Social System Reaction

The reaction that people have within the social system of the victim can be very important in the degree of disruption the victim experiences in task performance. Of course, this reaction will depend on the victim's telling the school officials or her employer about the rape. We have seen reactions of officials who have been told of the rape and, in turn, have been very helpful or have not been helpful.

In one situation, a victim reported her employer's reaction:

I am so excited. I have been promoted. My supervisor knew of the situation and asked if I was ready for a change. She said she didn't want to put me under too much stress but wanted to know if I would consider a transfer to another store where I would be a supervisor. I said I would be glad because it helped to keep me busy.

In contrast, some employers react negatively. For example, in the following case which occurred on the job, a female cab driver was robbed by three men she had picked up for a fare and later raped by one of the men. On hospital interview, she was afraid she would lose her job and that this incident would make it hard for other women who might want to drive a cab. On follow-up, the victim said that the cab company had changed its rules—women would only be allowed to drive for the company until 8 P.M. This victim found she was unable to go back to her job because of the psychological reaction. She said, "I have to get another job—just can't go back into a cab again." This victim also discussed the rape as a "double blow" by saying:

This is doubly hard. The rape is one thing, but the financial loss is equal. I lost my rent money because I was ripped off of my $50 pay check that I had just cashed. The guys took $60 cab fares that I have to pay back to the company. They smashed my glasses in the fight, and the lens costs $60. Lost my job and had to move as well as being raped.

Counselors have a constant role in assisting people within social systems to more fully understand the disruptive aspect of rape in terms of task performance. Support that is given in the first few weeks can be of major influence in the overall settlement of the total crisis.

Discussion

Despite the serious disruption in task performance at varying points in the life cycle as evidenced in the victims of rape trauma, the ability of victims to resume or develop a coping strategy within a relatively short period of time was impressive. For example, when victims felt the need to leave their job, they did not simply remain at home. For the most part, victims were able to relocate into another employment setting. Thus, they were able to stay within the work force and be gainfully employed.

Children, however, had considerably more difficulty resuming their task of school performance. Their resiliency to cope and adapt was not, on the surface, as successful as adults who had the freedom to move or to change to another setting. In studies involved with coping and mastery of life cycle tasks, one needs to become concerned when reviewing findings of task performance in childhood and adolescence. A study by Finger and Silverman (1966) showed that approximately 50 percent of students entering junior high school who experienced a drop in performance were rarely able to improve at a later point in a career. A study by Hamburg (1974) points out the entry into junior high school as a critical task of early adolescence. It is our belief that further study needs to be made as to the developmental crisis interacting with the external crisis of rape, and the potential results in school performance and later career development over time (Burgess and Holmstrom, 1974b).

It is noted that victims who receive active assistance from their family and social network cope and adapt more quickly. This assistance was behavior that we tried to encourage within the counseling follow-up. We believe that recovery from rape trauma is a social process that can best be handled when it is shared and assisted by others—family as well as concerned counselors, school authorities and administrators, and employers.

References

Burgess, A. and Holmstrom, L. Rape trauma syndrome. *American Journal of Psychiatry*, 1974a, 131: 981-986.

_____ and _____. *Rape: Victims of Crisis.* Bowie, Md.: Robert J. Brady Co., 1974b.

_____ and _____. Sexual trauma of children and adolescents: Pressure, sex and secrecy. *Nursing Clinics of North America*, 1975, 10 (3): 551-563.

Finger, J. and Silverman, M. Changes in academic performance in the junior high school. *Personnel and Guidance Journal*, 1966, 45: 157-164.

Hamburg, B. Early adolescence: A specific and stressful stage of the life cycle. In G. Coelho, D. Hamburg, and J. Adams (Eds.), *Coping and Adaptation.* New York: Basic Books, 1974, p. 113.

Holmstrom, L. *The two-career family.* Cambridge, Mass.: Schenkman, 1972.

4

Rape at Work

Carroll M. Brodsky

Work Is Dangerous to Your Health is the title of a recent volume describing the hazards of work (Stellman and Daum, 1973). Trauma as a result of falls, blows, fumes, noise, and mutilation are listed among the hazards that make work dangerous to health. For women workers, a unique work hazard exists: the threat of rape. The frequency of rape in work situations is unknown. Since rape in other settings is greatly underreported, we must assume that some of the attacks at work are unreported. Law enforcement agencies do not issue special statistics distinguishing rape at work from rape in other settings. Yet according to the laws governing workers' compensation, work-incurred injuries, including rape, are compensable. A worker who incurs an injury on the job, whether physical or psychological, is entitled to medical care for the injury and for any conditions that it precipitates or aggravates. If a worker is disabled as a result of that injury, he or she is entitled to temporary disability benefits and, if there is any permanent impairment resulting from the trauma, to continuing disability benefits as well.

In some states, applicants for workers' compensation benefits are advised to obtain the services of an attorney. The compensating agency, either a private insurance carrier or a government-established agency (such as the State Compensation Insurance Fund in California), arranges for extensive medical evaluation of the applicant. These carriers are interested in determining what impairment and disability the applicant has, how much is due to the accident in question, and what is necessary to repair the damage. The applicant's attorney seeks answers to the same questions, but often refers the applicant to different physicians to gain the benefit of study by physicians who are not biased in favor of the insurance carrier. As a result, most applicants accumulate an extensive medical dossier containing detailed information, enabling those studying the problems of work-incurred injuries to follow the course of impairment, disability, and recovery from the time of the injury until a final examination and/or until the case has been settled or closed.

Workers' compensation plans provide a guarantee of medical services, including psychiatric treatment from private sources for industrial injuries. Such treatment is readily available and is continued as long as there is any residual trauma. Usually the treatment is provided by the most highly skilled therapists in the community. This contrasts with the services available to the indigent in public hospitals where treatment is often provided by trainees or paraprofessionals. The disability benefits for the victim of rape at work last as long as she is disabled mentally or physically. The availability of benefits may sometimes interfere with the relationship of the helping person and the patient, compared to the private physician or therapist who has sole responsibility for the patient's care. The possibility of an award for "permanent" damages must also be considered a factor that affects conscious and unconscious motivation to recover from industrial injuries, including rape.

Those who examine accident victims have come to recognize a syndrome known as the "compensation neurosis." The term "neurosis" is, of course, a misnomer. It does not fall into any of the usual categories of neurosis. Actually, the syndrome called compensation neurosis is a bit of the psychopathology of everyday life. A person involved in an accident tends to behave in a way that will maximize the benefits from that accident. A person who believes that he or she has been injured hopes in some way to be compensated for that injury. The person might tend to perceive the effects of the injury as being far greater than others judge them to be. As long as certain benefits are forthcoming, such as care, sympathy, drugs, and relief from onerous burdens, the person might continue to see himself or herself as being a sick person.

In a typical compensation neurosis, one would expect that when the litigation is finally resolved and there is no further advantage to maintaining the symptoms, the person will improve partially or fully. A construction worker who is judged to be disabled because of an industrial back injury and was rehabilitated for light-duty hospital work returned to his heavy construction work almost immediately after the settlement. He continued to work in the heaviest of all construction work, using a jack hammer, and stated that he had no symptoms during the three years until he was the victim of a cave-in—at which time he had all the same symptoms in spite of the fact that there were again no physical findings.

This author did not have the impression that the symptoms described by the women who had been raped, or on whom rape was attempted, were those of a compensation neurosis. In only one of the cases did it seem that there might be some elements of this. The author made the same predictions about these cases as about cases of muggings, which, generally speaking, also did not contain large elements of compensation neuroses. To the contrary, settlement seemed to produce no changes, and in several instances the author recommended against settlement in the belief that there would be a prolonged course of psychiatric symptoms. The victim would therefore need psychiatric treatment, compensation for which would have been precluded by early settlement.

The true traumatic neurosis which most of these women suffered is not a compensation neurosis and unfortunately is not ameliorated by a termination of litigation but only by time, psychotherapy, and activity.

Five case histories illustrate the nature and consequences of rape or attempted rape in work settings. These women were raped at work and filed claims for medical benefits, temporary disability benefits, and permanent disability awards. The author examined and reviewed the records of these five women approximately 6 to 24 months after the rape occurred. In each case an extensive medical record had already accumulated. These records included the results of previous psychiatric examinations as well as reports from treating psychiatrists, gynecologists, family physicians, and law enforcement agencies.

Cases

Ann

Ann, a widowed white woman, was 48 years old when she was attacked. She worked as a substitute cook at a juvenile detention home where she was assigned to some of the outlying camps maintained for male juveniles. One evening while she was working at one of these camps, Ann was attacked by one of the inmates. At first she told him to stop. Then she started to scream, and he put his hand over her mouth. The more she fought him, the worse it seemed to get. The boy dragged her to the top of the hill adjacent to the kitchen. While dragging her, he tore off all her clothes. At the top of the hill, he raped her. She remembers that he entered her vagina and ejaculated. Ann managed to escape by sliding down a hill and running to a nearby building, where she located an attendant.

Ann was taken to a hospital for a medical check-up. She complained that the hospital authorities took a specimen from her vagina but paid no attention to any of her physical complaints. She said her body was "skinned" from one end to the other, and she had many bruises. She was given no medical treatment for this. She complained that she had to douche and shower at home because the hospital personnel did not properly cleanse her. No one suggested that Ann receive any kind of follow-up treatment from her own physician. She was told she was all right and was sent home.

Two days later, Ann went to the emergency room of a neighborhood hospital where she was given a tranquilizer for nervousness. Ann felt that she could not return to work at the place where she had been attacked. For a while, she could not work at all. She was very angry. Some friends advised her to sue the county because of the negligence of the authorities. She and her friends both felt she had not been properly protected.

Ann had returned to work at the time the author saw her, but had not worked in the same kind of unprotected situation in which she was attacked. The fact that Ann could not work in places where she would be alone with young inmates made it difficult to obtain full-time work. She still worked only when someone else was ill or vacationing. Whereas previously she had been able to work in a number of different facilities, after the attack she could work only at the central facility which had a large staff.

Well over a year after the attack, Ann still has many problems, including a "rectal muscle disorder," which she attributes to the rape. If she works a full 5-day week, Ann is so stiff that she develops pain in the rectal area. When she works a full week, she is exhausted physically and mentally. Ann would leave this job except that she has to support her household and cannot take a chance of being unable to find another job. She takes 30 milligrams of Valium a day, and sometimes she takes another Valium at night to sleep.

Ann remains active socially but is hesitant about going places at night; formerly she never thought about this. Even when she leaves home, Ann is always on guard, afraid something will happen to her. She is fearful and nervous even in her own home. At first Ann lost weight; she has since regained it. She has noticed no special effect on her sexual desires as a result of the rape.

Ann does not blame herself for the rape. She can think of no way in which she could have prevented it. She is angry that her employers had not provided better protection. As a result of the attack, Ann feels she could not work in places where she would be risking another attack. She feels uncomfortable about going places where she might be vulnerable, even in her own home.

Betty

Betty is a married 27-year-old woman who worked as an eligibility technician for a welfare department and liked her job. One day Betty left her office in an agency automobile to make a home visit. At her destination Betty parked the car and climbed out. Just as she slammed the door, a man approached her and asked for directions. She does not recall exactly what he asked. The man was somewhat inarticulate in his question. She asked him to repeat it and turned to hear him better. The man said he had a gun and she was to do what he said or he would kill her. She could not recall whether the man in any way forced her physically, but he led her into an alley beside a vacant house. He warned her again that he would not hesitate to kill her. Then he raped her.

Betty is not certain or clear about the details of the rape. Her back was to him, and her hands were on the wall of the house. She described the rape as "very quick. One, two, three, and over. It was not like having regular sexual intercourse." At first he wanted to have anal intercourse, but she begged him not to do that. She is unable to recall details. She does not recall whether he actually penetrated the vagina or ejaculated. All of it happened very quickly. He left quietly, telling her to stay where she was or he would kill her.

At first Betty was relieved that the experience had not been worse. When she was sure the man was gone, she left the alleyway. After running in the wrong direction, away from her car, she finally oriented herself and ran to her car. Then she drove to the welfare agency lot, which was directly across from a police station. By this time she felt relatively calm and entered the police station to report the assault. She did not want to tell the officer on duty about the nature of the crime because another man was standing nearby; she did not want to "shock" this other man. When the officer on duty insisted she explain, she told him and started crying.

The police made her wait for two or three hours while they checked out her story. Finally Betty called her sister-in-law, who drove her to a nearby hospital. An examination found no sperm in her vagina. Betty was concerned about possible pregnancy from the assault. She was not using birth control, and she did not believe in abortion. The doctor in charge gave her some medication which he said would prevent impregnation. Later Betty learned from another physican that this medication would not prevent pregnancy. Her concern about pregnancy increased. She continued to worry until she had a menstrual period.

Betty received little support directly after the rape incident. Her husband was a heavy drug user, and after a few days he said he couldn't handle this and was leaving. Betty went home to the East Coast to stay with her parents and try to forget. She also thought of going back to work at her old job but felt she could not do so. She decided to stay in the East. Life in California was associated with the pain of the incident and with the disappointment in her husband. She thought of asking for psychiatric treatment but decided she would handle it alone.

Betty had taken no medication and has actually had less alcohol since the rape than she had before. At first she was very depressed, but now is improving daily. She lost fifteen pounds after the rape incident, but gained back five of those pounds after about six months. Shyness and modesty caused her to understate the incident when she complained to the police. She received little support from them, little support from the medical authorities, and less support from her husband. She finally went home to her family.

Immediately after the attack Betty had no interest in sex. Six months later she was experiencing the beginning of some sexual interest. She has yet to have sexual intercourse. Betty felt she could never go back to the same kind of work, though the work was not related to the rape. It was only after six months that Betty began considering returning to work at all. She is again looking for work but avoids the area in which she has experience, namely social work.

Carla

Carla, a black woman in her mid-forties, was working as a nurse's aide at a hospital. Going from one building to another at about 11:00 in the evening, Carla heard someone behind her. She assumed the footsteps were those of nurses who were coming to work. Carla never learned whose footsteps they were; instead, she was struck from behind and knocked unconscious. When she gained consciousness, she was being attacked sexually. Carla did not open her eyes until the sexual attack was over. She did not report the attack to the police, her employer, a physician, or her husband. When asked why she did not report it, Carla said, "I was embarrassed." It was only much later that she informed others about what had happened.

The rape occurred at a time that was very stressful for Carla. She was returning from a session with her superior in which she had just been evaluated. Carla was angry because she believed the evaluation was unjust and that it should have been made by someone who knew her better. Immediately after the evaluation Carla had talked to another supervisor who agreed that she had been unjustly criticized.

The evaluation had been devastating. She was described as moody, sloppy, not giving herself to patients, and indicating she did not like her work. The performance report also suggested that she might be having outside problems. Carla felt she was being discriminated against. Several days after this evaluation, Carla was asked to resign. She refused and was terminated.

Carla felt that her vision had been impaired as a result of the rape. She was concerned about future employment because of her poor vision. Eight months after the incident Carla still has problems with her eyes. According to Carla, she is "practically blind" and needs glasses. She says that every doctor tells her a different story. One physician told her she needs glasses. Another physician said it was all psychological and she is becoming far-sighted as she becomes older.

Shortly after the attack Carla had nightmares and still has one occasionally when she is alone at night. When her husband is in bed with her, Carla feels safe. Carla is also afraid to leave home at night. She visits her relatives because they will escort her from the car to the house. She will go places at night with her husband. Still Carla is afraid of taking a job where she would have to park and walk to or leave a building.

At first Carla found sexual intercourse with her husband distasteful. As time passed, she was no longer adverse to it. After six or eight months Carla noticed her desire for sexual intercourse had returned.

Carla's case is unusual, because she was raped while in the midst of an employment crisis. She was too embarrassed to tell anyone about it, even her husband. It was only some days later that she could report it. Initially Carla had nightmares. She developed a functional impairment of vision and an aversion to intercourse. She feared going out at night. After eight months Carla still has visual problems and is still afraid to go out, but seems to have improved in other areas. Because she has child care responsibilities, Carla can work only at night, and she cannot go out at night because she is afraid.

Denise

Denise is a 25-year-old white woman who had recently moved to southern California at the time of the attack. She had four years of teaching experience in a New Jersey community close to where she had been born, raised, and attended college. Denise found a job soon after she arrived in the Los Angeles area. She was assigned to a predominantly black school. Denise had no problems with her students or with the parents and was happy with her assignment.

One morning Denise arrived at her classroom, which was at the end of the school away from the central office. She found no one else there. Because it was raining, one student came to the door, and Denise let him inside. Suddenly a young black man entered the classroom and told the one child who was in the classroom to stand facing the wall. He then took a gun from his pocket and threatened Denise. The man told her if she did not let him do what he wanted, he would kill her. He then proceeded to rape her, after locking the door so no other children could enter.

When the man left, Denise called the school authorities; they called the police. Denise was taken to the hospital where she was examined. Then she was sent home. Denise stayed home for three weeks in a state of shock. She was especially upset when asked by the police to view pictures of black males who had been involved in sexual offenses in an effort to identify her attacker. Denise recalled the procedure as being as traumatic as the initial attack.

After a month Denise returned to work. She was given a classroom close to the central office, but was able to work for only three days. She could not drive to work herself because she was too nervous; she would jump whenever she heard a loud noise. Even in her own apartment, she would hide if she heard someone walking up or down the stairs. One evening when her husband returned from work, Denise met him at the door with a gun they owned. She herself was frightened by this, and they decided to get rid of the gun.

Denise experienced nightmares repeatedly. She would awaken in terror and profuse perspiration. As so often happens, the nightmares were not of rape but of other fears, fears of mutilation, fears of falling. She would wake up in the morning feeling sick and would begin vomiting. Denise was not sure whether this was a psychological symptom or whether it was the result of drinking too much. Before the rape Denise never had more than an occasional single drink. After the rape she drank more in an effort to sedate herself. She was given tranquilizers, but they did not seem to help. Prior to the rape incident, Denise and her husband had what they considered an excellent sexual relationship. After the rape incident she could not tolerate the thought of sexual intercourse. She feared being alone and was especially anxious in the presence of a young black male.

Denise was referred to a psychiatrist. Slowly over a period of several months her startle reactions lessened. Her nightmares diminished in intensity and frequency. Her sexual relationship with her husband resumed, but remained less satisfactory with occasional feelings of aversion. After two months Denise was able to drive alone. Her psychiatrist believed she would be able to return to work for the next school year, but he thought it would be a very bad idea for her to return to school for the remainder of the present year. Denise believed and the psychiatrist recommended that, if possible, she should seek work in an integrated school rather than in an all-black school. Denise returned to teaching but continued to be insecure and anxious. Whenever she saw a man who reminded her of the attacker, she jumped. She had problems in relating to her husband sexually and emotionally.

Fourteen months after the attack Denise's psychiatrist thought she had overcome the "traumatic neurosis" which had resulted from the rape. She continued to have an aversion to working in ghetto schools, but she did well in her teaching. She continued to have marital problems and started having gynecologic problems. Denise was assigned to a school that was not integrated and received high ratings there. Eighteen months later her therapist noted there were times when she was symptom-free. However, Denise was still afraid of being alone and had a panic reaction whenever she noticed a black man approaching.

Edna

Edna was a white divorcee, who had been working at an institution for young female delinquents for ten years when the institution was phased out. Edna had few choices available if she wanted to continue working for the state. She chose to work in a detention facility for young male delinquents. She was unhappy with the choice she had to make. She did not want to work with male delinquents. Also, she had to leave her home community and move to a more isolated community some 100 miles away. However, her previous job experience as a ballroom dancer and as a clerk did not prepare her for entrance into the employment market at the age of 46.

Several months after Edna arrived at the facility for males, a young black 19-year-old inmate tried to rape her. He had written notes telling Edna how much he loved her. At first the notes were anonymous; later, he signed them. She reported the young man to the authorities, but in spite of this, he managed to get on a work detail with her. Using the ruse that he had left an article of clothing behind, he knocked on the door. Although Edna knew she should not let him in, she did. He dragged her into a closet, kissed her, bit her on the neck, and choked her. She fought and screamed for what seemed like "forever." Finally there was a noise outside, and he released her for a moment. She rushed out of the closet and pushed a "panic button" which was available. Help soon came. Her attacker left and returned to his dormitory.

Following the attack Edna was taken to the hospital on the grounds. A doctor gave her some medication and sent her home. She wanted to return to work to demonstrate that she was not afraid, as there had been some resistance to taking women into a men's facility. However, the physician would not allow her return to work, and insisted she go home. She stayed in bed all day. The next day she went to work, but found that she was too jumpy. When a maintenance man entered the room from behind her, she "jumped a foot" and screamed. At that point she asked for a few days off. Edna became terrified when she realized that the inmate who had attacked her could have killed her.

Shortly after the attack Edna returned to her home community to be with her friends and family. She was anxious, depressed, and angry. She had no job and could no longer work in the only system in which she had seniority and training. Shortly after Edna returned home, her youngest son had a nearly fatal automobile accident in a distant state. Edna visited him daily and provided him with assistance. Finally when he was able to travel, she brought her son home and spent her time nursing him and helping him readjust. Then Edna decided to learn some new skills. She began attending an adult educational center to become a medical assistant. However, Edna had been unable to mobilize enough energy to accomplish her goals.

Edna becomes depressed and feels she is stagnating. She had savings, but used all the money to support herself since leaving work and to travel to where her son was hospitalized. Edna is angry at the man who attacked her. She is resentful of the state's inconsiderate and unsupportive treatment. She has lost weight, drinks much more than formerly, and has trouble sleeping. Edna has no interest in sexual function. She likes to talk and dance with men, but is "turned off" sexually. For Edna the attack at work made her realize that the work was dangerous and that she risked not only sexual attack but also possible death. In spite of her wish to keep the job and in spite of an urge to prove that a woman could work in a male detention facility, Edna decided that the risk was no longer worthwhile and left, giving up many benefits. Two years after the attack Edna still has many of the symptoms described above, is in psychological pain, and has difficulty in relating to men, a condition which she had never had before.

Differences between Nonwork and Work-related Rape

One might speculate that the effect of rape at work might be different from that of rape in a nonwork setting, such as in a public park, on the streets, or even in the victim's home. Each of us compartmentalizes the world into safe and unsafe zones. There is a difference in the impact of an attack on one's person if one is walking through a dangerous section of town or participating in some activity in which violence is expected and if one is attacked on what one considers to be safe ground. Home is safe ground. Work is safe ground. Each of us is outraged when our safe ground is invaded. The author has seen persons who were almost psychotic following the discovery that their homes had been burglarized. Some became depressed; some went into a state of shock, because they discovered that what seemed to be "absolutely safe" was vulnerable.

This reaction increases the intensity of the reaction to rape at work. Work was a safe place. One did not go to work fearing attack. The victim did not take the special precautions nor was she as vigilant as she would have been in a high-risk setting. She felt deceived and tricked, and may begin to distrust her own judgment generally.

There is, however, less self-blame for the victim involved in work-related rape. A woman raped on the street may be angry with herself. She may condemn herself for having walked in a certain neighborhood at a certain time or for having been friendly with a certain person. The woman raped at work is engaged in a necessary activity, on what she had reasonably thought was safe ground, and has less tendency to blame herself for any aspect of the attack. The employer can be blamed for an unsafe environment and for not providing the employee with adequate means of protection.

Another major difference between cases of rape at work and of rape occurring elsewhere is the difficulty that women who were raped at work have in avoiding the site of the assault. Most jobs require a repetition of routine activities in fixed locations. It is almost impossible for the raped worker to continue on the job and to avoid the places and activities which made her vulnerable to attack in the first place. She must not only return to the same place, but must also work with people who may know about the assault. She will encounter co-workers who recall the incident, who are curious about it, who possibly blame her, and whose questions make it difficult for her to repress the unpleasant event. The only way the victim could avoid all such reminders of the traumatic event would be to leave work, and either remain unemployed or find another job.

Postrape Symptoms and Reactions

The postrape symptoms in these five cases were similar to the rape trauma syndrome described by Burgess and Holmstrom (1974). There was profound anxiety at not having dealt successfully with the rape situation and profound fear of being alone or of having someone behind them. In both groups of women, nightmares persisted at least six months after the attack. Also, there were psychophysiologic symptoms and hypochondriacal symptoms, the latter focusing in the rectal-genital area.

There seemed to be no guarantee of resolution for the victims. Not even the younger women could avoid the effects of the experience. All the victims were constantly reminded of their experiences by the inability to continue in their jobs. One year after the rape, four of the five victims were still not working or not working full time. Only one woman went back to her old job; she was the one who had psychotherapy. This woman expressed her financial plight. The temporary disability benefits she received did not replace the salary she lost. The other victims preferred a loss of salary and benefits to the alternative of returning to the place where they were raped.

The prerape problems of the victims help one understand their reactions to the rape. Four of the five workers were unhappy in their jobs and in their nonworking lives and relationships prior to the rape; the experience was less devastating for these victims. The woman most content with her home and work life prior to the rape was the one whose symptoms persisted longest and were the most severe. It was almost as if the rape incident had shattered her very satisfactory existence, and had converted what seemed perfect to something that was irrevocably imperfect.

Comparison with Reactions to Other Attacks

One might compare rape in work situations to other traumas such as falls, whiplashes in automotive accidents, or muggings. The reactions to rape are most similar to those following a mugging. Twelve cases of muggings at work were reviewed and compared with those of the rape victims.

All those mugged were male. Among them were an insurance salesman, an insurance adjuster, a bus driver, a high school teacher, an apartment manager, and a bank clerk. The men had all the symptoms evidenced by the rape victims. They did not return to their jobs. They had fears of being alone and walking on city streets. They always drove with their car doors locked. Several of the men even purchased guns or dogs. All had nightmares, avoided people, and had prolonged periods of sexual dysfunction. They became aware of fears seemingly unrelated to their mugging—namely, fear of heights or confining spaces or of riding as a passenger in a car.

One explanation of these reactions is that people live statistically, that each person programs himself or herself for a given set of probabilities based on predictions about the future. Changes in these programs are reflected in mood, in the shift to depression with its negative predictions or to mania with its irrepressible positive predictions. When a rape or mugging falls outside the set of events for which the individual is programed, the entire program is brought into doubt. Is anything in the set then valid? Is there anything bad from which one is safe? Does not one have to guard against every possible danger—danger of bodily attack by a rapist or mugger or of attack from disease, infection, or cancer?

Certain traumas engender what Keiser (1968) has called aphanasis, the fear of annihilation. In the rear-end accident, that fear is experienced for several seconds—from the moment of impact until the victim discovers that he or she is alive. A mugging continues for several more seconds, but seldom for more than a minute. The victim suffers the fear of annihilation during the attack and until he or she is reassured that the attackers are gone and that her/his wounds, if any, are not fatal or maiming.

The rape victim suffers for a much longer period. Although we have only rough estimates of the time from attack until departure of the rapist, the range extended from an estimate of 2 to 5 minutes. The reader may consider 2 to 5 minutes a short period of time, but to the person who is faced not only with sexual attack but also with the prospect of being beaten or even killed, that brief period is experienced as eternity. An experience of this kind can change the course of one's life and one's relationships with others and sensitize one to anything that might carry a similar threat.

Helping the Rape Victim

Helping the rape victim requires an understanding of the difference between postrape symptoms and reactions and those accompanying other kinds of trauma. Most persons cannot empathize with the "near miss," with the plight of the person who comes close to death and, although remaining physically unscathed or unharmed, is severely traumatized emotionally. All of us can feel for the person who loses a loved one; we can anticipate suffering such a loss or have already experienced it. All of us can empathize with pain. We have experienced pain; we know how excruciating it can be. We react to someone who is suffering from physical pain by helping in whatever way we can and by giving empathy, a facial expression or a shudder. Only the person who has suffered a psychic trauma such as rape or mugging can empathize with the prolonged reaction that the victim has.

In most instances, the rape victim is not damaged physically. The physical trauma is minor. Helping persons tend to urge denial and suppression of the memories. They would like to help the victim feel that it had never happened, to help her feel as she did before it happened. The helping person's intentions are good but psychologically unsound. Those women who are able to repress and deny the impact of the rape will not need therapeutic assistance; those who cannot repress and deny cannot forget.

In order to help rape victims, one must accept their reactions as being the "objective ones" in the sense that they are the ones who are really experiencing the reactions. It is the helping person who is having "subjective reactions" and who must subordinate those reactions to those of the victim. The therapist should not assume that the source of the victim's troubles is really something else, something deeper, something earlier. Rather, the attacks themselves should be given causal credibility. The victims must be helped to integrate the experience, to find a place for it in their lives, to deal with their feelings about it, and to restructure their defenses so that they can continue coping with life.

Recognizing this, the helping person must permit the rape victim to do more than ventilate. She must be permitted to ruminate. Victims of rape do not dispose of or deal with their feelings and their reactions by talking about them once. Obviously there is a difference in how individual victims of any trauma react. There is no evidence that these reactions can be predicted. Therefore, we must take our cue from the victim herself. We should not assume that the woman who copes with the rape and doesn't seem overwhelmed or violently angry really feels more than she is reporting, and we should not urge her to say more. On the other hand, we should not dismiss as excessive another's seemingly catastrophic reaction. The effects of being stuck in an elevator or caught in a fire or raped cannot be predicted, and the victim must be given as much time as she needs to work through the effects of that trauma to the maximum degree possible.

The victim of rape in the work setting may need vocational counseling in order to help her plot a future vocational course. Therapists and employers need to consider the advisability of having the rape victim go back to the job on which she was raped. Persons who are attacked on the job never again see their jobs in exactly the same way as they saw them before the attack. The worker starts thinking and feeling that his or her job is truly dangerous. The intellectual awareness of danger, the probabilistic awareness of danger, is converted into the emotional awareness of danger which is fear. Some people can never go back to their former jobs simply because they have discovered that those jobs are truly dangerous, and they choose not to risk the loss of life or the destruction of physical integrity again. Some workers have gone through profoundly life-threatening episodes and gone back to work the next day seemingly without any adverse effects. Others tried to return and perspired and itched, were anxious, had headaches, and spent their time worrying about whether they would survive the day.

Counselors of all sorts might take a counterphobic approach and urge the victim to return to work. When an attack produces a traumatic neurosis, a counterphobic approach—facing the fear—does nothing but exacerbate the symptoms. It eliminates that period of respite during which the victim can consider and reconsider the attack and her reactions to it. Instead of facilitating a resolution of the neurosis, it overloads the patient's cognitive and affective systems and disturbs her even further.

For this reason, employers, relatives, and counselors should make every effort to help the victim return to work in a job which she does not consider to be dangerous. Although there are no jobs in which one is free from the risk of being attacked, or in which a woman is free from the danger of being raped, there are jobs in which the worker *feels* that the risk is lower. Victims should be helped into such positions at least during the early months after an attack. As fears subside, and if motivating factors are present, the traumatized worker might again try to return to a job as it appears more manageable in the victim's mind. If the prospect of returning to that place of work is intolerable, then the services and support of vocational rehabilitation agencies are as necessary and as justified for the rape victim as they are for the victims of any other industrial injury and impairment.

Helping the Victim and Others Involved

In addition to helping the raped woman, the psychotherapist must also assist the woman's husband, her family, and her employer to reintegrate the victim into their living systems. Often the victim herself believes she is unlucky. Family members and employers may have the same feeling. The notion of being unlucky has special connotations. The unlucky person feels she is marked. Others also fear that her ill fortune, her unluckiness, might be contagious. The unluckiness might "rub off"; others might catch it. Consequently, one would do well to stay away from the unlucky person. In addition to dealing with the employer's mistrust in the victim, one must help her/him understand how profoundly the victim has been traumatized and how necessary it is to restructure her employment situation, if only temporarily, in order that she feel more comfortable, better protected, and safer.

If the rape victim is married, the husband must be helped too. When the rape victim is attacked, the husband feels raped. It is he, more than the victim herself, who feels his partner has been damaged or spoiled. The wife is no longer a "virgin" in that she has been ravaged by an undesirable person. The husband usually reacts in one of two ways. Either he avoids sexual contact with his wife, or he tries to force it almost contraphobically. The former makes the wife feel undesirable and unwanted. The latter makes her feel that she is being used and has lost her autonomy.

Conjoint sessions with the victims of trauma can be most helpful. Often the therapist will be surprised to learn that in spite of the fact that time has passed and the victim has had ample opportunity to talk to the spouse, in fact the victim has had very little contact. The spouse learns more about the victim's feelings in one hour of conjoint therapy than he had learned in all the previous weeks and months. The conjoint therapy has the dual effect of humanizing both the victim and the spouse. The spouse starts seeing the victim not as a victim but as a human being who is reacting in ways that are understandable. The victim comes to see the spouse as a person who has fears of his own, who has been traumatized too, and who is trying to cope with the effects of what he considers to be an invasion of himself. As with so many family problems, each spouse feels that the other does not know the pain and dissatisfaction that he or she suffers. A conjoint session is no panacea for the problems of the traumatized victim, but it does alleviate misunderstanding between the spouses and enables them to recognize that they may have come to treat each other in a dehumanizing way.

Employers are not disturbed by the fact that their female employees have been spoiled or contaminated, but they are concerned that this employee might make for further "trouble." Employers want peace. They do not want workers who disturb the tranquility of the organization in any way, not even as a result of bad luck. Employers whose workers are raped would like to have the victim disappear and to forget about this complication of the smooth functioning of their organizations. Most often no one can stop them from doing this. However, insurance carriers and company physicians who have access to employers can help them to understand that they can reemploy the rape victim and that there is no evidence she will be a less competent employee or that she will in any way disturb the workings of their organizations.

Prevention of Rape at Work

One reaction of those raped at work is anger at the employer for not providing a safer environment. Unfortunately, the economic cost of making a work setting safe from all human hazards makes such precautions impractical. Employers can place abrasives on floors so that workers will not be as likely to slip and metal screens can be placed around dangerous machines, but hiring enough security guards to prevent attack makes the cost of the service prohibitive. We must assume that there are certain risks to every job and that these risks should be minimized to the extent that it is economically feasible. In considering rape and assault prevention, we must remember that certain preventive measures would change the relationships between clients and helping persons. For example, a welfare office which had many security police and in which each client was checked for weapons, as is done before one boards an airplane, would create an atmosphere which would make any relationship between client and welfare worker very difficult at best. Similarly, police in the classroom or barriers between female correctional personnel and male inmates would interfere with the very relationship that such persons are trying to establish with the students or the inmates.

This does not mean that we should encourage workers in potentially dangerous situations to ignore the risk. The hazards of the job, including the possibility of a physical or sexual assault, should be discussed. Conditions and attitudes which may encourage assault should be examined. Precautions that might minimize the possibility of an attack should be described and taken, and employees should be alerted when others notice they are becoming careless.

In order to evaluate the risk of rape at work, rape must be recognized as part of a continuum of sexual harassment. At one end of the spectrum is teasing. It is common to all age levels and all social classes (Sperling, 1953; Bernard, 1972). It can be from male to female or vice versa. It is benign and mutually pleasurable. Healthy teasing is part of a sociocultural ritual for approaching a topic such as sex respectfully. The teasing is a recognition that sexual interaction is more than just the fulfillment of an appetite, but instead represents the beginning of a very complex, even when short-lived, relationship. The anthropological literature of almost every culture describes the forms of sexual teasing and its important function in the evolution of a relationship between a male and a female.

Successful and satisfactory teasing, whether about sex or about any other topic, requires sensitivity, skill, and deftness in the participants. If one or the other is clumsy, the interaction cannot reach a successful conclusion and is terminated either by separation or by an escalation of the teasing into harassment.

In contrast to teasing, harassment is not mutually satisfactory and is not enjoyable to all the persons engaged in it. Harassment is an interaction in which one person purposefully seeks to discomfort another person.

Sexual harassment is not as widespread as teasing. It has less widespread social approval, and almost any person asked would respond by saying that it was not kind or proper or tolerable. Disagreement might arise about the intention of the harasser: was he really harassing or was he only teasing?

The lightest forms of sexual harassment are the "little rapes" of which Medea and Thompson speak in their book *Against Rape*. These represent the invasion of females by males: invasion by suggestion, invasion by intimation, invasion by confronting the target with her helplessness. The woman who is the victim of the little rape knows that she can do nothing. By the time she calls the police, the aggressor either will be gone or will make a joke of his intentions and her reactions. If she engages in banter with him, there is a probability that the unpleasant experience will be prolonged. If she hits him on the head, she will be reacting with "unnecessary force."

Teasing occurs at work. Little rapes are frequent in work environments. Sexual extortion also occurs at work in the form of efforts to induce a female worker to prostitute herself, not for money but for work favors such as an easier, higher-status or higher-paying job. The author has examined several women who have filed claims against employers alleging and describing just such harassment.

A woman at work is in many ways a fixed target for all the forms of sexual harassment. If a woman joins a social group and finds the environment unpleasant, she can leave. If she goes to a bar and is harassed, she can depart. She cannot leave work or give up her job as easily. The woman at work is a "sitting duck" in the sense that in all probability she will return to her place of employment, and she will not raise much of a fuss about sexual harassment.

Rape itself is, as nearly as we can determine, a low-probability event in work situations. Rape marks not only the victim but also the attacker. There are very few males who are willing to be identified as rapists even if the charge is not proved. The rapists whom we describe were not coworkers or superiors. They were outsiders; in two instances they were inmates in penal institutions, and the victims were both older and in superior positions. In each of these two cases the rapist had a positive "transference" toward the woman. In one of the cases he had at first attempted teasing. This teasing continued although it was unpleasant for the woman. It continued after she asked him to stop and ultimately went on to become attempted rape. We must assume that in these cases the transference factor, the projections onto the superior older woman from a deprived, disturbed young male, established the setting for the rape. We do not, of course, know what was in the minds of these two young men. From having talked with others, we might assume that their fantasies of what the rape interaction would be like did not include violent force and violent resistance. In these cases, at least, one might assume that the fantasy of the rapist was that once the woman was faced with her helplessness she would submit and enjoy it.

Our attitudes toward sexual harassment, toward little rape, affect reactions to rape itself. If we accept rape as part of the continuum of sexual harassment, then in order to be outraged by rape we must be at least a little outraged by sexual harassment. Because we resist considering sexual harassment to be an outrage, we reduce the opprobrium we attach to rape.

A heartening change in attitudes is taking place. Women in some work organizations are redefining the rules for their interaction with their male co-workers. They are competing for the same jobs, and they insist on paying their own way. They are making a statement that they are not going to take anything from their male co-workers, not subordination, not material favors, and not sexual harassment. So far this change in attitudes affects co-workers most directly, and co-workers are not usually the ones who become rapists. But it is possible that this change in attitude will lead to a general societal change so that women will no longer be seen as objects to be teased, harassed, and even assaulted, but rather as equal members of society.

References

Bernard, J. *Sex Games: Communication between the Sexes*. Englewood Cliffs, N.J.: Prentice-Hall, 1968.

Brodsky, C. Antecedent sexual factors delaying recovery in compensation cases. *Journal of Occupational Medicine*, 1970, 12(8): 299-303.

_____. Compensation illness as a retirement channel. *Journal of the American Geriatrics Society*, 1971, 19(1): 51-60.

_____. Social psychiatric consequences of job incompetence. *Comprehensive Psychiatry*, 1971, 12(6).

Burgess, A., and Holmstrom, L. Rape trauma syndrome. *American Journal of Psychiatry*, 1974, 131(9):981-986.

Foxe, S. Sutherland, and Scherl, D. Patterns of response among victims of rape. *American Journal of Orthopsychiatry*, 1970, 40(3): 503-511.

Keiser, L. *The Traumatic Neurosis*. Philadelphia: J.B. Lippincott Co., 1968.

Medea, A., and Thompson, K. *Against Rape*. New York: Farrar, Straus and Giroux, 1974.

Sperling, S. On the psychodynamics of teasing. *American Psychoanalytic Association Journal*, 1953, 1:458-483.

Stellman, J., and Daum, S. *Work Is Dangerous to Your Health*. New York: Vintage Books, 1973.

5

Medical Treatment for the Victim: The Development of a Rape Treatment Center

Dorothy J. Hicks
and Charlotte R. Platt

When a group of feminists concerned with rape victims marched down the main street of Miami in 1971, the concept emerged of a rape treatment center in Dade County, Florida. Two years later in December 1973, the Metropolitan Commission, the governing board of the county, gave Jackson Memorial Hospital, the 1,200-bed county hospital and the teaching hospital for the University of Miami School of Medicine, a mandate to establish a treatment center for the victims of sexual assault and to have it operational by January 1974. On January 9, 1974, the Rape Treatment Center opened. The first patient was treated during the ribbon-cutting ceremony.

The need for the center was great. In 1973, 51,000 rapes were reported to the FBI. Law enforcement agencies estimate that at best 1 in 4 rapes is reported, and the figures may be as low as 1 in 10. The number of rapes in Dade County was increasing. In 1973, 370 cases of alleged rape were reported to the Dade County police departments. In 1974, the first year the center was open, 659 patients were treated.

The early meetings to organize the Rape Treatment Center involved members of the county's Rape Task Force, hospital administrators, representatives from the departments of gynecology and psychiatry, the psychiatrist in charge of the Crisis Intervention Program, and the director of nursing in the Emergency Room. The chiefs of the four police departments which conduct homicide investigations in the county also attended these meetings. These departments investigate the county's rape cases. General policies were established, and the cooperation of disciplines was assured. A 24-hour "rape hot line" was established.

Educational sessions were scheduled for personnel who would be involved directly with patient care. Not all police officers, not all hospital personnel, and not all people wearing white uniforms are sensitive to rape. To some members of the hospital staff this program only added another group of patients to the already heavy workload; an average of 500 patients were treated in the Emergency Room within a 24-hour period. Sensitivity sessions, under the direction of the psychiatrist in charge of the crisis intervention area, were attended by doctors, nurses, crisis workers, rape task force volunteers, police officers, and anyone else involved with the Rape Treatment Center and its patients. The nurses, in particular, were amazed when their lack of sensitivity to women and their problems in the area of sexual assault was uncovered. At the end of these sessions, those people who felt they could not cope with the rape victim and her problems were excluded from the treatment team.

Treatment Rationales and Activities

The program was designed to give comprehensive quality care to the victims of alleged sexual assault, both male and female, and includes psychological as well as physical treatment. (Males have been treated in the center, but the vast majority of patients are female.) The program serves the following functions: (1) provides the patient with immediate care including gynecologic, traumatic, psychiatric, and nursing; (2) provides the necessary assistance and encouragement in aiding the patient to speak to the proper law enforcement agency; (3) provides necessary care and appointments for long-range psychological treatment for not only the patient but the family or friend if necessary; (4) instructs and provides necessary follow-up for either private or clinical gynecologic care in 6 weeks to prevent pregnancy from this type of conception, and to be sure that any venereal disease has been controlled; (5) provides the patient/victim with the necessary care and information by a staff specially trained for this purpose.

Originally, the hub of the center was the Emergency Room; now it is a separate area. The center includes all the facilities needed to care for the victim of sexual assault: consultation room, examining room, conference room, laboratory, and offices. The area is separate from, but adjacent to, the Emergency Room. This proximity retains the capacity to treat any trauma involved as rapidly as indicated but gives the quiet, secluded atmosphere necessary for proper care of this patient/victim.

A "floating team" concept is used in the program. The team consists of an examining physician, a counselor from the crisis center, and a nurse from the Emergency Room staff. There is a panel of six physicians who have been trained to examine the patients and properly collect the evidence. They are gynecologists who are paid on a fee-for-service basis, not the "resident on call." The physician is expected to examine the patient within 45 minutes. If the doctor cannot respond immediately, the next physician on the roster is called. Once the center is notified that a victim of sexual assault is on the way to the hospital, the team is alerted.

Physican and Nurse Procedures

When the individual enters the hospital, she is no longer considered a "victim" but is referred to as a "patient." Physicians and nurses must protect the interests of the patient, of justice, and of themselves. Every instance of sexual abuse is a potential court case, and physicians should expect to be subpoenaed to justify their statements on the medical record. Whether rape or sexual molestation occurred is a legal matter for the court to decide and is *not* a medical diagnosis. Therefore, the physicians and nurses use the terms "alleged sexual assault."

During the hours the Crisis Intervention Center is open (8 A.M. to 12 midnight) the "hot-line" telephone is answered by the crisis workers. At other times it is answered by the charge nurse in the Emergency Room. Only persons who are trained to cope with any emotional problem of the caller are allowed to answer calls. The number is for the use of victims only. The police and ambulance drivers notify the center through the usual channels when they have a patient who needs treatment. The person handling calls: (1) provides initial supportive contact for the rape victim; (2) asks basic data questions and completes the telephone log sheet, including date and time of call, name of person calling if they will give it, nature of call, recommendation and/or referral of caller, and time spent on call; (3) encourages victim to come to the Emergency Room for treatment and gives information regarding services that will be provided; and (4) arranges transportation for victim by police if requested and available.

If the center is notified that a patient is coming to the hospital, a nurse meets her at the front door of the Emergency Room. Those patients who arrive alone are necessarily asked why they have come. Except in these instances the word "rape" is not used in the hospital. The term "M.E. Case" is used because the Medical Examiner's office previously handled these problems. Since M.E. cases can be of many types, there is no stigma.

When the patient is met by the nurse, she is taken into the consultation room of the center. Only minimal time is taken to begin a chart: name, address, birth date, and whether she has been a patient at the hospital are the only questions asked. These charts are not forwarded to the general record room but are kept in a locked file in the center office. The records, therefore, are confidential. The nurse stays with the patient until the counselor or physician arrives. As soon as the physician arrives, the patient is taken into the examining room.

Many times the alleged sexual abuse will have been the first sexual contact for the patient. In addition, the patient may have had no experience with gynecologic examination. Physicians carefully explain the procedure to be used in the gynecologic exam and are as considerate as possible. A child victim may or may not desire the family to be present during the exam. The physician asks the patient, when they are alone, if she prefers the family member be present or absent, and relays this information to the family.

The protocol for the physician's examination essentially follows the guidelines set by the American College of Obstetricians and Gynecologists, but it is tailored by the circumstances of the assault, the emotional condition of the patient, and the degree of trauma. Sometimes the portion of the examination related to the vaginal area is done when the patient is in the operating room under anesthesia being treated for injuries serious enough to require immediate surgical repair. Fortunately, the number of patients with severe trauma is few, but all the victims of sexual assault have psychological damage of varying degree.

The protection of the patient is an important duty of the physician and nurse. Psychosexual trauma must be recognized and minimized. Emotional support and sympathetic understanding of both the patient and family are very important. The family is given understanding and guidance. They are warned specifically against magnifying the situation. The patient's emotional reaction to sexual molestation is often far less damaging than that arising from the imposition of society's values upon the episode.

If at all possible, written consent (witnessed) is obtained for the following procedures: examination, collection of specimens, and photographs (in cases which include assault and battery).

The physician's history is brief but contains the facts pertinent to the assault. These facts include the time of the assault, the time of the last menstrual period, the time of the last sexual intercourse before the assault, whether the patient has douched or bathed since the attack, and the number of assailants. To some observers, the time of the last intercourse might seem irrelevant. However, if the patient was raped only a few hours after voluntary exposure, the presence of sperm may not be as significant, and the material must be typed in an effort to identify the source.

During the general examination any physical trauma, i.e., bruises, lacerations, foreign bodies, etc., are described accurately. Signs of external trauma are documented. The oral and anal as well as genital areas are examined when indicated. When appropriate, photographs are taken. If there was a struggle during the incident, scrapings are taken from under the patient's fingernails, are carefully placed in a clean envelope, and the envelope is sealed. Combings from the pubic hair area are treated in a similar manner. At times it is possible to recover pubic hair belonging to the assailant. The vulvar area is inspected for lacerations. The condition of the hymen is described. A Woods lamp is sometimes used to locate seminal fluid on the skin.

Before a bimanual pelvic examination is done, 2 cubic centimeters of saline solution are introduced into the vaginal vault. The resultant washings are recovered and placed in a sterile test tube. A culture for gonorrhea is taken from the cervical os and immediately planted on the chocolate agar slant in a carbon dioxide-filled Transgrow culture bottle. If indicated, a Pap test is done. Bimanual and rectal examinations are performed unless the patient objects. If there is bleeding and the area cannot be identified, the patient is taken to the operating room and the examination conducted under anesthesia. All injuries are repaired at this time. This is particularly true when the patient is a child. Forcing a pelvic examination on these patients would be tantamount to rape and should never be done under any circumstances.

The patient then chews a small square of clean cloth which provides a sample of the victim's saliva. The cloth is then placed in a clean box. The cloth is never handled by anyone except the patient and is checked by the crime laboratory for secretor substance. Two samples of venous blood are taken from the patient. One tube is sent for serological test for syphilis, and the other is given to the police officer. All specimens are properly labeled so that they are clearly identifiable as being from this patient/victim. They should be handed to the police. Care is taken so that the chain of evidence is not broken. The specimens are ultimately taken to the Metropolitan Crime Laboratory, the single laboratory that services all the police departments in Dade County.

After the examination is finished, the physician talks with the patient and discusses her possible exposure to venereal disease and pregnancy. Prophylactic treatment is offered. No patient is forced to take medication. The physician explains the situation, the possibilities, the short- and long-term effects of the therapy. The patient then makes the decision. If she accepts and is not allergic to penicillin, the drug of choice, she is given intramuscular Aqueous Benzanthine Penicillin G to protect against syphilis and Probobenemid and Ampicillin by mouth to protect against gonorrhea. If she is allergic to penicillin, the patient receives Spectinomycin by intramuscular injection. Since this will protect her from gonorrhea but not syphilis, she is urged to take Tetracycline by mouth for several days in addition to the Spectinomycin. The percentage of patients contracting venereal disease after sexual assault is low, but the patient should be offered protection.

If the danger of conception is present, the patient is offered DES (diethylstilbesterol) as a contraceptive. This is the "morning-after pill" approved by the Federal Drug Administration. DES is offered unless the patient is examined more than 72 hours after the exposure. After that time interval, DES is no longer an effective contraceptive. Tigan is given to combat any nausea that may occur as a result of the DES. If the physician suspects the patient may be pregnant, a pregnancy test is done before DES is given. Psychologically, prevention of pregnancy is a much better solution than abortion after the fact. If she accepts treatment, the patient must stay at the center for at least half an hour after being medicated to guard against any untoward reactions to the drugs.

Once the physican has completed the examination, she or he examines the vaginal washings for presence and activity of sperm and tests for acid phosphatase. The reports of the tests and the examination, as well as the evidence collected, are given directly to the police officer.

The medical record contains the patient's statement. It gives descriptions of the physician's procedure and findings. It also contains information as to what specimens were taken and to whom they were delivered. Because the medical record may be used in investigation of a case of rape or sexual molestation, and may become evidence in a court of law, full information should be given in it. All information should be exact and detailed to avoid any misinterpretation. Negative findings are as important as positive ones and may assist in the protection of an alleged assailant who has been falsely accused.

At this time, the counselor again becomes active. If necessary, sedatives or tranquilizers should be prescribed. She talks with the patient and stays with her as long as needed. The patient should be calmed and reassured. This may take several hours. Before leaving the patient, the counselor makes arrangements to contact the patient by telephone within 48 hours.

The patient is allowed to remain in the center as long as she wishes. Before leaving, she is given a printed sheet of instructions which explains the need for a physical examination 6 weeks after the attack. The examination may be performed by her own physician or by a physician at the center. The examinations suggested are a cervical culture for gonorrhea, a serological test for syphilis, and a pelvic examination for pregnancy. The importance of this examination is stressed.

Counselor Procedure

The main purpose of the counselor is to provide psychological support to the patient. They, she, or he elicit the history that the patient wishes to volunteer. When a victim of sexual assault arrives at the hospital, Crisis Intervention is notified. The first available trained staff member responds immediately and reports to the Rape Treatment Center. After reporting to the Emergency Room, the crisis staff member (1) assumes case management for the victim's psychological problem and provides immediate support; (2) accompanies the victim during all procedures including police questioning if the case is reported to police, at the request of the patient or if the counselor feels the support is necessary to the patient's welfare; (3) arranges to contact relatives and/or friends if the victim so desires; (4) contacts the parent(s) or guardian for nonadult victims; (5) counsels the victim's family and/or friends if they are present and advises them concerning the victim's psychological needs.

When Emergency Room procedures are completed, the crisis staff member assesses the case and discusses with the victim the availability of further psychological assistance. When circumstances warrant and the victim concurs, an appointment will be arranged for the victim in the Crisis Outpatient Clinic. The victim is given a normal crisis appointment referral slip and told which instructions on the slip (if any) need compliance. Appointments will be scheduled for the nearest working day without regard to the maximum appointment limit normally observed. These visits will now take place in the Rape Treatment Center instead of at Crisis Intervention.

The crisis staff member ensures that the victim has been given all information and has had all questions answered before the victim leaves. The victim is instructed to telephone the Rape Treatment Center if problems arise between the Emergency Room discharge and the Crisis Intervention Outpatient Clinic follow-up.

When the victim has left the Emergency Room, the crisis staff member will complete appropriate records on the case and see that the Crisis Intervention Outpatient Clinic is informed of all pertinent data.

Police Cooperation

Before the center was established, rape victims were not eligible for examination and treatment by the Medical Examiners unless they reported the assault to the police. The hospital has taken the position, and the police agree, that treatment can be given without the patient's reporting the case to the authorities. We urge the patient to report, but if she or he is adamant, an anonymous report is given to the police department in whose area the crime was committed. If the patient is reporting the case to the police, she is now taken back to the consultation room. The detectives are waiting for her there and continue their investigation. Dade County police officers have been cooperative and sympathetic to the problems of the rape victim. We have not had many of the problems with law enforcement described by others working in this field. Even in those cases in which the victim does not want to report the assault, the police will transport her to the hospital and to her home after the examination and counseling are completed. The police helped develop the hospital forms used for the reports. Two of the City of Miami detectives have written a series of instructions "How to Talk with Victims of Sexual Assault." These instructions are excellent and are provided to the officers and to the cadets at the police academy.

Conclusion

The services of the Rape Treatment Center were needed by the community; this has been proved. The attitude of the community, police, attorneys, and judges toward the problem of sexual assault is changing. Florida now has a Sexual Battery Law instead of the old rape law. In the new statute, the sexual background of the victim is no longer admissible in court. People in our area are finally beginning to realize that forcible rape is a violent crime which has more emphasis on aggression than sex. They also realize that the psychological damage to the victim is a serious complication that must be properly and sympathetically treated.

Present and Future Measures of Victimization in Forcible Rape

Lynn A. Curtis

"Let us sit on this log by the roadside," says I, "and forget the inhumanity and ribaldry of the poets. It is in the glorious columns of ascertained facts and legalized measures that beauty is to be found. . . ."

"Go on, Mr. Pratt," says Mrs. Sampson. "Them ideas is so original and soothing. I think statistics are just as lovely as they can be."

O. Henry
The Handbook of Hymen

One of the most positive functions of research is to provide objective, reliable measures by which the effects of action programs can be evaluated and around which theoretical understanding can be contoured. For many persons engaged in action against rape, the ultimate measure of success is reduction in the incidence of the crime. But even for those with other objectives—such as improving the treatment of rape victims—reliable and valid statistics on the incidence of rape and its variation from year to year are an important gauge by which the phenomenon is assessed. The purpose of this chapter is to review briefly the kinds of social statistical indicators of rape victimization that are presently available, as well as those which may be used in the future.

The traditional official measures have been reports by the police based on victims who contact them. These figures are published yearly in the FBI's *Uniform Crime Reports*. Criticism of police data is well known. Only a fraction of the rapes committed are reported, and there are many differences in recording objectivity and crime classification among different police departments.

The variability among police departments in reporting is nicely illustrated by Chappell, et al., who examined the forcible rape reports from two of the seventeen cities in a study the present author conducted for the National Violence Commission. The Boston reports were terse, formal, laconic, and vague about what happened. They were pressed into a seemingly preordained formula. But the Los Angeles reports were richer in detail, tending "to be in the nature of Dostoevskian endeavors, with a goodly amount of Mickey Spillane added in . . . Bras, capris, and other garments are often ripped asunder . . . and the attack is apparently carried on with a fair bit of gusto." It was also "patently obvious that what each department regards as the kind of case to be classified as forcible rape and forwarded to the *Uniform Crime Reports* for tabulation as such is far from equivalent."[1]

The question of bias in police data on rape is particularly volatile when one compares the races of offender and victim. For the seventeen cities as a whole in the National Violence Commission study, we found that 60 percent of the reported rapes where an arrest was made were by blacks on blacks, 30 percent by whites on whites, 10 percent by blacks on whites, and a negligible percent by whites on blacks. The proportion of rapes by blacks on whites was higher in cases where no arrest was made.[2]

In a follow-up to the 1967 survey, more recent figures on race of offender by race of victim have been collected from police departments with available data. This allows for trend comparisons over time. To the extent that there was any consistency in the reported trends, it was found in rape by blacks on whites. In most cities which sent data, there was an increase in the relative percentage of reported rape by blacks on whites. When there was an increase, it ranged from slight to dramatic. For the most part, the exceptions to this trend were instances where there was little change in the relative black-white percentage rather than a substantial decrease in the proportion (Curtis, 1974).

These conclusions should be treated with extreme caution. Some of the increases were insignificant in any statistical sense. The sample sizes were low in certain instances, and the data were from only a limited number of cities. Often an upward trend was based on only two discrete data points. Some of the changes may have been due to variations in victim reporting to police as well as police recording and disclosure to the public. However, until the more refined statistics that are urgently needed become available, the considerable uniformity of the reported black-white increase across a number of cities provides some reason for attaching significance to the pattern, at least in certain places.

The reported statistics on rape may raise the contention that American police have given new meaning to Claude Rains' classic order at the end of *Casablanca—* by rounding up blacks as the usual suspects. Yet available evidence from reputable scholars—for example, Black (1971), Skolnick (1966), Tiffany, McIntyre, and Rotenberg (1967)—does not necessarily underscore the assertion of racial discrimination by police in making arrests and sometimes dismisses the significance of the issue.

However, the negligible percent of reported rapes by whites on blacks undoubtedly reflects police reporting bias. White males have long experienced and imposed nearly institutionalized sexual access to nonwhite women. Black autobiographers living in the nineteenth-century American South testify that, "often through 'gifts,' but usually through force, white overseers and planters obtained the sexual favors of black women. Generally speaking, the women were literally forced to offer themselves 'willingly' and receive a trinket for their compliance rather than a flogging for their refusal and resistance" (Blassingame, 1972, pp. 82-83).

There are no objective twentieth-century data on the exploitation of black women by white men, but descriptive accounts and participant observations are not difficult to find. Access to domestic house servants illustrates a continuity with the slave experience. Another institution providing ample opportunity for white-black rape is the police. Here is a black Chicago streetwalker of the 1930s telling her pimp about providing services demanded by two white policemen to avoid being booked:[3]

"Blondie" pushed my head down to his lap. Then I got on the back seat with him. That freak bastard, Max, turned around and kept his flashlight on us the whole time. I made "Blondie" holler. I finished with "Blondie." Max got back there with me. For a half hour he called me filthy names. He punched me. I'm sure sore all over. "Blondie" begged him to stop. My ass feels like he split something back there. I had a rough time.

Here is a chronicler of the 1970s visiting a friend in Harlem and watching two white policemen entering the apartment of a recently jailed man who had left behind a young daughter (Guy, 1972, pp. 74, 80).

Neighbors were standing at windows and stoops all around looking toward that building. Wasn't anyone going to do something? "Look," (the friend) said. "Those cats leave their cars and hitch up that big gun bulge on their hips. They come out and hitch that bulge again before they get in their cars. They know as long as they hitch that bulge they got us."

With whites in control of the institutions, there are good reasons why a black woman would not report. Thus, in one study an informant disclosed that "no black woman would report being raped by a white man to the police in Oakland. They might report it to the Panthers, but never to the police" (Agopian et al., 1974, p. 15). It is a near certainty, then, that the negligible reported white-black rape rate would rise if all rapes were reported to the police.

As an alternative to crime statistics filtered through the police and the criminal justice system generally, there has been a dramatic development of community victimization surveys over the last ten years. Respondents drawn randomly from the general public are asked in personal household interviews to list any crimes which may have been committed on them. Rates of victimization can then be projected from the sample population to the general population. The outcome is an estimate of the "true" incidence of crime, which can be compared to the reported incidence.

In terms of scientific reliability, validity, and objectivity, two victimization studies stand out. The first, conducted by Ennis and the National Opinion Research Corporation, is based on 10,000 interviews in all parts of the United States for the year 1966. It was estimated that 3 to 4 rapes are actually committed for every rape reported to the police (Ennis, 1967).

The second survey, a National Crime Panel study jointly undertaken by the Law Enforcement Assistance Administration (LEAA) and the Bureau of the

Census, is much more ambitious. Unlike the one-shot Ennis study, this is a continuous effort costing $10 million per year in which close to a half million Americans will be interviewed annually. Thus, a survey sample approach to indicators of crime which avoids the contamination of criminal justice institutions is now being applied yearly, just as surveys of the population have long been used to estimate unemployment figures which bypass the potentially biased reports from industry, unions, and welfare agencies (Burnham, 1974).

Preliminary figures from the LEAA-Census survey in eight large cities for 1973 estimate that 2.1 rapes are committed for every rape reported to the police. This is lower than the estimate by Ennis for 1966. It is difficult to determine the extent to which the discrepancy reflects such disparate factors as a real change in incidence over time, an increase in reporting by women, a sampling concentration on cities rather than the entire rural-urban continuum, and a change in methodology. In 1973 this estimated ratio of true to reported crime for rape (2.1 to 1) was lower than for robbery (2.3 to 1) and burglary (2.7 to 1) but higher than for auto theft (1 to 1) (Burnham, 1974).

Informed research and action on rape should place more reliance on these indicators than on any other source. Yet this is often not done, particularly in the feminist literature. For example, Medea and Thompson assert that ten rapes may be committed for every one reported. Lear writes of police estimates "that at least four out of five victims, and probably more, stay silent" and concludes that "what is important is that rape is the *least reported* of all crimes" (original emphasis) (Medea and Thompson, 1974, p. 4; Lear, 1974, p. 43). In each case, these claims are made without any supporting citation. Ratios of 5 to 1 or 10 to 1 may well apply to certain places. However, until better data become available, the more scientifically accurate National Crime Panel figures ought to be used, and the newly fashionable assumption that rape is always the least reported of the major violent crimes cannot necessarily be made.

The LEAA-Census National Crime Panel study and many other studies of rape victims are asking women who did not report why this was so. In a New York City study, women who *did* report rape were asked why they did so and for what reasons they might not have reported (Cottell, 1973). Such information can be useful in reforming the police response to rape—for example, through publicity campaigns encouraging women to contact rape crisis centers or female-staffed police units. In turn, these reforms promise to increase the rate of reporting to police and so decrease the "gap" between the reported police rape rate and the estimated rate calculated from victimization surveys. More systematic—though, of course, discreet—use of information on reporting from women who call rape crisis centers might also be used to this end.

The LEAA-Census National Crime Panel Study has significantly expanded the recorded universe of behavior which can be labeled "forcible rape," yet victimization surveys still have many shortcomings. Concentration on the victim misses much valuable information on the criminal event, yields very little on the offender, and depends on the unsubstantiated testimony of the voluntary respondent.

One useful, albeit expensive, way of substantiating interview data is a "reverse records check," in which disclosures from the survey are correlated with information on the same events from other sources. Thus, known rape victims from the files of the San Jose, California, police have been interviewed, ostensibly as part of a general crime survey (LEAA, 1972). Two-thirds of the known victims reported to the interviewers that they recently had been raped. This figure was higher than in assault (where only half of the known assault victims reported being assaulted) and thus again suggests that rape is not necessarily always beset with more reporting problems than any other serious crime. Nonetheless, the reverse records check shows that, even when they report to the police, rape victims often will not disclose the incident to a survey interviewer. If only two-thirds of those rape victims who *do* report to the police tell interviewers about the event, what proportion of victims who *don't* report to police will disclose this very personal and painful experience? One must presume the proportion to be even lower.

The true size of the statistical universe of rape victimization will never be known, but refinements in surveying methodology can continue to expand it.

Rape victims are often embarrassed to relate their experience to an interviewer and are suspicious of the motives of government-sponsored interviewers. Victims may not even define, or want to define, an act as rape. Validation studies have shown that such discrepancy between victim and official definitions is more frequent for violent than for property crimes. This is especially so if a prior relationship existed between victim and offender. The relationship may partially obscure the criminal aspect of the act in the mind of the survey respondent. Thus, 84 percent of the known victims who were raped by strangers disclosed the encounter to interviewers in the San Jose reverse records check, but only 54 percent of the known victims who were raped by nonstrangers (LEAA, 1972; Biderman, 1973). Compared to the victims of strangers, the victims of nonstrangers may have been more embarrassed to disclose the rape to interviewers and more reticent to implicate the offender—but some also might have perceived or preferred to remember the incident as not really involving behavior proscribed by law.

In response to these and many related problems, Biderman, among others, is developing an alternative question format from the one used by interviewers in the National Crime Panel. The question sequence begins by asking about injury rather than crime and very much follows the pattern in the United States National Health Survey. If the respondent has suffered any injuries over a recent specified period of time, the query moves to whether another person was involved. This establishes "an objective universe of pertinent incidents of actual interpersonal violence toward which subsequent questioning in the interview [is] directed for information on those more subjective, inferential, judgmental, and transactional matters involved in defining events as crimes" (Biderman, 1973). If another person was involved, follow-up probes address intent, culpability, whether the act was perceived by the victim as reportable to the police, whether in fact it was reported, and, if so, what the outcome was in the criminal justice system.

By using these less obtrusive methods and by avoiding the word "crime," the universe of known crime may be expanded. It is possible that such an injury orientation will direct the expansion more in the direction of nonsexual attacks, such as those labeled "aggravated assault" or "assault and battery" by the criminal justice system, rather than in the direction of sexual attacks, such as "forcible rape" or "statutory rape." Yet many rapes are correlated with injuries (see, for example, Curtis, 1974). It is possible that the victim not uncommonly chooses to frame the memory of these experiences in terms of physical or psychological injury, rather than as sexual "crime."

Instead of a questioning sequence oriented to injury, it might also be feasible to focus on sexual activity. After some initial questions on sexual experiences generally, a respondent might be asked if any episodes had been "forced" on her, again without any mention of the word "crime." In such an approach, contemporary victimization surveys would begin to merge with the early work of Kinsey (1953).

These innovations hopefully will work toward more accurate annual estimates of the real incidence of rape. Yet, beyond more sensitive rates per 100,000 population, a great deal remains hidden about the rape victimization process that, for the time being, must be uncovered through special studies.

One topic of crucial importance is "victim precipitation." To what degree, if any, is the victim responsible for bringing on the act? In the National Violence Commission study, we followed Amir in defining victim precipitation as a situation ending in forced intercourse where a woman first agreed to sexual relations, or clearly invited them verbally or through gestures, but then retracted before the act. Whereas Amir judged 19 percent of the rapes studied in Philadelphia from 1958 to 1960 to be precipitated by this definition, our figure was only 4 percent for the seventeen-city aggregate in 1967. (For Philadelphia alone, 2 percent of the rapes were judged to be precipitated in 1967 (Curtis, 1974; Amir, 1971).) Amir has used his findings to give the victim a considerable role in his theorizing on rape; by the same token, the National Violence Commission findings have led us to place much more singular, conceptual emphasis on the offender (Curtis, 1975; Amir, 1971).

A host of definitional, conceptual, methodological, and empirical questions must be answered to resolve this controversy. Elsewhere (Curtis, 1974) we have suggested that future research on victim precipitation should avoid police reports and other institutional filters. Instead, the need is for detailed clinical interviewing and projective testing of incoming victims and offenders on a scale large enough to retain a significant and stratified sample. Whenever possible, the developmental history of any prior relationship between offender and victim should be reconstructed from accounts by the participants as well as by significant others. Teams of researchers with different personal attributes should be used for interviewing. Will, for example, conclusions by investigators of the same race and sex of the offender or victim be greatly different from what is now mainly viewed through the eyes of white male scholars?

Eventually, such special studies of victim precipitation and other important topics (such as the very ill-defined process by which encounters with nonstrangers in social or quasi-social circumstances escalate into reports of rape) may crystallize concepts and reliable question sequences which can be added to annual victimization studies. Such information is not only useful to the theorist, but also helps guide policy. For example, if, as now seems the case, victim precipitation is more applicable to homicide and assault than to rape (Curtis, 1974), caveats in victim compensation schemes for withholding funds as a function of victim culpability will need to be structured with this disparity in mind.

Whether from special studies or annual surveys, measures which uncover more and more of the rape experience, quantitatively and qualitatively, will serve the action interests of feminists and criminal justice practitioners. Further, they will contribute to the new movements for objective social indicators in the United States and for the study of "victimology" as an integral part of criminology.

Notes

1. Chappell et al. (1972). For a broader critical review of police statistics, see Mulvihill and Tumin with Curtis (1969).

2. Nonwhites other than blacks were eliminated from these figures. See Curtis (1974).

3. Iceberg Slim (1969, p. 177). Of course, white prostitutes are not immune from such situations; yet a white woman going into prostitution may have a better chance than a black woman of becoming a call girl or otherwise working in a way to avoid the greater abuse encountered on the street.

References

Agopian, M., Chappell, D., and Geis, G. Interracial forcible rape in a North American city. In I. Drapkin and E. Viano (Eds.), *Victimology.* Lexington, Mass.: Lexington Books, 1974, pp. 93-102.

Amir, M. *Patterns in Forcible Rape.* Chicago: University of Chicago Press, 1971.

Biderman, A. "When Does Interpersonal Violence Become Crime?—Theory and Methods for Statistical Surveys." Paper prepared for a meeting on Access to

Law, Research Committee on the Sociology of Law, International Sociological Association, Girton College, Cambridge, England, September 25-28, 1973.

Black, D. The social organization of arrest. *Stanford Law Review*, 1971, 23: 1087-1111.

Blassingame, J. *The Slave Community*. London: Oxford University Press, 1972.

Burnham, D. Federal surveys to gauge crime levels in big cities. *New York Times*, 27 January 1974, p. 1.

Chappell, D., Geis, G., Schafer, S., and Siegel, L. Forcible rape: A comparative study of offenses known to the police in Boston and Los Angeles. In L. Curtis, "Criminal Violence: Inquiries into National Patterns and Behavior." Ph.D. dissertation, University of Pennsylvania, 1972.

Cottell, L. New York Police rape project. Proposal submitted to the Police Foundation, Washington, D.C., February 1973.

Curtis, L. *Criminal Violence: National Patterns and Behavior*. Lexington, Mass.: Lexington Books, 1974.

_____. *Violence Race and Culture*. Lexington, Mass.: Lexington Books, 1975.

Ennis, P. *Criminal Victimization in the United States: A Report of a National Survey*. Field Surveys II, President's Commission on Law Enforcement and Administration of Justice. Washington, D.C., February 1967.

Guy, R. Black perspective on Harlem's state of mind. *New York Times Magazine*, 10 April 1972, 74-80.

Iceberg Slim. *Pimp: The Story of My Life*. Los Angeles: Holloway House, 1969.

Kinsey, A., Pomeroy, W., Martin, C., and Gebhard, P. *Sexual Behavior in the Human Female*. Philadelphia: Saunders, 1953.

Law Enforcement Assistance Administration. San Jose Methods Test of known crime victims. Statistics Technical Report No. 1. National Institute of Law Enforcement and Criminal Justice, Statistics Division. Washington, D.C.: LEAA-NILECJ Publication STA-1, June 1972.

Lear, M. The American way of rape. *Viva*, November 1974, 43.

Medea, A. and Thompson, K. *Against Rape*. New York: Farrar, Straus and Giroux, 1974.

Mulvihill, D., and Tumin, M., with Curtis, L. *Crimes of Violence*. Task Force Report on Individual Acts of Violence, National Commission on the Causes and Prevention of Violence. Washington, D.C.: Government Printing Office, 1969.

Skolnick, J. *Justice without Trial*. New York: John Wiley & Sons, 1966.

Smith, C.A. (Ed.). *Selected Stories from O. Henry*. Garden City, N.Y.: Doubleday, Doran, and Co., 1933.

Tiffany, L., McIntyre, D., and Rotenberg, D. *Detection of Crime*. Boston: Little, Brown and Co., 1967.

7 History of Women's Movement in Changing Attitudes, Laws, and Treatment toward Rape Victims

Mary Ann Largen

During the period of 1967 to 1972, the rate of forcible rape in the United States increased 62 percent. During that same period of time, women began meeting in homes and apartments across the country to participate in group discussions called consciousness-raising sessions. It was at these consciousness-raising sessions that the issue of rape was loudly voiced in the women's movement. As women at these sessions discussed the problems of being female, there was an astonishing frequency of descriptions of being raped. In some groups more than half the women had been sexually assaulted, as either an adult or a child; the majority had never told anyone before.

Finally, in 1971 the New York Radical Feminists sponsored a Speak Out On Rape, at which some of these victims spoke out publicly for the first time. The stories they told of verbal abuse and insensitive treatment by police, doctors, lawyers, and the courts were the same stories still often told by victims today. The isolation and fear were understood by the women present. In 1971 it was quite brave and bold to speak publicly, as the publicity generated by these disclosures was often sensationalized.

Among women of all ages and occupations, however, there was a growing awareness that rape was far from an isolated act among certain groups and that the continued threat of this danger had restricted their very life-styles from childhood into the adult years.

Small protest groups began forming throughout the country, usually in wake of a rape or a series of rapes in local communities. Organized around the principle that rape is not an isolated act of an aberrant individual, but a crime against women encouraged by a sexist society, young and old, black and white banded together in determination to assist the victims and each other. It was here that the formal war against rape was born, with many groups taking the name Women Against Rape—WAR.

Although this movement started in the large cities and university towns where the more mobile life-styles of women made them a more visible target for rapists, many suburban and rural women viewed the 1972 establishment of crisis centers in Los Angeles, Washington, D.C., and Ann Arbor as models on which they, too, could develop a rape assistance and prevention program in their communities.

The initial purpose of rape crisis centers, staffed in part by victims themselves, was to provide empathetic support for rape victims by either hotline counseling or escort services. In hospitals, police stations, and courts the staffers served, in effect, as a buffer between the victim and the negative experiences she encountered there. The philosophy of the original crisis centers was "I do for you. You do for others." In addition to offering alternatives to women, centers sought to assist rape victims in regaining the self-determination denied them by their assailant and often by the very institutions which were supposed to aid them.

During the past two years many centers have been able to increase their services by providing medical, legal, and psychiatric referrals; group counseling sessions for both the victim and her family; and self-defense workshops open to the public at large. Hundreds of centers now exist from coast to coast providing either limited hotline and referral services or the full services of support, counseling, prevention, and public education programs.

In the beginning, communicating the center's existence to women in the community was difficult. The activities of these groups were mainly reported by the underground press and a few feminist writers. Although Germaine Greer had scored a first on network television in 1971 when she interviewed a rape victim on ABC TV, historically rape had been viewed as a taboo subject by the "establishment" press. By 1972, however, some journalists and commentators were beginning to address the issue in varying degrees.

In the early 1970s, members of the National Organization for Women had been working in coalition with other feminist groups on the issue of rape. Approximately 15 local chapters had actively involved themselves as an organization. By 1973 one author expressed, "Like the women's movement itself, it was an idea whose time had come." In February of that year, the Sixth Annual National Conference of the National Organization for Women (NOW), meeting in Washington, D.C., voted by acclamation to establish a National Task Force on Rape—the only resolution passed by acclamation of the conference body.

During the following year, the number of chapters actively involved in the issue grew from 15 to 85. By the end of the second year, the number grew to over 200 chapters from Maine to Hawaii. The special problems of rural areas were represented as well. Originally centered in the large urban areas, activity spread to isolated regions in the Northwest and small, conservative regions in the Deep South.

As the number of organized women's groups has grown in strength and number of members, public awareness of rape and the surrounding issues has also grown. Governors' and mayors' task forces on rape have been established in response to the concerns of women. Many community institutions are beginning to rethink the desirability of their own existing procedures and training programs and to experiment with innovations. Working with women's groups, these communities are experimenting with such programs as assigning all women officers to rape cases and establishing special hospital units for the treatment of rape victims. Though such projects are relatively few in number at the present time, they will encourage other areas to take like action. State legislatures are beginning to take action on the revision of their rape laws, and federal monies are being spent on limited rape research and action programs. Public education programs in the form of rape conferences, workshops, and symposia are being conducted nationwide by women's groups, universities, and community and professional groups.

In many respects, the goals of the women's antirape movement are slowly being met. In the area of legislation, it is clear that the women's movement is providing the impetus for rape law reform. The charges of "raped by the courts" emanate from the existing criminal laws which, unlike those in other crimes, often require victims to furnish corroborating evidence of their victimization to a degree frequently impossible to obtain. Likewise, rules of evidence which permit the past personal life of the victim to become the central issue in the trial, rather than the commission of a criminal act, pose unwarranted invasion of the victim's right of privacy and lead to an unprecedented number of acquitted or dismissed criminal charges. The prevalent legal definition of rape as vaginal penetration alone reinforces societal misconceptions about the crime and denies equal protection under the law to victims, both female and male, subjected to other types of sexual assault.

While these are probably the major inequities in rape laws, they are only a portion of the overall problems. Women's groups have been lobbying and conducting public education campaigns about rape nationally. They have been joined by a growing number of supporters from within the community at large and the judicial system itself. Partial rape law reform measures have been undertaken in numerous states. Due to the organized efforts of women in Michigan, that state enacted in 1974 an almost total rape law reform—the first one on record.

Public education in terms of news coverage of women's activities has improved to the point of being an invaluable assistance. In the beginning, as mentioned earlier, coverage centered on the sensational or the controversial. Many women invited to tape a show by a local television station found themselves confronted with a fellow guest loudly proclaiming women were hysterical, neurotic, vengeance seekers. Victim appearances were described as "A rape victim recounts the horrors of her ordeal." Journalists attempted to relate rape to prostitution and pornography or relegated the opening of a crisis center to the society page. While in many parts of the country, antirape activities are still banished to the society pages, for the most part local news media are now providing constructive coverage of issues, actions, and services in their community. National coverage, though still relatively sparse, is improving. Magazine coverage is still slight; and when in fact they take on the subject, the result is often similar to *True Confessions*. On the other hand, in a recent publication of a magazine with a large homemaker readership, all mention of the enclosed article on rape was omitted from the cover of the magazine. Overall, the news media have played an invaluable role in public education. As rape becomes a less sensationalized and a more commonly discussed subject, it will be interesting to see if media interest continues, or moves on to what will then be a more controversial subject.

In the wake of a rising crime rate, tremendous community involvement, and increasing public attention, Senator Charles Mathias of Maryland in September 1973 introduced a bill to establish a National Center for the Prevention and Control of Rape. The impact of this bill would be to provide a focal point within the National Institute of Mental Health from which would be undertaken a comprehensive national effort to research, to develop programs, and to provide a national clearinghouse of information leading to aid for the victims and their families, to deal in a rehabilitative way with the offenders, and ultimately to curtail the crime of rape. It represents an acknowledgment by Congress that the crime has reached immense national proportions and has created a major national concern not only for safety but also for the health and mental health problems which the crime produces. Moreover, it is an acknowledgment of the issues raised by the women's movement and seeks to emphasize the plight of the victim—an emphasis seldom seen in criminal cases.

The bill was passed by overwhelming vote of the 93rd Congress and then vetoed by President Ford. Despite the veto, there is no doubt that in the future this bill will be enacted and will establish a center to coordinate and develop national programs on rape. Sponsor of the Rape Prevention and Control Act, Senator Mathias credited the Congressional passage of the bill to the National Organization for Women. It is evident that the women's movement has brought the attention of the highest levels of the federal government into rape concern.

Congress, however, cannot legislate rape out of existence. Some feel that the women's movement has accomplished near miracles within the space of a few years. The women themselves feel that gains have indeed been made. Attitudes are slowly changing; institutional procedures are changing; laws are changing. Reeducation of society is always difficult under the best of circumstances, and the destruction of myths and misconceptions as old as the human race is an enormous task. As the movement against rape begins to make gains, it also begins to confront new and unanticipated problems.

While the women's movement continues to focus upon the societal sexism inherent in rape, society itself is taking up the rape issue under the "law and order" banner. This banner provokes emotion but fails to deal with the source of the problem; it is a Band-Aid solution to an injury which requires major surgery.

National interest in the issue has given rise to a wave of "entertainment" shows and movies, saturated at best with a wealth of misinformation and at worst with the historical emphasis on the sensational or the bizarre. Shows range from the realistic "A Case of Rape" on CBS to the semi-X-rated "Rape Squad" shown at neighborhood theaters.

In the wake of increasing public attention, self-styled "experts" on rape are touring the country with self-aggrandizing lectures on rape prevention which perpetuate sex role stereotypes and generally denigrate women.

The training and education programs sought by women for police and prosecutors are becoming a reality. Some programs are producing sensitive personnel with raised consciousness. A new phenomenon has arisen, however, within the past year—the training format utilizing *Playboy* jokes. The undermining of women and victims as presented in such programs (where the victim is called Millie Mini-Skirt, or some such) is quite unlikely to produce any change of attitude in the attendant personnel.

In the surge of research and community involvement stimulated by the women's movement, the victim of rape is now often overlooked. While concern for the health, mental health, and social service needs of the victim initiated the antirape movement, those priorities are now often being replaced by other concerns. The goal of self-determination for victims is being lost in the trend to determine the victim's needs for her.

As rape continues to become a "popular" national issue, institutions are surging to compete for the limited funds available for community services—often squeezing out the lifeline of rape crisis centers. As federal action funds begin to be distributed, the years of developed expertise of women's groups is being overlooked in favor of the current interest of other groups. The potential effectiveness of women's groups is being severely limited by finances. In short, problems are arising out of progress.

Despite the problems, however, the antirape movement continues to grow. Local units are organizing into state units. National action is underway. Women are organizing in Canada, England, Australia, Ireland, and Belgium. The movement against rape is becoming international in scope.

The ultimate goal of the society relatively free from rape is still in the distant future. The war, however, goes on.

8

Prevention of Rape: Deterrence by the Potential Victim

Stanley L. Brodsky

Two kinds of advice typically are given to women to avoid being the victim of rape. One advice pattern deals with avoiding the situation in the first place. That is, women have been told how to dress, where to go, and whom to see. This advice has been viewed on a mixed basis by feminists. While police and citizens can indeed identify dangerous places for women to be, the critics point out that women have their freedom restricted, and thus in effect are punished for the possible actions of others.

The second approach deals with what the potential victim can do at the time of the attack. Police have often suggested that the potential victim acquiesce to prevent severe bodily harm. This advice is consistent with Henry Fieldings' cynical comments in *Jonathon Wild*: "He in a few minutes ravished this fair creature, or at least would have ravished her, if she had not, by a timely compliance, prevented him." Prevention of bodily assault through submission to rape perhaps is contradictory. However, acquiescence as prevention will be considered further.

One prominent aspect of preventive approaches has been to instruct women in self-defense methods. A number of martial arts schools specialize in direct instruction, as well as in written information, on how women can best defend themselves from rapists.

How do women successfully interrupt or prevent attacks by potential rapists? In one study of rape in the Denver area (Giacinti and Tjaden, 1973), it was reported that 319 out of 915 rape offenses studied were interrupted rapes. Of these, 66 percent were prevented through the victim's active resistance. The most successful methods of prevention were fleeing from the potential assailant (successful by 24 percent), physically attempting to fight off the attack (18.4 percent), crying aloud (15 percent), and verbally refusing (10.5 percent). The remaining preventive events consisted of another person coming to the victim's aid (10.5 percent), the police arriving (6.3 percent), and other interruptions (14.5 percent).

In MacDonald's book *Rape: Offenders and Their Victims* (1971), screaming aloud was attempted to prevent the attack in six cases. In three of these, in which screaming was combined with physical attack, the attack was successfully aborted. There were ten reported cases of physical resistance alone, and none of these were successful in preventing the rape.

If the behavior of the victim or potential victim is to be changed and the responses to each situation optimized, such an effort would call for both training and dissemination of information. As Feldman-Summers (1974) has pointed out, "this would require additional research focused on the characteristics of the victim and her actions immediately prior to the assault."

The characteristics of both the assailant and the victim have been reported in the book *Against Rape*. In their study of 60 rapes, Medea and Thompson (1974) categorized the attitudes of the rapists into six major groupings: hostile, 32 percent; contemptuous, 28 percent; angry, 22 percent; frightened, 13 percent; matter-of-fact or calm, 42 percent; self-righteous, 22 percent. Many of these attitudes appeared in combinations; thus the totals are over 100 percent. By far the greatest incidence of violence associated with a rape occurred with hostile and contemptuous rapists: 48 percent violent rapes and 20 percent nonviolent rapes by hostile assailants, 50 percent violent rapes and 11 percent nonviolent for contemptuous assailants. The lower proportion of the violent rapes occurred with matter-of-fact and angry rapists. It was also found that the chances of encountering a hostile and contemptuous rapist were greatest when the victim did not know him at all.

The present research issue was the difference between a rape victim and a successful rape resister. If there is some technique, trait, or response that a successful rape resister uses, this information ought to be shared and distributed to women in general and particularly those who might become potential victims. In a substudy of 305 rape cases in Denver in 1973, the Violence Research Unit of the Colorado Division of Psychiatric Services (Selkin and Hursch, 1974) reported that "about half of the offenders who approach a rape resister were indeed carrying weapons and about 42 percent of the total number of resisters faced a man with a gun or a knife." In the search for successful resister characteristics Selkin and Hursch found no differences in age and experience in man-woman relationships between rape victims and rape resisters. They conducted intensive interviews with both victims and successful resisters. Among other techniques used in the interviews were administration of the California Psychological Inventory. On that test, resisters had significantly higher scores on the *dominance, sociability, social presence,* and *achievement via conformance* scales. Resisters were found to be lower on *communality* than the victims, suggesting "that the resisters are less patient and conscientious than the victims."

The present investigation was concerned with situational aspects and victim responses. (1) Given a particular attitude presented by a potential assailant, what is the range or repertoire of responses of the potential victim? (2) Which response would have the highest payoff in likelihood of interfering with successful completion of the rape? (3) What women's actions do convicted rapists report as most personally preventive? Some actions found in the Denver Research Studies to be effective included fleeing, and under certain circumstances physical fighting. However, these two responses were beyond the scope of the present investigation. The present investigation was concerned primarily with verbal responses in the interpersonal prerape situations.

Method

The Taxonomy

A thorough literature review of rape resisting and rape prevention was conducted. Particular attention was directed toward case reports of verbal responses by women in the prerape situation (e.g., MacDonald, 1971). A preliminary taxonomy of these verbal statements was constructed from a content analysis of published reports in books and journals. The prototypical responses of the victims and potential victims fell into the following nine categories:

1. Self-punitiveness ("I'll kill myself if you do this"; "I'll never be able to live with myself.")
2. Body weakness (statements of illness, cancer, pregnancy)
3. Verbal attack ("Get the hell away from me.")
4. Interpersonal liaison (an effort to communicate and become personally known)
5. Virginity
6. External influence or distraction ("My boyfriend will be here any moment.")
7. Moral appeal or conscience-surrogate ("It's the wrong thing to do"; "What would your mother think?")
8. Simple acquiescence with appeal ("I'll do anything you say; please don't hurt me.")
9. Ambivalent refusal with acquaintances (present only with men known to the victim and considered to be primarily a product of the ongoing interaction)

The Rape Videotapes

The second procedure consisted of videotape recording of twenty scenes portraying these nine response categories. Sixteen actors and actresses and a faculty member from the University of Alabama Theater prepared for this filming during five weeks of intensive imagery and rehearsals. The imagery consisted of constructing mental images and participating in role playing related to being the victim or perpetrator of aggression and sexual assault.

The exercises by the actors were of sufficient intensity that both actors and observers were frequently moved to crying and great emotional involvement. As the role playing and rehearsals moved closer to the specific rape situations, a sex difference was observed in involvement of the actors and actresses. The actresses were easily able to accept the role of victim and to play it with great facility and spontaneity. Considerable ambivalence was observed on the part of the actors in assuming their roles. Several stated that they could not picture themselves as rapists under any circumstances. Others struggled to modify the script or instructions in ways so they could assume such a role. This sex difference was apparent in the videotaped performances as well as in the rehearsals. The women were more realistic than the men.

Because almost all the actresses played the roles with considerable emotional display, three scenes (numbers 18, 19, and 20) were shot using nonactresses. These individuals simply played themselves and presented more matter-of-fact victim responses.

Two types of camera scenes were shot. The first eight scenes were interactions between the potential assailant and the potential victim. The last twelve scenes used the "subjective camera technique," in which the actress spoke directly to the camera. The viewer is assumed to be the other party to whom she is speaking. The transcripts of the rape situation videotapes are shown in Table 8-1.

In all scenes minimal background information was given, and no outcome of the interaction was shown. That is, the films were stopped or edited prior to an indication of whether the woman's effort to deter the rape had succeeded.

Judgments by Rape Conferees

The relative deterrence effectiveness of the prototypical responses was evaluated by showing all twenty scenes at a conference on "Rape: Research, Action, Prevention." One hundred ninety-nine persons working at rape crisis centers, conducting research into rape, or in attendance for related reasons completed a rating sheet after seeing each of the scenes. They indicated on a 5-point scale whether the woman's response was highly effective in deterring the rapist (5 points); medium-high in effectiveness (4); medium in effectiveness (3); medium-low in effectiveness (2); or low in effectiveness (1). The same group also offered comments about the scenes as related to prevention of rape.

These videotapes were played consecutively; on a few of the scenes up to 20 members of the audience did not have the time to make a judgment or chose not to make a rating. Thus the sample for scene 1 was 199; it dropped to as low as 172 on other scenes.

Judgments by Forensic Treatment Personnel

The videotapes were viewed and the relative effectiveness of the deterrence strategies was assessed on the same five-point scale by eighteen staff members

Table 8-1
Transcripts of Stimulus Videotapes

Scenes 1 to 8: Objective camera scenes: Both man and woman are shown.

1. External influence: (Man asks woman if person lives there)

Woman: I don't know him.

Man: You don't? (grabs woman) Well, I want your money.

W: (screams) What are you doing?!

M: I want some money.

W: I don't have any money.

M: What do you mean you don't have any? You live in a place like this and you don't have any money?

W: Leave me alone!

M: You don't have any money?

W: No!

M: I think you're just gonna have to give me something.

W: (crying) My husband will be here in a minute. I am expecting him.

M: Oh, sure, now that's a bunch of bull.

W: No, he's coming! He really is!

2. Interpersonal liaison: (Man and woman sitting down next to each other)

Woman: I really appreciate your taking me home. My car doesn't usually stall, and I . . .

Man: It's all right. I don't mind it really. It really isn't very far.

W: I've often thought of taking those silly courses they have for women, you know, mechanics for women. My husband will fix the car as soon as he gets home. (He grasps her hand.) Uh . . . uh . . .

M: What's the matter?

W: Nothing, uh . . .

M: What's the matter!

W: You're hurting my hand.

M: I'm not hurting your hand.

W: Yes, you are!

M: I'm not hurting you; I'm not going to hurt you.

W: Yes, you are.

M: I don't want to hurt you.

W: You *are* hurting me!

M: I like you, you're very nice. I don't want to hurt you.

W: Well, if you like me, then don't hurt me. That *does* hurt. (More argument back and forth with simultaneous speaking)

M: Your husband's not gonna know. Your husband's not here. Your husband's not even in town. I know that. I heard you say that on the phone tonight. So what's to worry about? He's not going to know anything at all. (She starts screaming and struggling.)

W: Uh, oh, hey, I just read this book.

M: Shut up! Do you want to get hurt?

W: It's the most terrific thing I have ever read. Of course I don't want to get hurt. I want to tell you about this book I read. The name of the book is *Jonathan Livingston Seagull*, and I just read the book.

Table 8-1 (cont.)

M: Shut up!

W: It's a really terrific book. Look, I got it right here in my purse. It'll only take a minute. I want to read some of it to you out of this.

3. Virginity: (Man seizes woman, placing one hand over her mouth, and holding one of her arms behind her back)

Man: Okay, just be quiet, real quiet. Now go ahead and open the door. Open the door! Come on. Come on! Take it easy. All right, where is your bedroom? Where's your bedroom?! (She is crying.) Take it easy, I'm not going to hurt you.

Woman: Listen, listen to me, please. I'm going to be married next week . . .

M: It doesn't matter whether you get married.

W: No!

M: Now, come on! Are you going to cooperate? Where's the bedroom? Let's go.

W: I've never had sex before. Please! Don't do this to me!

M: It doesn't matter whether you've ever had sex before.

4. Acquiescence: (Man stops woman on street, asking for the time)

Woman: No, I sure don't, but it's getting pretty late.

Man: Well, do you have any idea what time it is?

W: Uh, no. Maybe 11:00, 11:30, I don't know.

M: I'd like to talk to you for a minute.

W: What is it?

M: Do you mind?

W: Well, I don't know, there's people waiting for me at home.

M: I know you. Yeah, I know you. I mean, you don't know me, but I know you. I've seen you around, places.

W: Oh.

M: Yeah, and I knew you were coming by here. Yeah, that's why I'm here—because I wanted to talk to you.

W: Well I have to go.

M: Could you step over here for a minute. Just step over here with me, for a second.

W: Well, listen, I've never seen you around . . .

M: Yeah, I know, I know, but would you step over here and talk to me for a minute.

W: Well, what is it you want?

M: I *want* you so step over here and talk to me, all right? Now if you'll take it easy and be quiet, you won't get hurt. Otherwise you might. I want to have sex with you.

W: What?

M: I want to have sex with you.

W: That's ridiculous!

M: I want to have sex with you, and I'm going to have it right now. Now go down on your knees. I said go down on your knees. (Resistance) Go down on your knees! Now! (She is forced to her knees and whimpers.) Shut up, shut up!! Shhh. Now I'm going to let you go. I want you to lie back, and don't say anything, okay? Okay?! (She cries.)

W: Okay. Look, I'm not going to fight you. I don't understand this. Why are you doing this to me?

5. Ambivalent refusal: (Couple in loose embrace)

Woman: Ed, what are you doing? (laughing) Ed! Ed, look, come on.

Table 8-1 (cont.)

Man: (continues to hug and kiss her)

W: Ed, what about Julia!? Ed! Ed! Ed, come on. Come on, we don't want to do this.

M: Why not?

6. Self-punitiveness: (Couple embracing, with woman sometimes pushing man away)

Woman: Ed!! Ed, Ed, Ed, come on, cut it out! What are you doing? Come on, cut it out!

Man: Oh, come on . . .

W: No! No! I'm not just a piece of meat that you can just make on the floor!

M: I don't think you're a piece of meat.

W: I, I don't love you. I could never live with myself if this happened! (crying) Stop, please!

7. Moral appeal: (Apparently hurt, man holding his head)

Man: Excuse me, Miss, I've had a kind of an accident. A car hit me outside. Can I just . . .

Woman: Oh, my God!

M: I just want to lay down.

W: Let me call the hospital.

M: No, no, no. It's okay, he just knocked me down.

W: Oh, my God, let me call the hospital.

M: No, can you just sit here?

W: Let me get a washcloth. My God, who hit you?

M: Well, it was a car. He didn't see me and I wasn't thinking.

W: Let me call the hospital . . .

M: No, no, no! If you'll just hold me . . . (He places arms around her.)

W: Be still, relax, relax.

M: I just need someone to hold onto.

W: I'm here. I'm here. Let me call the hospital, and I'll be right back.

M: No, I can't.

W: It' all right. Listen. (Struggle starts. He forces her to the floor with him atop her, stroking her.)

M: No, it's going to be okay now. (They continue to struggle.)

W: Listen, listen, please. I'll help you. I'll help you. Believe me, I'll help you.

M: No, I don't want any help. I just want you.

W: Listen, listen, you don't want to hurt me.

8. Verbal attack: (Man and woman on couch. Woman sits back with arms crossed. Man sits sideways looking at her.)

Man: So, what have you been doing lately?

Woman: Nothing.

M: Nothing? That's what you call fucking around then, huh?

W: Sure.

M: Well, that's funny. That is really funny.

W: Hysterical.

M: Listen, you went with me for three months, and I never got anything.

W: So?

Table 8-1 (cont.)

M: So now as soon as we break up I find out you've been fucking half the people in the the goddamn town. Oh, that strikes you as humorous too, doesn't it?

W: Yeah, that's pretty funny.

M: Oh, that is really funny. Listen, what do you think I am? Do you think you can just play around with me? Do you think I'm a little kid? One of your faggot friends? Listen, I'm not. Listen, I'm a man. You may not think it, but I'm a man. Listen, goodamnit. (He grabs her.)

W: You get your fucking hands off me!!!!

Scenes 9 to 20: Subjective camera scenes: Woman looking at audience from the screen, as if viewer is assailant.

9. **External influence:** Sam Billings does not live here. I don't know who he is. What are you doing? Leave me alone! You can't do this. I don't have any money. My husband will be home any minute. I called him. He'll be here.

10. **Interpersonal liaison:** Please let go of me. You are hurting me! Hey, listen, I just read this book, and the name of it is *Jonathan Livingston Seagull.* It's really a fabulous book. I just got through reading it, and I think you are the type that would really love this book. Just a minute. I've got it right here in my purse.

11. **Virginity:** Please don't do this to me. Please, I've never had sex before. I'm begging you. It's the most important thing in the world to me. Please don't do this to me, please.

12. **Acquiescence:** Hey, okay, I'm not going to fight you. I just don't understand this. Can't you tell me why? I don't love you, and you don't love me. You don't even know me. What is sex without love?

13. **Ambivalent refusal:** Please, no, listen. Listen, we're just friends. Come on. I'm not just something that you can just screw. No, Ed, please, what about Julia?

14. **Moral appeal:** You don't want to hurt me, right? You don't want to hurt me. You know this isn't the right thing to do. You know it. So don't do it. Please, you know this isn't the right thing to do. You know it. So don't do it. Please, you know that this isn't the right thing to do. You don't want to hurt me and I don't want to hurt you, and . . .

15. **Verbal attack:** (stated with great emotion) Get out of here! I don't like the sight of you. Get out! Out of this place! I'm tired of seeing you. Get out! I don't want to see you again. Get out, you son of a bitch! Get out of my life!

16. **Body weakness:** (said almost crying) Please don't do this to me. I've just gotten out of the hospital. I've only been out of the hospital a week. I don't understand. Please, if you rape me, I'll never have a baby.

17. **Body weakness:** (said with moderate calm) Now, wait a minute. Listen, Why don't you take a second thought and consider just what you're doing. Look at me. I'm not exactly big, you know, and I just got out of the hospital, and I'm not in any condition to do any of that sort of stuff, so could you just leave me alone. Just leave me alone.

18. **Interpersonal liaison:** (woman smiles) Listen, you don't really want to do this. I mean, let's be friends, okay? We'll talk to each other and get to know each other, and then, you know, we may become really good friends. My name is Becky. What's your name?

19. **Moral appeal:** If you do that, you'll go to hell. It's against Christian principles. What are you? I mean, you know it's wrong. You just don't do that to people. Christians don't do that.

20. **Verbal attack:** (stated firmly, evenly) You've got a lot of nerve. Get out of here. Who the hell do you think you are? I'm going to call the police if you're not out of here in ten seconds.

employed in a forensic unit at a large southeastern state mental hospital. They included psychiatrists, psychologists, social workers, nurses, attendants, and graduate students.

The staff had gathered to hear a presentation on rape research by the author. The videotapes were shown at the very beginning of the presentation, prior to any formal lecture or discussion. Most of the staff were themselves actively involved in the therapeutic programs for rapists and other forensic patients, and had personal contact or knowledge regarding the confined rapists.

Deterrence from Rapists' Perspectives

Thirty-nine men involuntarily confined at this forensic unit also served as subjects. Almost all were admitted and convicted rapists; a few reported that they weren't certain if the rape occurred. The majority were confined for treatment under the provisions of a Mentally Disordered Sex Offender Act, and were engaged in an active group psychotherapy program.

Two procedures were used. The men came in three separate small groups and viewed the videotapes. They were asked to rate the effectiveness of each videotaped prevention effort, as it applied to them personally. There was an attrition of two subjects during the viewing. One man became upset and nervous. He asked to be excused and explained afterward that his own case and memories were sufficiently similar and painful that he did not wish to view the scenes. A second man was excused when it became apparent that he was unable to pay attention to the testing situation. He was apparently hallucinating, staring into space, and writing first names in the questionnaire response spaces. Other confined rapists who were openly psychotic and unable to converse were prescreened and not requested to participate.

The second procedure with the rapists was to ask their opinions about what prevention efforts might have worked, and did not work, for the women they encountered themselves. They were specifically asked the following questions. The answers were then categorized for common themes and responses.

1. Based on your personal experience, what statements or efforts by the woman might have successfully stopped the rape?
2. Why?
3. What statements or efforts were unsuccessful?
4. Why?
5. Please describe your own experience.

A note about the nature of these rapists is in order. Their mean age was 26.2 years and mean educational level 11.9 years. The largest number were convicted rapists who were in the mental health control system; a few were rapists found not competent to stand trial or not guilty by reason of insanity.

Results

Deterrence Effectiveness: The Ratings

The means of the deterrence ratings by the conferees are shown in Table 8-2. The three highest rated responses, in which more than a medium level of deterrence effectiveness was achieved, used verbal attack or active discouragement by the potential victim. The highest rating of 3.60 was for a woman actively and profanely telling the man to stay away from her. The next highest in effectiveness were an emotional description of recent hospital release (scene 16, $\overline{X} = 2.50$) and the subjective camera statement of virginity (scene 11, $\overline{X} = 2.40$). The lowest rated techniques for effectiveness were the two acquiescence scenes (scene 4, $\overline{X} = 1.35$; and scene 12, $\overline{X} = 1.51$).

The treatment personnel means and standard deviations are also shown in Table 8-2. None of the mean ratings were as high as 3.00, the indicated point of medium effectiveness. The rapist treatment personnel placed an especially high value on the development of a personal relationship in the verbal prevention of rape. The three interpersonal liaison scenes were assessed as first, third, and seventh most effective among the twenty scenes. The two very vigorous verbal attacks, which were rated first and second by the rape conferees, were similarly viewed as effective by the treaters (ranks of fifth and second). The body weakness videotape, scene 16, was viewed by both groups as a powerful prevention measure. This particular scene was played tearfully with much emoting by the actress. The actress pleaded that she had just been released from the hospital and was fearful that she would never have a baby.

The rapist subjects similarly attributed considerable weight to the deterrence potential of this same approach and scene (16). It may be seen in Table 8-2 that the rapists assigned a mean value of 3.72 to this vignette; the next highest mean rating was 2.81. Both this second highest rating and the fourth highest were for scenes of acquiescence and ambivalent refusal, rated low by the other two subject groups. The accompanying comments of the rapist subjects indicated that they perceived much genuineness and meaningful personal contact in the responses. The rapists also produced substantially lower ratings for the category of verbal attacks. This result was produced by strong feelings by a sizable portion of the rapist sample that such a response was provocative and exciting.

The Rapists' Suggestions for Deterrence

Success through Interpersonal Liaisons. A substantial number of the rapists indicated that development of an interpersonal relationship between the potential victim and themselves would have made a difference. Two reported that they had been successfully deterred from some rapes in the past as a result of the women's comments. Typical statements by these men were:

Table 8-2

Deterrence Effectiveness Ratings by Conferees ($N = 199$), Treatment Personnel ($N = 18$), and Rapists ($N = 37$)

Scene Number	Response Type[a]	Rape Conferees		Treatment Personnel		Rapists	
		Rank	$\bar{X}$[b]	Rank	$\bar{X}$	Rank	$\bar{X}$
8	Verbal attack	1	3.60	5	2.56	14	2.03
15	Verbal attack	2	3.47	2	2.78	19	1.83
20	Verbal attack	3	3.06	10	2.28	11	2.16
16	Body weakness	4	2.50	4	2.61	1	3.72
11	Virginity	5	2.40	14	2.05	5	2.64
14	Moral appeal	6	2.20	9	2.28	3	2.78
2	Interpersonal liaison	7	2.19	7	2.44	20	1.76
6	Self-punitiveness	8	2.08	17	1.83	6	2.63
7	Moral appeal	9	2.08	6	2.52	9	2.27
1	External influence	10	2.04	13	2.17	7	2.36
10	Interpersonal liaison	11	2.03	1	2.89	16	1.89
5	Ambivalent refusal	12	2.01	20	1.50	13	2.10
9	External influence	13	1.98	11	2.22	15	2.03
17	Body weakness	14	1.98	8	2.33	10	2.24
13	Ambivalent refusal	15	1.96	12	2.11	4	2.75
18	Interpersonal liaison	16	1.96	3	2.61	8	2.31
3	Virginity	17	1.70	15	1.89	17	1.87
12	Acquiescence	18	1.51	16	1.89	2	2.81
19	Moral appeal	19	1.50	19	1.56	18	1.84
4	Acquiescence	20	1.35	18	1.72	12	2.15

[a]Scenes 9 to 20 were subjective camera scenes.

[b]Rating scores are based on a 5-point scale ranging from 5 for high deterrence, 3 for medium deterrence, and one for low deterrence. Standard deviations are not shown. The range of standard deviations was from .66 to 2.28, with a modal standard deviation of .97.

"the woman talked to me calmly, and it sort of got to me on my softness . . . this was successful."

(by talking to me, the woman) "kind of got to my head, and I found out what I was doing."

(she reasoned with me and) "it worked on the occasion it was used . . . in crying, a sympathy resulted."

"talking with me would get my mind off the rape (and) tell me how it would affect her and that she would help if I wanted it."

"a true trust would be what I needed."

(if she had shown) "caring: attempt to understand (my) loneliness," (I would not have gone ahead).

Two of the men spelled out in detail the specific kinds of talking which would discourage them. Thus one man reported that it would be:

calm talking, asking "why are you doing this to me?" and try to establish in the rapist's mind that she is a real person with real feelings and not just an object . . . in doing so it makes a realization in your mind that you are doing something wrong to a real person. If they scream, usually it frightens you away. If screaming doesn't do it, then talk, talk, and talk.

The other man explained that the best way to deter him would be:

by talking to me and telling me I did not want to really do this and by showing no fear. I don't mean by fighting, but by words . . . I believe each rapist is a little emotional and really don't want sex but companionship and someone to talk to . . . I broke into a house and was going to rape her. I had a knife. She started talking to me, telling me I didn't want to do this. She finally talked me out of it, so I left.

A total of nine of the thirty-seven responding rapists indicated that this interpersonal liaison either was effective or would be effective in preventing their rapes. Thus 23 percent would have been deterred by this approach.

Verbal Attacks and Refusals. In the earlier discussion, verbal attacks and outright refusals had been grouped together, considered to fall in the category of strong, unequivocal statements of unwillingness to participate in the sex act with the potential rapist. Eleven men, or 30 percent, indicated that a flat, unequivocal refusal, a firm no, would have deterred them. Examples of these responses are:

In my case it could have been stopped if the woman would have put up a little more struggle . . . I was just as scared as she was.

Flat refusal, running and screaming.

If she'd put up a fight or screamed, it probably would have been effective. She would have scared me.

To make as much noise as possible and make the rape hard by not doing what I want.

Her saying no would have stopped it.

If the woman would've stood up for herself, said no, and begin to cry out, most of the rapes wouldn't have happened . . . because most rapists is lonely and need someone to talk to.

The way they can stop rape because they could tell a man to stop it all . . . they could do it all over again and they could stop it at all times and tell the man not.

Express to the raper that he or she is doing something against their will.

Two men indicated that very strong verbal abuse directed toward them would have deterred them. In one case a man indicated "getting very angry" would have deterred him, and still another that "fighting, yelling, not showing fear, get out of here you jerk, asshole . . . if I suspected the fight I wanted no part of it."

Other Suggestions

Three men indicated that there was nothing that the woman could do under any circumstances to deter them. Two more suggested that signs of great weakness and distress would deter them. Among the remaining subjects there were a variety of responses. They include victim-blame responses, such as:

If they didn't wear short dresses and hitchhike along the highway, and be out late hours walking along the highway or streets . . . because most of us believe that the woman is out looking for some sex if they flash or be out like this.

Unsuccessful Efforts. Eight of the men reported that the women they attacked had actively tried to resist by verbal attack. Fighting, screaming, cursing, and threatening the rapist were all reported as being unsuccessful. As one man reported that it made no difference when the woman was:

playing the tough bit if her act came off phony . . . because it would make me mad. I'd have been up anyway.

Another man reported that fighting him would only make him more violent, and still another that trying to fend him off only increased his determination. Another rapist's reaction to a woman's threat to have him picked up by the police was:

I am not scared of being picked up by the police, and I have a hate toward women.

Nine men reported that crying, passivity, acquiescence, and other signs of weakness were ineffective. One man explained:

These are things a rapist gets off on. He usually seeks domination, and those things bring out his domination.

Other men reported that the women being submissive made it all the easier. One man reported, "Any pleading would only increase my urge," and still another that passivity was very close to consent, as he saw it.

Several men were highly suspicious of women who would be "running a line" on them, that is, women who would be inventing a story to deter them. Most of these men reported that such deceit infuriated and angered them. They were ready to believe legitimate reasons, but were resentful of women who would lie to them. Indeed, one concern of this investigator was that some of these dangerous men when released would be less likely to be deterred by otherwise successful efforts by women. That is, the rapists might become sufficiently sophisticated in detecting different ploys, that they would persist more than before in persevering in the rape attempt.

Discussion

Matching Response to Type of Potential Assailant

In the discussions accompanying both the videotapes and the personal statements, it appeared that two types of psychological stances were present. On the one hand was the dominant, aggressive, highly assaultive rapist. This man indicated that resistance and verbal attacks by the women only served to sexually excite him more and encourage him more to violence. A few of these men indicated that passivity, crying, signs of great personal weakness and distress would distract them or turn them away from their act.

On the other hand, almost an equal number of men reported that the signs of weakness, personal distress, and passivity served to increase their sexual excitement. They had been very tentative in their approaches toward the women. These are predominantly the men who stated they would have been stopped by aggressive or forceful refusal by the women. The question then arises, how does a woman differentiate between the two types of men?

After the interviews with the rapist subjects were concluded, one man asked to see the investigator. This convicted rapist stated that the best thing that could be done for women was to provide them with a checklist so that they would know in what way they should respond. Based on the very preliminary findings in the present study, a strategy is suggested.

If the rapist approaches with great verbal or suggested physical aggression or antagonism, then crying, signs of weaknesses, protests about body difficulties, and open exhibition of great personal distress may be useful. For these men there is a much lower success likelihood for active, verbal resistance. On the other hand, for the men who are highly tentative, relatively more polite, and who have preceded the actual rape threat with a number of preliminary conversations and tentative judgments about the woman, then the woman may be well advised to try active rejection and verbal or physical attack. These results are consistent with Selkin's report (1974) that explicit unavailability, communicated from potential victim to assailant, is an effective rape prevention method.

The preventive prototypical responses are distillations, and as such they also represent simplifications. A number of successful rape resisters described a much more complex process than a single response, sometimes trying five or six methods until one worked. Thus one woman reported waking up in bed at 4 A.M. with a man on top of her. Over a long period of talking with him she agreed not to report him to the police, provided he would see a psychiatrist, and eventually he was deterred. Another woman assessing the scenes reported, "I interrupted my assault by saying that we could go to the bank (which was nearby) and get all my money which would enable him to hire a prostitute. He agreed, and when we left the house he stepped out in front and I slammed the door."

It is apparent that victims' responses in isolation are not as meaningful as they are in the context of the nature of the attacker and his behavior and attitudes. The needed next step is to develop a grid in which patterns of attacker behaviors and victim responses are presented, with optimal and worst possible combinations listed. It is clear that the tactics rated highest on success are valid only in certain situations. Subsequent research should validate when they work and when they do not. It may be that the development of the prototypes is as important as the specific results of the study. Now that the major styles and patterns of responses are identified, further investigation and program development may be built upon them.

It was observed that other messages are embedded in the content of these films. Tone of voice, amount of confidence, volume of the voice, and physical postures from the women may be of equal importance with the actual words used. While these variables were not studied in the present investigation, they are clearly an additional direction to be pursued in the future.

A future application for this research is a public education campaign. If one has a reasonable expectation that certain verbal or nonverbal responses successfully deter potential rapists, then this information ought to be distributed, at least experimentally, to a substantial number of women for their own protection. The provocative question might be raised of whether this information also would be available to potential rapists, who would then be less deterred. While this is a possibility, it would seem that the behavior of the potential rapists would be far more influenced by the woman's immediate responses than by any publicized advice.

Summary

This investigation utilized four sequential procedures. First, nine major categories of verbal responses to deter rapists were identified from the literature. Second, a series of twenty film vignettes were made utilizing actresses and actors who portrayed these prototypical responses. Third, these vignettes were shown to an audience of informed judges, who rated their differential effectiveness. Fourth, a group of rapists were asked for their judgments about what would deter them.

This study represented a preliminary effort to study the verbal interactions between potential victim and assailant. While it is recognized that looking primarily at the woman's role takes her response out of context, this procedure is seen as gathering information for use in deterrence of rapists.

Proposals are often made for changing the nature of society as well as changing the behaviors of convicted rapists so that rape will disappear. While both proposals are important, neither deals with the problems of a woman who is immediately confronted with a potential sexual assault and has no opportunity to physically flee or resist. The present study posed the questions, What is it that successful rape resisters do in their resistance? Can these actions be identified and validated? and Can they be distributed so that other women will benefit? The preliminary findings were that active verbal attack or discouragement, successful interpersonal contact, and arousal of sympathy were the most successful deterrents, depending upon the nature of the rapist.

Note

1. Phyllis Brister, Joan White, and Teresa G. Earnhart generously offered their aid and advice in this research.

References

Feldman-Summers, S. "Research Dimensions in the Area of Sexual Assault." Paper presented at the meeting of the American Psychological Association, Montreal, Canada, August 1974.

Giacinti, T., and Tjaden, C. "The Crime of Rape in Denver." A report submitted to the Denver High Impact Anti-Crime Council, Denver, 1973.

MacDonald, J. *Rape: Offenders and Their Victims.* Springfield, Ill.: Charles C. Thomas, 1971.

Medea, A., and Thompson, K. *Against Rape.* New York: Farrar, Straus, and Giroux, 1974.

Selkin, J. Rape. *Psychology Today*, 1975, 8(8): 70-76.

_____, and Hursch, C. Rape Prevention Project—Quarterly Report. Department of Health and Hospitals, Denver, Colorado, July 1, 1974.

9

The Rapist in Treatment: Professional Myths and Psychological Realities

Asher R. Pacht

Myth 1: Expertise of Professionals

The border between myth and reality is often diffuse. Properly clothed, even myths can seem real. Therefore, the first myth may well be the myth of my expertise, or, for that matter, anyone's expertise in this area with the possible exception of the rapist and the victim of rape. If expertise is based on a foundation of solid research, then there are few who can claim to be experts, particularly with respect to treatment of the rapist. Most individuals who have done work in this area have focused on a rather narrow section of the broad spectrum involved in a study of the offense of rape. In the specific treatment area, most of the available information is experiential rather than research-based.

Much of what is written about the rapist or the victim of rape is frequently based on either subjective impressions or descriptive studies of highly selected subgroups. Very little information results from well-designed experimental research. Given this, the reader should accept what follows with caution and skepticism. Recognize that this material is based on a mixture of experience, twenty-plus years of working with sex offenders in a direct clinical and administrative fashion, along with some limited hard data. Recognize, however, that the hard data comes from a selected group, i.e., the convicted rapist. That group clearly is not representative of the general class of rapists.

Myth 2: All Rapists Have Similar Characteristics

Given those disclaimers, let us examine the second major myth surrounding the rapist, i.e., that all rapists have similar characteristics. If we are going to attempt treatment, we should be able to delimit our population. Who, then, is the rapist? The most honest answer is that it probably depends of whom the question is asked. If one believes much of the popular literature, for example, most rapists would be seen as oversexed, stupid, animalistic, psychopathic monsters. Perhaps some are, but certainly, based on the Wisconsin data, not the majority.

If rapists were asked who they are, they would produce a variety of answers. One frequent response would be that it was a "bum rap." They might add that they are nothing more than fun-loving guys who were really seduced and felt it would be dishonorable to disappoint the woman involved. That also might be true, but in terms of our Wisconsin data, certainly not very often. As an aside, it is interesting that a version of those words were used by one sex offender where the seductress was a "woman" who had reached the grand old age of four years and three months.

Professional literature is both helpful and confusing. It is helpful in that some meaningful, descriptive characteristics about individuals involved in rape, as well as demographic data about the victims of rape, begin to emerge. Some of the information is useful—age of rapist, relationship to victim, degree of aggression, marital status, etc. It is confusing, however, because the data sometimes appear inconsistent and usually lack generalizability because they are so closely related to the specific population sampled. One example should serve to illustrate this problem. In the Amir (1971) work, which has been cited repeatedly and is probably the single most complete and significant study of forcible rape available, the rate of rape by blacks was roughly 5 times more than that by whites. Indeed, in that study 82 percent of all persons arrested for forcible rape were black. Amir's data are based on cases found in the files of the Philadelphia Police Department for the year 1960. By contrast, in the Wisconsin data on convicted rapists, over 6 times more whites than blacks were convicted of rape. Similar discrepancies appear when we compare other data and other studies. Which study should be believed? The differences between Amir's study and the Wisconsin data can probably be accounted for most simply by recognizing the fact that the populations studied were markedly different. There are apt to be significant differences between arrested rapists as contrasted with convicted rapists. Further, a large Eastern city with a large black population is probably not comparable with a Midwestern state which has a relatively small black population. These kinds of discrepancies, which appear with some frequency in the literature, make it essential that extreme caution be used in interpreting results.

Confusions about the rapist become even greater in the examination of some of the alternative explanations offered in the literature for understanding rapist behavior; e.g., do they really hate their mothers, are they psychopaths, are they psychotic, are they morally deficient, or is it one of the myriad of other alternatives? One thing seems evident. Rape is a legal term, and not all individuals who commit rape fit neatly into the same personality or behavioral classifications. Indeed, there may be more differences between two rapists than there are similarities.

A number of researchers have attempted to set up classifications for rapists in an effort to organize the differences that seem apparent. Most of these classifications, including the one that was used in Wisconsin for a number of years, appear to have built-in inadequacies. The Wisconsin classification system was relatively simple and was devised in an effort to differentiate from the larger group of sex offenders those who were in need of specialized treatment. It was an operational concept "based on a continuum which is bounded on one side by the crime committed primarily as a result of sociological or cultural factors, and bounded on the other extreme by crimes committed almost entirely because of the psychological determinants. At the one end of this continuum is the criminal who shows no evidence of mental illness and who commits a crime because of the inadequate moral standards or controls in his social milieu. At the other end is the individual who is obviously mentally ill and whose criminal sexual act appears clearly to be a product of that illness" (Pacht, et al., 1962, p. 804). In practice it was easy to separate the two extremes of criminal sexual behavior, i.e., the psychotics and the psychopaths; there were very few of either. The difficulties arose "... with the many shades of gray along the continuum of criminal sexual behavior that are neither entirely culturally nor psychologically determined" (Pacht, et al., 1962, p. 804). In Wisconsin, a definition was necessary in order to comply with the statute (Wisconsin, 1951) which required that specialized treatment be offered to those sex offenders who were considered "dangerous" and in need of treatment. The Wisconsin definition was modified in 1967 in order to deal more directly with issues of sexual psychopathology, treatability, and dangerousness (Jesse, 1967).

Most researchers would probably agree that it is a myth to think of the rapist as a member of a homogeneous group. It is particularly important to recognize this lack of homogeneity in order to develop treatment programs that are effective for the rapist. It is clear that some rapists do not show any indications of psychological pathology and should not be subjected to those treatment programs which are oriented toward the elimination of pathology. Others appear to have significant emotional or behavioral problems, but, even with those cases, blanket labels do not suffice since it is essential to tailor programs to meet the treatment needs of the specific individual involved.

Before looking at such treatment programs, what can be said about the original question. Who or what is the rapist? It is probably not possible to answer that question in a significant fashion. In the Wisconsin data, the convicted rapists were not oversexed fiends, nor were they stupid, nor were they psychotic, nor did they fit into a specific psychiatric diagnosis. Some needed psychological treatment; others did not. Clinically, many of them appeared to be emotionally immature and sexually inadequate. In addition, most of them were married or had been married, had a history of moderate to heavy drinking, had been drinking at the time of the offense, had worked in skilled and semiskilled trades, and were not at all provoked by their victims. It might be added that there are probably a lot more similarities between them and us than there are differences between them and us—a fact about all offenders that is frequently forgotten.

Myth 3: Sex Offenders Are Not Treatable

The third myth—that sex offenders are not treatable—relates to sex offenders in general and rapists in particular. Most of the treatment of sex offenders had been conducted in an institutional setting under the provisions of some special state statute. There was a rash of these laws enacted in the late 1940s and early 1950s. Most are atrocious, and like the sexual psychopath statute recently declared unconstitutional in Alabama, are little more than preventive detention laws. Some, like the Sex Crimes Law enacted by Wisconsin in 1951, are more adequate. The Wisconsin law recognized the psychological nature of many sex offenses and was established to provide treatment for the treatable and security for those who did not benefit from treatment and who remained a danger to society. It paid special attention to the constitutional protection of the offender which the Alabama law did not do. It also provided for the administrative and clinical machinery which was essential for effective diagnosis and treatment. Finally, it built in flexibility for change as new knowledge developed. It also had, and continues to have, many problems, not the least of which was the location of the Sex Crimes Treatment Center in the middle of the state's maximum security prison.

Rapists, as a group, along with most sex offenders, are usually seen as highly dangerous. The treatment they have received, if any, has usually taken place in a security setting. Very few rapists are put on probation, and relatively few are offered treatment. There is some evidence that most sex offenders, including rapists, who are in the need of treatment can benefit from some form of specialized treatment (Roberts and Pacht, 1965). This requires, however, not only careful assessment but also the availability of a continuum of treatment approaches from which to select the most appropriate treatment.

Although there are a variety of treatment approaches which can be utilized, virtually all these were developed in working with other psychiatric groups. There is, unfortunately, little information available which relates to the effectiveness of these approaches when they are applied to sex offenders. The treatment issue is made even more difficult by the fact that the artificial environment of the typical correctional institutional setting is not the most conducive for achieving meaningful psychological change. It is incongruous for an individual who may have primary problems in his relationships with mature women to be sentenced to the all-male environment of the typical prison. That is hardly an ideal atmosphere for the development of the social-sexual skills necessary for establishing such relationships. If institutional treatment is to have any chance of being effective, efforts must be made to develop "... flexible programs which encompass all modalities of psychological treatment, increased utilization of women as therapists, provision for early release and continued treatment in an outpatient setting, a close effective working relationship between clinical and legal personnel, and programmatic research which makes possible definitive studies of the variables related to treatment. Without research, we may continue treatment programs that have little impact on the behavior of the sex offender" (Pacht, 1976).

Both traditional and innovative approaches have been utilized in the treatment of sex offenders. The following is a brief review of some of the typical efforts. It should be emphasized that despite descriptions in the literature, basic research has yet to establish the effectiveness of any of these approaches. Among the available approaches are those which involve the use of castration or hormones. Stürup (1972) has been a leading advocate of castration for sex offenders, which is a legal approach in a number of countries. This approach has been criticized on humanitarian, ethical, and scientific grounds. Even with highly specialized selection, which is claimed, it is difficult to understand how rapists, who may already feel inadequate sexually, can be aided by a process which may serve to enhance their sense of inadequacy.

Individual therapy has been used on selected cases by therapists from most therapeutic orientations. My personal bias is that the skill of the therapist may be far more important than his or her specific orientation. Although some success has been claimed for this approach, it is not economically feasible to expect that individual psychotherapy will become a primary treatment approach in correctional settings. Group psychotherapy appears to offer more potential on theoretical as well as on economic grounds. Several writers (e.g., Peters and Roether, 1972) have described programs utilizing group approaches with sex offenders which they claim are effective. The varieties of group approaches will not be described here. Suffice it to say that there are many different and creative group approaches (e.g., Anderson, 1969). With few exceptions, however, the data which indicate that these approaches work are experientially rather than research-based.

A helpful technique used in Wisconsin is family therapy. In this approach the entire family is seen as operating in a maladaptive fashion. It is the dysfunctional family rather than the individual that is helped to develop the requisite social climate which will lead to offender rehabilitation. Similarly, for married individuals with no children, couple therapy based on a similar social systems model may have some advantages. Unfortunately, we tend to build our institutions as far from civilization as possible. It is, therefore, often difficult for families to participate in these programs.

The most promising techniques of the past few years have been the maligned behavior therapies. Despite the adverse position of the popular press and the publicity given *A Clockwork Orange*, behavior therapy is not synonymous with the aversive conditioning approaches. The behavior therapies involve a number of approaches (aversive therapy included) geared to helping the individual modify his or her behavior. Although the aversive approaches have been used with sex offenders (their use has been both attacked and defended), there are still no specific, well-designed research studies which demonstrate their effectiveness with sex offenders. No less authorities than Serber and Wolpe (1972) point out that most of the present information comes from case descriptions.

The same lack of research base for the use of behavioral approaches with sex offenders is true of both systematic desensitization and social skill training. The latter approach is particularly intriguing in the treatment of sex offenders because it is in part directed toward teaching the individual the skills necessary for establishing mature interpersonal relationships. Despite the theoretical promise of this approach, it, too, needs considerable research before definitive statements can be made about its effectiveness.

Are rapists treatable? There is some evidence that they are despite the paucity of controlled research. Our experience clearly suggests that where approaches are available that can be tailored to fit the needs of a particular individual, those approaches will have an impact on his future career as a sex offender. It is important to recognize that all individuals involved in the treatment of sex offenders should be required to follow rather rigid ethical guidelines. Basic to these guidelines are such things as voluntary participation in treatment programs, informed consent, termination without penalty, and peer review. Such guidelines are particularly important if we are to combat the coercive qualities present in all correctional settings.

Conclusions

It should be emphasized that the psychological reality that would do most to counter both the professional and public myths which surround the rapist is the need for more controlled research. Until a sufficient number of controlled research studies have been completed, we shall continue to use approaches which may be invalid in our efforts to provide appropriate treatment for the rapist. Only through information obtained from such studies can we make the determinations necessary to provide not only what is needed for treatment of the individual but also what is needed for the protection of society.

References

Amir, M. *Patterns in Forcible Rape.* Chicago: University of Chicago Press, 1971.

Anderson, R. The exchange of tape recordings as a catalyst in group psychotherapy with sex offenders. *International Journal of Group Psychotherapy,* 1969, 19(2): 214-220.

Jesse, F. Criteria for commitment under the Wisconsin sex crimes act. *Wisconsin Law Review,* 1967, 1967: 980-987.

Pacht, A. Treatment of the sex offender. *International Encyclopedia of Neurology, Psychiatry, Psychoanalysis and Psychology,* 1976, in press.

_____, Halleck, S., and Ehrmann, J. Diagnosis and treatment of the sex offender: Nine-year study. *American Journal of Psychiatry,* 1962, 118: 802-808.

Peters, J., and Roether, H. Group psychotherapy for probationed sex offenders.

In H. Resnik and M. Wolfgang (Eds.), *Sexual Behaviors.* Boston: Little, Brown, 1972, 255-266.

Roberts, L., and Pacht, A. Termination of inpatient treatment for sex deviates: Psychiatric, social and legal factors. *American Journal of Psychiatry*, 1965, 121: 873-880.

Serber, M., and Wolpe, J. Behavior therapy techniques. In H. Resnik and M. Wolfgang (Eds.), *Sexual Behaviors.* Boston: Little, Brown, 1972, pp. 239-254.

Stürup, G. Castration: The total treatment. In H. Resnik and M. Wolfgang (Eds.), *Sexual Behaviors.* Boston: Little, Brown, 1972, pp. 361-382.

10 Psychological Treatment of Rapists

Gene G. Abel, Edward B. Blanchard, and Judith V. Becker

In recent years a variety of therapy techniques have been described for the treatment of rapists. These methods have been outlined in various publications, but there has been no attempt to organize the literature into a composite of the treatment components common to these programs. We will attempt such an organization as well as assess the evidence that supports the effectiveness of these treatment components.

Psychological evaluation and treatment of rapists has been impeded by both the lack of accessibility of rapists for evaluation-treatment and the failure of the psychological community to develop effective, efficient therapies for them. Accessibility of rapists for therapy has been, and continues to be, a major roadblock because traditionally rape has been viewed as a crime. The disposition of rapists has been through legal channels such as trials, prison, etc. Evidence that the criminal justice system has failed to convict most rapists is accumulating. For those convicted, recidivism rates have been relatively high.

The second major impediment to evaluation-treatment has been the failure of the psychological community to provide practical, effective treatment for rapists. In the last ten years, however, numerous new treatment methods have appeared for rapists, primarily based on treatments developed for the broad range of sexual deviates, such as voyeurs, exhibitionists, etc., who have been more accessible for treatment than rapists. With the guidance of methods developed for treating other sexual problems as well as a number of therapies already applied to rapists, a sufficient body of components for the treatment of rapists exists.

The Process of Psychotherapy Evaluation

There are differing levels of confidence or of validity of the evidence supporting the effectiveness of any particular treatment component. Some treatments have been extensively researched, relying heavily on the scientific method to confirm that the treatment is definitely effective. Other components have never been evaluated using the scientific method; and, although developed by competent clinicians, there is no scientific proof of their effectiveness. Understanding the levels of scientific inquiry enables the reader not only to be aware of the components, but also to appreciate the extent of scientific proof indicating the effectiveness of the treatment.

Bergin and Strupp (Bergin and Strupp, 1972; Strupp and Bergin, 1969; Bergin, 1971) have outlined three levels of increasing sophistication in evaluating the effectiveness of any treatment intervention. These levels include case reports, controlled single-case experimental design, and controlled group outcome.

Case Reports

Most conclusions that a particular component of treatment for rapists is effective are based on clinical judgments derived from a therapist's experience. The therapist believes he or she is using a particular treatment strategy to produce behavior change. If the rapist improves, the therapist concludes it must have resulted from the therapy methods applied. However, since no experimental method is used and no dependent measures of progress are systematically collected, the rapist's improvement may have resulted for reasons completely unknown to the therapist. The confidence one can have in the validity of treatment effectiveness from such case reports is very low. Nonetheless, hunches derived from case reports are some of the best sources of treatment techniques to be investigated more thoroughly by using experimental methods.

Controlled, Single-case Experimental Design

A more sophisticated means of evaluating a treatment method involves planned, single-case experiments. The therapist first identifies dependent measures that he or she expects will be altered by the treatment. For a rapist, these measures might include the frequency of thoughts of rape and nonforced sexual intercourse, the subject's ongoing erection responses to rape and nonrape cues (Abel, Blanchard, and Mavissakalian, 1974; Abel, Barlow, Blanchard, and Guild, 1975), and his report of how arousing thoughts of rape and nonforced sexual intercourse are. After establishing the occurrence of these dependent measures in a rapist before treatment begins, the therapist then introduces, withdraws, and reintroduces a *single* treatment variable. If that treatment variable is effective, improvement as measured by the dependent variables will occur as the treatment is introduced, stop as it is withdrawn, and reappear as it is reinstated.

The single-case experiment is very powerful at identifying the effectiveness of one treatment method; however, it cannot compare the relative effectiveness of one treatment with another. A large number of treatments have been validated as effective with sexual deviants using this method, and a few treatment results have used this design with rapists, primarily pedophiliacs. (See Hersen and Barlow, in press, for a fuller description of single-case design procedures.)

Controlled Group Outcome

If a treatment method has been found to be effective by single-case experimental design, it is next compared to another treatment method by a controlled group outcome study. Two groups of rapists, for example, would be equated in all ways and dependent measures obtained before and after the treatment being investigated. One group would be administered the new treatment; the other would receive a standard treatment or no treatment at all. The relative improvement of the two groups provides the therapist with a valid measure of the effectiveness of the new treatment. Although this method has been used with mixed groups of sexual deviates including a few rapists, no group comparisons of any treatment have been reported using groups of rapists only. Group outcome studies only occur in the final stages of a therapy's development but yield the strongest, most valid results about a therapy.

**The Treatment Components Common to
Current Treatment Programs for
Sexual Aggressives**

Our review examines the current treatment programs for sexual aggressives. The first objective is to identify those treatment components common to a variety of programs, assuming that frequent use of the same component suggests that the technique is critical for the rapist's improvement. Our second objective is to identify the level of research supporting the effectiveness of that treatment component.

*Empathic Relationship between Patient
and Treatment Agent*

Common to *all* programs is the establishment of a warm, accepting relationship between the offender and therapist. This relationship is especially critical in psychodynamically oriented treatments (Salzman, 1972; Karpman, 1954). The relationship (transference) becomes an essential vehicle by which the rapist's neurotic conflicts can be viewed, interpreted, and worked through to establish a more mature personality.

Pastoral counseling methods (Dates, 1972), milieu (Boozer, 1975a), and group therapy programs (Boozer, 1975b; Hendricks, 1975; MacDonald, 1974; Peters, Pedigo, Steg, and McKenna, 1968; Brancale, Vuocolo, and Prendergast, 1972) all stress the importance of the empathic relationship. Whether this relationship is established between patient and therapist or between patient and other offenders varies from program to program. Although behavioral modification programs tend to avoid discussions of the importance of this empathic relationship, those behavioral programs that have been effective also establish a deep regard and empathy for the patient.

The precise mechanism by which this empathic relationship actually produces change is unclear. Group therapists stress as essential the value of the offender being accepted by other offenders in spite of his sexual offenses (Peters, Pedigo, Steg, and McKenna, 1968; Hendricks, 1975). Others stress the opportunity for the open expression of emotions during the therapeutic alliance as critical for the breaking down of unresolved psychological conflicts, especially issues around anger and hurt (outlined more thoroughly by Brancale, Vuocolo, and Prender-gast, 1972). However, since no controlled research studies with rapists have systematically investigated the relationship of empathy to clinical improvement, the validity of the effectiveness of this factor is at the case report level.

Confrontation regarding the Responsibility for One's Sexual Behavior

It is difficult to separate the offender's denial of responsibility for his sexual acts, the confrontation methods used in treatment, and his understanding of the unconscious factors contributing to his rape behavior. Although the methods used vary widely from treatment program to treatment program, the goal of these techniques remains the same, i.e., that the offender accept the fact that *he* is responsible for his actions, that only he can stop his raping.

Pastoral counseling methods (for example, Oates, 1972) describe deviates' frequent attempts to justify their sexual offenses by considering "spiritual unity" or "mystical understanding" as a product of sexual misconduct and therefore not an appropriate behavior to change since the spiritual effects of the behavior would be lost. Some offenders use swift religious conversion as a testimony that they have changed the deviate behaviors. They attempt to avoid the issue of *how* they are going to prevent themselves from raping in the future, by attending instead to the strength of the religious insight and conversion. The pastoral counselor from the vantage point of an expert in religion not only must point out to the rapist the value of the rapist's religious convictions, but he must lead the rapist into specific therapeutic encounters with the treatment program to assist him in the specifics of how his urges to rape can be controlled.

Confrontation methods are more obvious in group therapy where denial, projection, and isolation are seen as early stages of therapy requiring confronta-tion between new patients and either the therapist or other offenders further along in the therapeutic process (Peters, Pedigo, Steg, and McKenna, 1968; Hendricks, 1975). The actual techniques of dealing with such resistance vary and may include such methods as marathon groups (Brancale, Vuocolo, and Prendergast, 1972), isolating the patient with other rapists so that he is more easily labeled as a rapist (Boozer, 1975a), sensitivity groups or video tape feedback (Brancale, Vuocolo, and Prendergast, 1972), or verbal feedback from a variety of staff or other rapists (Hendricks, 1975).

Similar objectives are reached by more traditional psychoanalytically oriented psychotherapy (Karpman, 1954; Salzman, 1972). Confrontation per se is replaced by nondirective exploration of the patient's unconscious motivations that have led to rape behavior. The basic premise of such a method, however, is that known or unknown (unconscious) to the patient, rape behavior follows situations or conflicts that have been experienced by the rapist. It is, therefore, his responsibility to understand and change these factors and subsequently change his proclivity to rape.

Behavior modification approaches also require the patient to take responsibility for his behavior. All such methods that directly attempt to alter symptomatology require the rapist's cooperation in the treatment on both ethical grounds (without the patient's requesting treatment for his rape behavior, no treatment should be instituted) and for treatment reasons (all behavioral treatments require the active participation of the rapist and, therefore, acceptance of himself as having problems controlling his rape behavior).

As with the previous component, no systematic, controlled studies have investigated the importance of confrontation to therapeutic improvement. The level of confidence in the importance of this component is thus only at the case report level.

Heterosocial-Heterosexual Skills Training

Under this category falls a variety of methods for teaching social interaction between the rapists and others, especially the rapist and adult females. The premise of such skills training is that rapists may be sexually aroused by women, but unless they can carry out the preliminary conversation, flirting, and other dating skills antecedent to a relationship, they will not have the opportunity to become involved sexually with the female (except by rape).

In those treatment programs surveyed, the majority included social skills training at some level. Basic social skills, for example, are a major goal of most group therapy programs. The shy, withdrawn offender has the opportunity to learn to relate to others by observing and trying out new social behaviors while in the supportive surroundings of the therapeutic group (Peters, Pedigo, Steg, and McKenna, 1968; Boozer, 1975a, 1975b).

Many programs go a step further, however, in an attempt to teach offenders heterosocial-heterosexual skills. Pacht (Pacht, Halleck, and Ehrmann, 1962; Pacht, 1975) attempted to teach social interactions in prison by *requiring* that offenders actually ask for and "go out" on informal dates within the prison walls with females, e.g., secretaries, clerks, aides, etc. Two problems, however, interfered with such a program. Administratively, the security hospital where treatment was initiated simply did not have sufficient numbers of females for the implementation of such a program. Furthermore, measures of the impact and effectiveness of such a program could not be obtained in the prison setting.

Pacht (1975) and MacDonald (1974) have both stressed the problems of implementing heterosocial skills training in the prison system. MacDonald has emphasized the countertherapeutic nature of our confinement system for sexual aggressives. Rapists, many of whom lack adequate heterosocial-heterosexual skills with women, are confined in security environments which actually isolate them from social contact with women. As a consequence, they have no opportunity to learn social skills and actually may become less adept with those skills they did have before incarceration due to lack of practice in prison.

Boozer (1975a), working with rapists within a state hospital, has also viewed heterosocial-heterosexual skills training as essential to treatment. She has hired *only female* attendants for her rapist treatment ward. Structured interactions between the rapists and the female staff are strongly encouraged. Boozer has also attempted to structure explicit sexual activity for the rapist. During the first year of hospitalization, no overt heterosexual behavior is allowed other than masturbation. During the second year, sexual behavior between the rapist and his wife is gradually reintroduced during weekend passes. Concomitant sexual counseling also occurs if problems are identified.

Sexual counseling in the form of sex education is also a component of the treatment programs at Atascadero State Hospital (Laws, 1974) and at the New Jersey Treatment Center (Brancale, Vuocolo, and Prendergast, 1974b), where offenders are acquainted with sexual information previously unknown to them.

Since the heterosocial-heterosexual skills training outlined above has never been separated from other components of treatment and since no controlled studies have been completed, the relevance and validity of such skills training for rapists is only at the case report level of confidence. Both controlled group outcome studies, however, have been conducted utilizing college students and psychiatric patients (non-sexual aggressives) as a subject population.

The problem of "minimal dating" among college males has recently been an area to which heterosocial skills training has been applied successfully. In these well-controlled studies, subjects have been non-psychiatric volunteer male college students (Martinson and Zerface, 1970; MacDonald, Lindquist, Kramer, McGrath, and Rhyme, 1973; McGovern, Arkowitz, and Gilmore, in press; Christensen, Anderson, and Arkowitz, in press; Christensen and Arkowitz, 1974). Goldsmith (1973) has also demonstrated the effectiveness of heterosocial skills training with psychiatric patients.

Hersen and Miller (1974), Eisler, Miller, Hersen, and Alford (in press), Hersen (1973), and Hersen, Eisler, and Miller (1973) have conducted a series of studies focused on the precise measurement of specific social skills deficits. Their results with nondeviant males suggest that treatment must focus on three response systems: (1) verbal and nonverbal (motor behavior) communication, (2) physiological concomitants (not feeling discomfort, e.g., anxiety in a social situation), and (3) the patient's attitudes and verbal reports on how he feels in the various stages of treatment or social situations.

The present authors conducted a series of studies to develop a systematic approach to the teaching of heterosocial-heterosexual skills. During these studies, it became apparent that minimal attention had been given to what behaviors actually reflected poor social skills and, therefore, what behaviors needed to be taught. We subsequently videotaped and observed the heterosocial skills displayed by sexual deviates who had indicated they historically had difficulty dating and clinically appeared to lack social skills. Their talking with a female assistant (as if trying to ask for a date) was compared with the performance of males of a similar age who were identified by their female friends as being very adept at heterosocial skills.

It became apparent that specific motor skills, the amount of affect displayed, components of voice, and flow of conversation clearly discriminated between the two groups, and a heterosocial scale was developed (Barlow, Abel, Blanchard, and Bristow, 1975). This scale can be used to assess any rapist's heterosocial skills with women. When the patient reports heterosocial skills deficits and these are confirmed by measurement with the heterosocial skills scale, treatment is initiated to correct the deficits.

Treatment, substantiated by single-case experimental design methods, begins by establishing the rapist's baseline skills performance. Thirty-minute treatment sessions involve videotaping the rapist's social performance. One element of the skills scale is corrected at a time, by verbal feedback as to how the rapist should change, by modeling correct behavior for him, by verbal reinforcement for improved performance, and by videotape feedback that allows him to see not only his deficits, but also his improved skills.

The most impressive aspects of such treatment are the lack of heterosocial skills displayed by some rapists and the rapidity with which the patients can acquire these skills with direct skills training (usually within two to three weeks). The current state of assessing the utility of this treatment component is as follows: numerous single-case and controlled outcome studies have demonstrated its effectiveness with nondeviants; controlled single-subject studies have recently been conducted with sexual deviates, but no controlled studies have been completed with rapists. Now that adequate dependent measures of social skills acquisition have been established, controlled studies are expected to accelerate. For the present, case reports strongly support the need for heterosocial-heterosexual skills, and single-case experiments have confirmed the effectiveness of skills training.

Increasing Arousal to Adult Females

Surprisingly, a number of sexual aggressives show little or no sexual arousal to adult females and/or to "normal" sexual intercourse with a consenting adult.

This may sound paradoxical at first, since most rapists are arrested for sexually forcing themselves on adult females. Many rapists, however, report that intercourse with a consenting female is not erotic. Forced sexual contact or actually sadistically raping the female, by contrast, is highly erotic.

These reports by rapists have recently been confirmed experimentally in the laboratory (Abel, Barlow, Blanchard, and Guild, 1975). Thirteen rapists and seven controls were presented rape or mutually enjoyable intercourse scenes while monitoring subjects' erections. Results indicated that only those subjects with histories of rape responded significantly to the rape scenes. Furthermore, when rapists were arranged along a continuum from few to many rapes, those with the highest incidence of rapes had very high arousal to rape scenes but relatively low arousal to mutually enjoyable intercourse scenes.

Other rapists fail to respond to mutually enjoyable intercourse with an adult female because they are exclusive pedophiliacs. Regardless of why a rapist fails to have adequate arousal to adult women, the psychoanalytic psychotherapy programs and behavior modification programs both have viewed development of such arousal as a critical element of treatment, a component ignored by other treatment programs.

Analytically oriented therapists such as Rado (1949), Karpman (1954), Ovesey, Gaylin, and Hendin (1963), Bieber, Bieber, Dain, Dince, Drelich, Grundlach, Kramer, Wilber and Bieber (1963), and Salzman (1972) have viewed heterosexual fear and avoidance as the underlying causes of sexual deviations such as rape. Treatment has involved exploration of the rapist's fears and phobias of women or female genitalia (castration anxiety) so as to allow genital union between the patient and a mutually consenting adult female. Since rape is viewed as an avoidance behavior that has replaced such consenting sexual union, it is assumed that once such adult genital union is completed, rape will no longer be necessary.

Although this conceptual model is used by the analytically oriented programs and is felt to be critical for treatment, no measures concomitant with analytic treatment have been obtained to substantiate that resolution of castration fears leads to increased arousal to adult females and to reduction of arousal to rape cues. Controlled studies are still needed in this area.

By contrast, behavioral programs have developed several methods of increasing normal heterosexual arousal as substantiated by well-controlled studies that have recorded the patient's increased erection to adult females as treatment progressed. The methods include masturbatory conditioning, fading, classical conditioning, and exposure, and have recently been summarized and reviewed by Abel and Blanchard (in press).

Of particular relevance to the treatment of sexual aggressives are the techniques of masturbatory conditioning (Abel and Blanchard, 1974) and fading. In the former technique the patient is taught to substitute normal heterosexual fantasies in place of his sexually aggressive fantasies used during masturbation. Marshall and his colleagues (Marshall, 1973; Marshall and Williams, 1975) have successfully used masturbatory conditioning as part of their treatment program for rapists and pedophiliacs. Abel and his associates (Abel, Barlow, and Blanchard, 1973; Abel, Blanchard, Barlow, and Flanagan, 1975) have used masturbatory conditioning as the exclusive treatment modality in two single-subject experiments with sadistic sexual aggressives. In these latter studies, not only did the sadistic aggressives develop arousal to mutually enjoyable intercourse cues, but concomitantly they both lost their marked arousal to sadistic cues without institution of a treatment method specifically to reduce that sadistic arousal. We have observed similar results in about one-third of those patients who once lacked, but later developed, normal heterosexual arousal. This finding points to the value of developing adequate heterosexual arousal before decreasing arousal to rape, since arousal to rape cues may simply extinguish while heterosexual arousal develops. It also stresses the need for continuous monitoring of arousal patterns throughout treatment so as to identify which treatments are actually needed (Barlow and Abel, in press).

Another promising behavioral method for developing heterosexual arousal is fading (Barlow and Agras, 1973). Based on the stimulus control literature, the method involves gradually changing the source of the patient's erection response from a deviant object (arousal to young children, for example) to a nondeviant object (an adult woman). Laws (1974a) has recently automated this procedure with some degree of success.

In conclusion, the behavior modification approaches have developed a number of methods to generate arousal to consenting adult females in rapists previously lacking such responses. Although no controlled outcome studies have been completed, numerous single-subject experiments have confirmed the effectiveness of these treatment methods.

Decreasing Sexual Arousal to Rape

This final component of treatment involves techniques to decrease the rapist's sexual arousal to thoughts and urges to rape. Reducing rape behavior is an objective of all treatment programs, although some programs have more explicit methods to accomplish this than others.

Psychoanalytically oriented treatment programs (Salzman, 1972) do not necessarily see reduction of urges to rape as the major goal of treatment since rape is viewed as but one expression of the patient's basic personality. Treatment is not aimed primarily at this symptom reduction (arousal to rape), but ideally involves resolution of the patient's castration anxiety and heterosexual phobia. Control of rape behavior is expected to follow reestablishment of his sense of self-worth.

Individual and group therapy programs attempt to improve the patient's self-control of his urges to rape by repeated confrontation, catharsis, testimonials, and numerous self-control methods.

Another method to reduce arousal to rape has been to reduce overall sexual drive by either surgical or chemical castration. Surgical castration has been completed in over 900 cases of sex offenders at the Herstedvester facility in Denmark (Stürup, 1968). Of 38 rapists housed at that unit from 1935 to 1961, 18 requested and were granted surgical castration. Information has been reported for 11 of these cases released one year after castration. Of these 11, no rapist has been rearrested for a sexual crime, but 6 of the 11 were arrested for non-sexually related crimes.

A form of reversible castration, the use of the drugs cyproterone acetate or medroxyprogesterone, has been more recently explored (Hoffet, 1968; Laschet, Laschet, Fetzner, Glaesel, Malland and Naab, 1967; Money, 1970). These agents functionally cause a depletion of testosterone which results in a decline in sexual drive and interest and reportedly with greater control over one's sexual behavior. These agents also produce side effects such as impotence and depression. This treatment has generally been used in a crisis situation, when the patient reports loss of control is eminent, and there is need for some immediate control of his desire to rape. Clinically, it appears that the acute reduction of overall sexual drive may be of therapeutic value in some cases, but the ultimate and more humane goal of treatment should be *selective* reduction of deviant arousal while nondeviant arousal is maintained. To date, such discrimination of arousal has not resulted from chemical castration.

The opportunity for ethical abuse using castration methods is fairly high, especially in view of the permanency of surgical castration. Of equal concern are the effects of castration on other treatment program development. If castration was seen as an easy method to reduce sexual arousal to rape, fewer programs might be researched to teach suppression of arousal to rape cues while maintaining arousal to normal heterosexual themes.

Behavior modification approaches to the treatment of sexual deviates initially focused almost exclusively on methods for decreasing excessive sexual arousal to deviant persons, objects, or activities. Hence, there is a fairly large body of literature on the use of aversion therapy with a variety of sexual deviates (summarized in Rachman and Teasdale, 1969; Barlow, 1972). Studies at all levels of sophistication, from case reports to controlled group outcome studies, have been completed with sexual deviates generally, although only case reports and single-subject experiments exist for rapists specifically.

Behavioral aversion methods do not vary theoretically from other therapies, in which thoughts of rape are associated with discussions of aversive consequences. They do vary in three significant areas however. First, behavior approaches use a greater variety of aversive stimuli to pair with rape cues. Second, these pairings occur over time, and the association between rape and aversive cues becomes more easily learned. Finally, as exemplified in prior sections, dependent measures are recorded during treatment to substantiate that with aversion, arousal (erection) to rape cues decrease while arousal to nonrape heterosexual cues continues (Abel, Levis, and Clancy, 1970).

Any variety of aversive cues such as offensive odors, pain delivered by electrical shock to the arm, or aversive images (such as fantasies of being arrested or shot in the process of attempted rape) may be used in such treatment. A variety of researchers (Abel, Levis, and Clancy, 1970; Marshall, 1973; Marshall and McKnight, 1975; Abel, Abel, Blanchard, Barlow, and Flanagan, 1975; Marshall and Williams, 1975) have reported electrical aversion as being successful at suppressing arousal to rape cues with adult rapists or pedophiliacs. This effectiveness has been confirmed by case reports and single-subject experiments.

Another aversive technique, covert sensitization (Cautela, 1967), has recently been shown to be as effective as electrical aversion (Callahan and Leitenberg, 1973). Covert sensitization has the added advantages of being less susceptible to ethical abuse and of requiring less equipment. The rapist is asked to imagine those situations that are most conducive to rape, including the circumstances preceding the act, the environment, the victim, her response, etc. Once these scenes are well in the patient's "mind's eye," aversive scenes such as being shot by the police, being beaten in jail after an arrest, are interspersed. Such pairings are repeated, and the rapist learns to use similar aversive scenes any time urges to rape are high. We have recently completed two single-subject experiments using covert sensitization. Its effectiveness has been confirmed by the rapists' markedly reduced erections to rape cues and by their verbal reports of decreased urges to rape.

Treatment Results

The process of psychotherapy evaluation and a review of the components of effective treatment for rapists indicate that evaluating total treatment outcome is premature. At this time, the elements of total treatment for the rapist are still being developed. Although attempts have been made to define the total treatment needs of sexual deviates in general (Barlow and Abel, in press), studies evaluating treatment for rapists have relied primarily on recidivism rates. Even comparing the effectiveness of programs using the simple measure of recidivism (in effect, reduction of arousal to rape cues) is filled with complications. For example, some centers report their treatment results with all types of sexual deviates, while other centers report treatment with rapists only. Unequal amounts of treatment are applied by different centers, making comparison difficult. Recidivism itself is frequently determined differently: some centers rely on rearrest, some rearrest for sexual crimes, some rehospitalization, etc. Finally, some centers have a limited follow-up period, while others carry out extensive follow-up for five years or more. In spite of these limitations, the following table summarizes the results from some of the treatment programs. (See Table 10-1.)

Of special note are the data from the Atascadero State Hospital. This information was obtained from patients discharged from 1954 to 1960 and involved the most detailed comprehensive follow-up available so far. Although the data do not represent the effectiveness of newer treatment methods initiated at Atascadero, they do suggest a relatively high recidivism rate (22 to 36 percent) five years following discharge from what was essentially a milieu and group therapy program at that time. Since other programs report recidivism rates ranging from 0 to 9 percent, such low rates may simply reflect briefer, less thorough follow-up periods. It is clear from the available publications that, except for the data from Atascadero, no treatment program has sufficiently developed a follow-up system to allow an adequate appraisal of treatment results at this time.

Experience from our own treatment program suggests that at the present, it is impossible to compare treatment results across programs. We are only beginning to define which components of treatment are needed and what objective measures confirm the effectiveness of a treatment method to alter that component. We find each rapist has a specific combination of treatment needs, requiring treatment of one, two, three, four, or all five of the components outlined above. Until group outcome studies comparing identical groups of rapists with identical components of treatment needs are completed, a comparison of results from treatment centers is only suggestive of their relative effectiveness.

The important point at this time is that the first step toward scientific inquiry—the development of objective measures of treatment progress—has been made. More single-case and controlled outcome studies will follow. In the meantime, perhaps our communities' attitudes toward the sexual aggressive will allow further application of newer treatment methods, rather than relying on the current incarceration techniques that have hindered the development of treatment methods for so long.

References

Abel, G., Barlow, D., and Blanchard, E. "Developing Heterosexual Arousal by Altering Masturbatory Fantasies: A Controlled Study." Paper presented at the Association for Advancement of Behavior Therapy, Miami Beach, Florida, December 1973.

_____, _____, _____, and Guild, D. "Components of Rapists' Sexual Arousal." Paper presented at American Psychiatric Association, Anaheim, California, May 1975.

_____, _____, _____, and Mavissakalian, M. Measurement of sexual

Table 10-1
Treatment Center Outcomes for Sexual Aggressives

Program	Treatment Population	Outcome
Atascadero State Hospital, Atascadero, California	106 sexual aggressives with adult or child victims	22 percent recidivism rate at 5-year follow-up for pedophiliacs, 36 percent for adult rapists
Center for the Diagnosis and Treatment of Dangerous Persons, Bridgewater, Massachusetts	82 physical or sexual aggressives	6 percent later committed assaultive crime
Herstedvester Center, Denmark	11 rapists	No recidivism for sex crimes at 11-year follow-up
New Jersey State Diagnostic Center, Menlo Park, Edison, New Jersey	200 sexual deviates, 29 percent of which were rapists	"Very small" recidivism
Philadelphia General Hospital, Philadelphia, Pennsylvania	92 sexual deviates, some of which were rapists	1 percent arrests for sex crimes at 2-year follow up
South Florida State Hospital, Coral Gables, Florida	75 rapists	7 percent recidivism at unspecified follow-up
Western State Hospital, Ft. Steilacoom, Washington	658 sexual deviates, 11 percent of which were rapists	9 percent rehospitalization rate at unspecified follow-up
Wisconsin Sex Offender	475 sexual deviates, some of which were rapists	9 percent recidivism at unspecified follow-up

arousal in male homosexuals: The effects of instructions and stimulus modality. *Archives of Sexual Behavior* (in press).

Abel, G. and Blanchard, E. The measurement and generation of sexual arousal in male sexual deviates. In M. Hersen, R. Eisler, P. Miller (Eds.), *Progress in Behavior Modification: 2.* New York: Academic Press (in press).

_____ and _____. The role of fantasy in the treatment of sexual deviation. *Archives of General Psychiatry*, 1974, 30: 467-475.

_____, _____, Barlow, D., and Flanagan, B. "A Controlled Behavioral Treatment of a Sadistic Rapist." Paper presented at Association for Advancement of Behavior Therapy, San Francisco, December 1975.

_____, _____ and Mavissakalian, M. "The Relationship of Aggressive Cues to the Sexual Arousal of Rapists." Paper presented at the American Psychological Association, New Orleans, Louisiana, September 1974.

_____, Levis, D., and Clancy, J. Aversion therapy applied to taped sequences of deviant behavior in exhibitionism and other sexual deviation: A preliminary report. *Journal of Behavior Therapy and Experimental Psychiatry*, 1970, 1: 58-66.

Barlow, D. Aversive procedures. In W. Agras (Ed.), *Behavior Modification: Principles and Clinical Applications.* Boston: Little, Brown and Company, 1972.

_____. The treatment of sexual deviation: Toward a comprehensive behavioral approach. In K. Calhoun, H. Adams, and K. Mitchell (Eds.), *Innovative Treatment Methods in Psychopathology.* New York: John Wiley & Sons, 1974.

_____ and Abel, G. Recent developments in assessment and treatment of sexual deviation. In A. Kasdin, M. Mahoney, and E. Craighead (Eds.), *Behavior Modification: Principles, Issues and Applications.* Boston: Houghton Mifflin (in press).

_____, _____, Blanchard, E., and Bristow, A. A heterosocial skills checklist. Unpublished manuscript, 1975.

_____, and Agras, W. Fading to increase heterosexual responsiveness in homosexuals. *Journal of Applied Behavior Analysis*, 1973, 6: 355-366.

Bergin, A. The evaluation of therapeutic outcome. In A. Bergin, and S. Garfield (Eds.), *Handbook of Psychotherapy and Behavior Change.* New York: John Wiley & Sons, 1971.

_____ and Strupp, H. *Changing Frontiers in the Science of Psychotherapy.* Chicago: Aldine and Atherton, 1972.

Bieber, B., Bieber, I., Dain, H., Dince, P., Drelich, M., Grundlach, R., Kramer, M., Wilber, C., and Bieber, T. *Homosexuality.* New York: Basic Books, 1963.

Boozer, G. Offender treatment: Programming (Workshop). Presented at Sixth Alabama Symposium on Justice and the Behavioral Sciences, University of Alabama, Tuscaloosa, Alabama, January 1975a.

_____. Personal communication, 1975b.

Brancale, R., Vuocolo, A., and Prendergast, W. The New Jersey program for sex offenders. In H. Resnik and M. Wolfgang (Eds.), *Sexual Behavior*. Boston: Little, Brown and Company, 1972.

Callahan, E., and Leitenberg, H. Aversion therapy for sexual deviation: Contingent shock and covert sensitization. *Journal of Abnormal Psychology*, 1973, 81: 60-73.

Cautela, J. Covert sensitization. *Psychological Reports*, 1967, 20: 459-468.

Christensen, A., Anderson, J., and Arkowitz, H. Beaus for cupid's errors: Practice dating as treatment for college dating inhibitions. *Behavior Research and Therapy* (in press).

_____, and Arkowitz, H. Preliminary report on practice dating and feedback as treatment for college dating problems. *Journal of Counseling Psychology*, 1974, 21: 92-96.

Eisler, R., Miller, P., Hersen, M., and Alford, H. Effects of assertive training on marital interaction. *Archives of General Psychiatry* (in press).

Goldsmith, J. "Training Psychiatric Inpatients in Interpersonal Skills." Paper presented at American Psychological Association, 1973.

Hendricks, L. *Some effective change-inducing mechanisms in operation in the specialized treatment programs for the sex offender*. State of Washington Department of Social and Health Services, Western Washington State Hospital, Fort Steilacoom, Washington, April, 1975.

Hersen, M. Self-assessment of fear. *Behavior Therapy*, 1973, 4: 241-257.

_____ and Barlow, D. *Single Case Experimental Designs: Strategies for Studying Behavior Change*. New York: Pergamon Press (in press).

_____, Eisler, R., and Miller, P. Development of assertive responses: Clinical, measurement, and research consideration. *Behaviour Research and Therapy*, 1973; 11: 505-521.

_____, and Miller, P. Social skills training for neurotically depressed clients. Unpublished manuscript, 1974.

Hoffet, H. On the application of the testosterone blocker cyproterone acetate (SH 714) in sex deviants and psychiatric patients in institutions. *Praxis*, 1968, 57: 221-230.

Karpman, B. *The Sexual Offender and His Offenses*. New York: Julian Press, Inc., 1954.

Laschet, U., Laschet, L., Fetzner, M., Glaesel, H., Mall, G. and Naab, M. Results in the treatment of hyper-or-abnormal sexuality of men with anti-androgens. *Acta Endocr.* (kbh.), 1967, 56: Suppl. 119.

Laws, D. "Non-aversive Treatment Alternatives of Hospitalized Pedophiles: An Automated Fading Procedure to Alter Sexual Responsiveness." Paper presented at American Psychological Association meeting, New Orleans, September 1974a.

_____. Personal communication, 1974b.

MacDonald, H., Lindquist, C., Kramer, J., McGrath, G., and Rhyme, L. Social skills training: The effects of behavior rehearsal in groups on dating skills. Unpublished manuscript, 1973.

MacDonald, J. *Rape—Offenders and Their Victims.* Springfield, Ill.: Charles Thomas, 1974.

Marshall, W. The modification of sexual fantasies: A combined treatment approach to the reduction of deviant sexual behavior. *Behaviour Research and Therapy*, 1973, 11: 557-564.

_____, and McKnight, R. An integrated treatment program for sexual offenders. *Canadian Psychiatric Association Journal*, 1975, 20: 133-138.

_____, and Williams, S. "A Behavioral Treatment Program for Incarcerated Sex Offenders: Some Tentative Results." Paper presented at Association for Advancement of Behavior Therapy, San Francisco, December 1975.

Martinson, W., and Zerface, J. Comparison of individual counseling and a social program with non-daters. *Journal of Counseling Psychology*, 1970, 17: 36-40.

McGovern, K., Arkowitz, H., and Gilmore, S. The evaluation of social skills training programs for college dating inhibitions. *Journal of Counseling Psychology* (in press).

Money, J. The therapeutic use of androgen-depleting hormone. *The Journal of Sex Research*, 1970, 6: 165-173.

Oates, W. Religious attitudes and pastoral counseling. In H. Resnik and M. Wolfgang (Eds.), *Sexual Behavior.* Boston: Little, Brown and Company, 1972.

Ovesey, L., Gaylin, W., and Hendin, H. Psychotherapy of male homosexuality. *Archives of General Psychiatry*, 1963, 9: 19-31.

Pacht, A. "The Rapist in Treatment: Professional Myths and Psychological Realities." Paper presented at Sixth Alabama Symposium on Justice and the Behavioral Sciences, University of Alabama, Tuscaloosa, Alabama, January 1975.

_____, Halleck, S., and Ehrmann, J. Diagnosis and treatment of the sex offender: A nine-year study. *American Journal of Psychiatry*, 1962, 118: 802-808.

Peters, J., Pedigo, J., Steg, J., and McKenna, J. Group psychotherapy of the sex offender. *Federal Probation*, 1968, 32(3): 41-45.

Rachman, S., and Teasdale, J. *Aversion Therapy and Behavior Disorders: An Analysis.* Coral Gables, Fla.: University of Miami Press, 1969.

Rado, S. An adaptional view of sexual behavior. In P. Hook and J. Zubin (Eds.), *Psychosexual Development in Health and Disease.* New York: Grune and Stratton, 1949.

Salzman, L. The psychodynamic approach to sex deviation. In H. Resnik and M. Wolfgang (Eds.), *Sexual Behavior.* Boston: Little, Brown and Company, 1972.

Strupp, H., and Bergin, A. Some empirical and conceptual bases for coordinated research in psychotherapy: A critical review of issues, trends and evidence. *International Journal of Psychiatry*, 1969, 7: 18-90.

Stürup, G. *Treatment of Sexual Offenders in Herstedvester, Denmark: The Rapists.* Copenhagen: Munsgaard, 1968.

11 Rape, Race, and Culture: Some Speculations in Search of a Theory

Lynn A. Curtis

Introduction

There is little theoretical understanding of forcible rape. The purpose of this chapter is to speculate on one framework which may have potential for understanding a portion of the forcible rapes committed in the United States.

Data from victimization studies and police reports show that a large volume of rape is committed by whites, yet nonwhite rates per 100,000 population are much higher. The proportion of all rapists who are nonwhite appears to be considerably larger than the proportion of the total American population that is nonwhite (U.S. Bureau of the Census, 1975; Curtis, 1974).

The disproportionate rates lead to the focus on nonwhite offenders in this chapter. Because most nonwhites are blacks in the United States, only this group will be considered at present, although much of what is speculated also can be applied to Hispanic males. Black male rapists tend to be of lower socioeconomic status and live in urban areas (Curtis, 1974). Consequently, poor black inner-city males will receive the greatest attention.

A formal theory of rape by poor blacks would be premature. Instead, some ideas are presented with the hope that they will provoke the kind of debate that is needed for such a theory to eventually emerge. A general framework is first presented, based on cultural responses by blacks to the structural inequalities in American society. The model is then applied to rape by poor black males—on other blacks, as well as on whites.[1]

A General Framework

Little agreement exists on the precise meaning of "culture." Kroeber and Parsons (1958, pp. 582-583) define the term narrowly, as "transmitted and created content and patterns of values, ideas and other symbolic-meaningful systems." Observers such as Hannerz (1969b) follow Tylor's classic perspective by treating culture very broadly, arguing that to concentrate mainly on values fails to embrace behavior, essential shared community meanings, modes of outlook, definitions of reality, and imagery of expectations.

In defining culture, a useful refinement is to follow Yinger (1960) in

117

distinguishing between subcultural and contracultural component systems. Subcultures have values different from but not in conflict with the dominant culture. Contracultures have values different from *and* in conflict with the dominant culture. These are conceptual poles: In practice, subcultural and contracultural elements are usually mixed.

With these general principles in mind, a dominant culture, black poverty subculture, and violent contraculture can be identified in the American setting.

Dominant Culture

The "dominant culture" will be associated here with the locus of power in the United States—the values, behaviors, and outlooks, of the persons most influential in making the laws, leading the country politically, and controlling the economy and society. This interpretation is consistent with the use of the term by Wolfgang and Ferracuti (1967). The attribute group of Americans which has the clearest shared expression of the dominant culture conceived in this way consists of older, white, middle- and upper-class males. They are hardly a single and homogeneous cultural package, but it can be argued that they have certain values, behaviors, and outlooks in common and that they exert a pervasive influence on the rest of the country.

Among the several attitude-value measurement instruments which seek to assess these American values, Gruen's (1966) perhaps has the most potential for measuring the dominant culture as defined here. The cluster of values, behaviors, and outlooks, which he identifies through factor analysis is typified by vigorous pursuit of status change, preference for external attributes of people and relationships, standardized behavior, and impulse restriction and control.

Black Poverty Subculture

A review of the participant observation and black studies literature on poor urban blacks in the United States (e.g., Ladner, 1971; Blauner, 1970; Rainwater, 1970a; Cole, 1970; Hannerz, 1969b; Schulz, 1969; Keil, 1966) yields the following as some of the most mentioned descriptive parameters of what might be characterized overall as a "black poverty subculture": a belief in determinism, a demonstrative expression in speech and action, an identification with forebearance and tragedy, an adaptive life-style, and an irreverence toward man's motives.

These parameters can be hypothesized as characteristic of a culture shared by many poor blacks, male and female, young and old. As with Gruen's operationalization of what is involved in defining the American dominant culture, the parameters represent a first iteration, an initial attempt at specifying some of the characteristics most commonly shared by many poor blacks. A comprehensive definition and operationalization of the sum total of poor black life experience is impossible to make. But there is more than enough material already in the literature with which to hypothesize "black poverty subculture" as a valid concept.

Note that it is *sub*culture being hypothesized. The adaptive emotional world view described is different from but does not necessarily conflict with or threaten injury to the dominant culture.

Violent Contraculture

The same participant observation literature combines with studies in crime and delinquency (e.g., Wolfgang and Ferracuti, 1967; Short and Strodtbeck, 1965; Yablonsky, 1963; Cloward and Ohlin, 1960) to document another set of values, behaviors, and meanings which, when adhered to at all, is not uncommonly characteristic of young poor black males. The following are some of the most frequently mentioned parameters or descriptive emphases in what might be characterized as a "violent contraculture": emphasis on physical prowess and toughness, on sexual prowess and exploitation, on shrewdness and manipulativeness, and on thrill seeking and change.

Consistent with the emphases on physical toughness as well as change in this cluster of values, Blumenthal, Kahn, Andrews, and Head (1972) found that black males in a national sample justify violence for social change more than white males. Such findings help argue that a contraculture as defined by Yinger (1960) is in fact being described by the parameters: Implicit is some threat to the present order.

Multidimensional Value Space

The ghetto literature (e.g., Hannerz, 1969b; Rainwater, 1970a), the theoretical literature on violence (e.g., Wolfgang and Ferracuti, 1967), classical black studies (e.g., DuBois, 1968), and empirical investigations of value orientations (e.g., Clark and Wenniger, 1963) can be cited to argue that poor black males who adhere to contracultural plus subcultural patterns also simultaneously carry dominant culture values. In a multidimensional version of Rodman's (1963) lower-class value stretch, poor young black males can be said to occupy a different place in value space than other groups, differentiated by race, sex, age, and socioeconomic status. Figure 11-1 hypothesizes the relative positions of poor young black males, poor black females, and middle-class older white males in such a value space. It is assumed here that operationalizations can be made of the parameters describing dominant culture, black poverty subculture, and

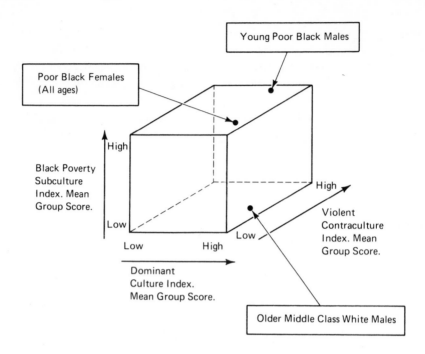

Figure 11-1. The Hypothesized Positions of Selected Attribute Groups in a Three Dimensional Value Space

violent culture. These operationalizations would form three indices, each measuring adherence to one of the three cultural levels. Each index forms one dimension on Figure 11-1.

The figure does not predict that all poor young black males would score high on a violent contracultural index. A very considerable group variance would be expected. Even individuals scoring high should not be thought of as spending most of their time expressing overt violence. The hypothesis being advanced is simply that poor young urban black males adhere to and approve of violent contracultural patterns more than most other American attribute groups when the measure is the kind of average group index suggested. *Importantly, all the statements about cultures and attribute groups in this chapter are meant to be operationalized in such terms.*

It is very possible that the mean contracultural score for poor young urban black males would be higher than for poor young urban white males. A central argument for more frequent and intense contracultural patterns by the blacks is that they have adapted to racial as well as class barriers and, unlike the European immigrant groups, that they have inherited the unique experience of Southern slavery and violence. The same reasoning would predict a significantly higher poverty subcultural score for the blacks.

Economic and Racial Determinism

Those who dispute the existence or impact of a shared and transmitted black poverty subculture (to say nothing of a violent contraculture) assert that the dominant culture has overriding meaning and that lower-class black behaviors are a direct outcome of structural economic constraints. Thus, for example, Liebow (1967) says that father and son are "independently produced look-alikes" forged in different generations by the same rigid cast. Similarities between the lower-class black father and son do not result from cultural transmission, says Liebow, but from the son independently experiencing the same failures, in the same areas, for the same reasons as his father.

This position has created a false dichotomy between economic and cultural interpretations. Anthropological theory acknowledges behavior that is both culturally inherited from past generations and shaped by a person's relationship with the environment. The argument therefore can be made that concepts of independent adjustment should be integrated with, not contrasted to, models of cultural transmission.

Not to allow theoretically for separately experienced encounters by each black generation may understate the sense of relative deprivation, ever counter-pointing one's status vis à vis the white man's, that is argued by many to be scored into black poverty. More basically, we might risk discounting the operation of racism—particularly, today, the institutional variety, which has managed relative immunity from reform. Some critics of black poverty subculture miss this point in thinking it merely class-based. A good case can be made for asserting that, at present, the central constraint evoking black cultural responses is none other than institutional racism. One definition points to the set of "policies, priorities, and functions of an ongoing system of normative patterns which serve to subjugate, oppress, and force dependence of individuals or groups by: (1) establishing and sanctioning unequal goals; and (2) sanctioning inequality in status as well as in access to goods and services" (Ladner, 1971, p. 271).

The argument, then, is that racial-economic constraints have causal primacy in determining black behavior, but that culture is a critical intervening variable.

Another way of saying this is that institutional racism blocks opportunities in the mode specified by Cloward and Ohlin (1960), creating economic marginality among blacks and inducing adaptations that include behaviors labeled conflicting and discordant by those holding power and institutionalizing the racism. Unemployment, underemployment, street-corner status: These are the disproportionately probable outcomes reserved for black males.

The Generation of Violent Contraculture

The blocked economic opportunities and institutional racism that coexist today are very real and can be seen as the most fundamental external factors generating contracultural responses. Some urban males, born poor and black, have the strength, luck, and ability to achieve middle-class or even upper-class status. From the perspective of the dominant culture, obtaining a higher education and showing competence in business or professional work are perhaps the most approved means. There are other more publicized and glamorous means, equally legitimate and straight (e.g., athletics); others are illegitimate and hip (pimping). But the relative absolute numbers of young poor black males involved in achieving such status remain small.

Many of the rest, one way or another, can be interpreted as rechanneling their expressions of masculinity into whatever avenues they perceive are still open, given closure of legitimate economic attainment, the quality that probably institutionalizes masculine respect and is associated with masculine success more than any other by the dominant culture. Even if opportunities remain blocked, subliminated or noncreative-but-nondestructive rechannelings can be useful in expressing masculinity. The same holds true for untolerated, discordant behaviors. Such activity need not be related to violence, but the fact is that a great many of the avenues of masculine expression still open have elements of violence. If one accepts the influences of the dominant culture on the behavior of poor black males; agrees that toughness, hard drinking, freely roaming sexuality, and the like are still more typically regarded as male than female characteristics in the dominant culture; concedes that the young poor black male faces fewer impasses against emulatively extending these patterns than attaining economic success; and finds the suggestion of masculine rechanneling a reasonable one—then an impulse process has been defined by which some individual personalities independently can develop the cluster of values and behaviors being interpreted as contracultural.

With only a limited number of avenues open, it is but a short theoretical step to think that some blacks have concentrated such expressions more than is acceptable in the dominant culture, so that a more distinguishable cluster highlighted by physical toughness and sexual exploitation emerges among some poor black males than among middle-class black or white males. The credibility of the process heightens when the quality of youth is added to blackness, maleness, and poverty. In certain ways, adaptive physical embellishments beyond subcultural patterns can be interpreted as coalitions of body and mind at the crest of energy and exploratory inquisitiveness.

At some period in the life of any particular large black American urban community, the summation of individual recourses to overt masculinity would seem to become large and visible enough to be characterized as contracultural. It may be correct to think of violence-related patterns as being "shared" at this threshold, if only in the very elementary sense that those accepting such values and behaviors would find it difficult not to be aware of others doing the same in the tight ghetto confine. Now a boy who does not opt for violence on his own faces a second hurdle. He is exposed to ghetto examples presenting violence-related patterns as necessary for acceptance by peers. A personality not inclined to an independent assertion of toughness may still find it attractive to conform to the displays of others. This is all the easier because group sharing and transmission institutionalizes the normative integrity of overt masculinity.

Applications to Rape by Blacks

We can now apply the general framework to forcible rape by American blacks in urban areas. This is not to deny that a large amount of rape is committed by white and Hispanic males in the urban United States. It is merely to reiterate that the best available data suggest that poor young black males are disproportionately involved in rape and to ask why. Rape by blacks on blacks and then by blacks on whites will be considered, in turn.

Rape by Blacks on Blacks

Sexual Values and Behaviors in the Ghetto-Slum. How well does the theme of sexual exploitation and prowess in the violent contraculture apply to poor young black males? What is the relative sexual posture of poor black females? How can these patterns lead to forcible rape in particular situations? The participant observation and black studies literature provides some answers to these questions.

In one of the more recent and thorough accounts of ghetto male sexuality, Rainwater (1970a) describes how great prestige and maturity within male street-corner life are attached to intercourse. Sex has psychological and social import for a male far above any sense of biological urgency. Rainwater's male sees the benefits of sexual behavior as far outweighing the costs. Most young men feel some responsibility in providing for mother and child if pregnancy occurs, but any felt loss of career opportunity is not a great deterrent because options are already perceived as limited. Everything that has been said about the impulse and transmission of contracultural behaviors can be reiterated for the single parameter of male sexual exploitation.

Clark (1965) and Staples (1972) say much the same. The marginal young black male is seen as identifying his masculinity with the number of females he can attract. In this "compensatory distortion of the male image," masculinity is equated with sexual prowess.

The theme of contracultural expression by black males as extended emulation of white males also comes through clearly in the area of sexual exploitation. Few would deny that today many white males sexually exploit women. Greer (1972) recalls how wealthy white males at one of the universities she attended competed for the number of women taken and disrupted their lives and expectations partly as a class prerogative, "like the hero of *My Secret Life*, but more callously." A superb portrait of how the ritual of quantity over quality, regardless of the cost paid by the women, fits some white American males was offered in the 1971 Feifer-Nichols film *Carnal Knowledge*. It is also interesting to note that from 1971 to 1973 at least twenty major films shown in the United States—like *A Clockwork Orange, Straw Dogs, Blume in Love*, and *Save the Tiger*—served rape to their audiences. The (predominantly white male) movie-makers say they are responding to the demands of the mass audience (Harmetz, 1973). We know that the mass is more white than black, and it is reasonable to accept the argument that women are not demanding such films.

Poor black men experience fewer restraints against expressing masculinity sexually than economically, so they may exaggerate the dominant culture pattern even more. There is reason to believe that the concern over sexuality by some black males is reinforced by the feedback of expectations by some white males. "The black man spends too much time trying to prove that he is the great lover that he is accused of being by the white man," said one black woman. It is possible that a need to live up to their perceived sexual role, regardless of whether they enjoy it, can be a source of anxiety to some poor black men (Hare and Hare, 1970).

Let us not exaggerate, however. Ladner, Hill, Billingsley, and others might argue that black males have been sensitive to their women, even within an acknowledged exploitative world view. Perhaps Liebow (1967) has set the most realistic modern cadence. His men present themselves as exploiters of women. Yet Liebow also notes a discrepancy between the words and actions of street-corner men. Women are divided into two classes, one for exploitation ("not nice girls"), the other for a more completely satisfying give-and-take relationship based on liking or love. Most other observers also report the distinction.

Consider, now, the sexual values and behaviors of poor black females, the disproportionate victims of reported rape (Curtis, 1974). The available information—for example, in the work of Clark (1965), Schulz (1969), Hannerz (1969b), Rainwater (1970a), Ladner (1971), and Staples (1972)—concentrates on premarital sexual patterns. The consensus is that it is more common than not for young poor black females to engage in premarital sex. The reasons include pressure from boyfriends, reinforcement from female peers, a subcultural association of sexual experience with womanhood, and an awareness that in a hostile environment personal identity and social security often can be acquired by exchanging sex for the thoughtfulness and attention of a male from and for whom there is real affection. Typically, teenagers and young women are concerned with their reputations, seek to protect themselves against being labeled promiscuous, carefully choose their sex partners, and regard intercourse as appropriate only at a certain stage in a relationship with a male. There is also reason to believe that the ultimate long-run ideal for the lower-class black female crystallizes on dependability, family, and home—even though practical realization is the future of an illusion. By contrast, black middle-class females are said to tie sex more singularly to permanency, status, and upward mobility.

A particularly subcultural style of nonmechanical sexual expression might be related to these young women. Staples (1972) generalizes that because virginity has been difficult to maintain for poor black women, they have learned to enjoy the intrinsic pleasure of sex without guilt and anxiety. But, for our purposes, the salient implication from this brief overview is the lack of evidence that the young poor black female typically plays sexual adventuress with a role intensity rivaling the emphasis by many of her male counterparts on sexual prowess and exploitation.

In effect, then, the hypothesis of similar poor black male and female loadings on subculture but higher male loadings on contraculture would seem to hold from the narrower perspective of sexual values and behavior. This conclusion helps support the very low percentage of "victim precipitation" for all-black forcible rape reported in a national survey (Curtis, 1974). The percent is considerably lower than Amir (1971) found in Philadelphia. That is, the observation and black studies evidence converges with national survey data to argue against giving black women a significant role, cultural or otherwise, in the genesis of rape by black men.

Offender, Victim, and Social Distance. This position can now be expanded by examining all-black rapes according to prior relationship between offender and victim.

One estimate is that about 40 percent of the urban rapes by blacks on blacks involves an attacker previously known to the victim (Curtis, 1974). There are few good interpretive analyses of such nonstranger rape. One exception is Goode's (1969) sensitive account of how heterosexual dating in the lower class (he does not specify blacks) can lead to reports of rape. Goode draws considerable attention to a "reciprocal failure to communicate" in situations where the male presses a resistant female for sexual favors. The male commonly believes that the female's apparent unwillingness to engage in sexual intercourse is only an effort toward appearing respectable, whereas the female feels that their previous relationship establishes "an agreed upon limit to the intimacy permitted, as well as a trust that her rejection will be accepted." Similarly, Weis and Borges' (1973) important contribution discusses how mutual misinterpretations and differential sex role expectations in male-female encounters can escalate to forced intercourse.

However, Rainwater's (1970a) observations imply that poor black males may communicate and show more patience than Goode, Weis, or Borges allow in their analyses. Often unlike the situation among whites, a young black male can talk openly about and suggest intercourse without implying that the girl is promiscuous. The boy asks for "a chance," rather than necessarily relying on unspoken physical escalations, and rarely automatically terminates a relationship if initially refused.

But it cannot be expected that those poor black males who are exploitative will always restrain themselves when sexually excited. On the spot and convinced that he wants (or should want) sex, a male may not feel like leaving a reluctant female for an alternative, even if there may be an abundant supply of more willing women. His greater physical strength and willingness to use it then presents a viable option. In addition, for some, rejection may be harder to sustain and rationalize to self and others in an inner-city setting that promotes male sexual prowess than in relatively more restrictive sexual climates. And just as black males may worry little about the financial-support consequences of impregnating a girlfriend, because the economic situation is already perceived to be rock bottom, so there may be relatively minimal fear of social reprisal for rape—a feeling that one has little more to lose.

In the majority of all-black rapes, not occurring within dating relationships and particularly those in which the offender is a stranger, the female is clearly less likely to be affectionate toward and protective of him. She is much more apt to be concerned with upholding her reputation and maintaining the convention of control. An official report is commensurately more probable (unless perhaps considerable fear of reprisal has been instilled). Correspondingly, the male is less disposed to assuage contracultural force with subcultural patience. There has been little emotional investment in the woman, and she may be perceived, rightly or wrongly, as the sexually "bad kind" for whom the double standard generates very little sympathy. Comparable thinking is all the more probable in the supportive context of group rapes.

One objection to this line of thinking may be that intercourse by force is unnecessary because of relatively easy access to women in the ghetto-slum. But the contention has less applicability to older street-corner men, especially when they want young women. Rapes by strangers, which are probably increasing in the United States (Curtis, 1974), may commonly point to such situations.

In sum, our interpretation of rape among blacks has an overriding concentration on the offender. In spite of very large variance among individuals, young poor black males as a group are viewed as often exploiting females in everyday contracultural sexual interactions, some of which emerge, in the most extreme form, as official statistics on forcible rape. A theory that fully accounts for this reported tip of the iceberg must begin with such crucial additional variables as reinforcement from white males, a black male's verbal skills and ability to isolate a victim, a black female's ability to control, and the prior relationship between offender and victim.

Amir. Amir's (1971) examination of rape supports the cultural interpretation of black-black encounters presented here, but falls short by assigning major roles to *both* men and women. Amir does not center his theoretical interpretations solely on blacks, but all-black rapes make up 77 percent of the 646 cases in his Philadelphia sample. He concludes that psychiatric and psychological interpretations do not adequately explain the epidemiology of rape.

Amir distinguishes between two categories of rapists. The first consists of men whose acts are idiosyncratic, for "psychopathic" reasons or special circumstances, and are therefore devoid of any socially explicable role. They are apt to be compulsive repeaters with no planned, conscious motive.

Yet the majority of rapes conformed to role expectations approved by the offender's peers. This is the second category: normatively acceptable behavior within a multiple-person ghetto-slum setting in which males exploit females and seek transitory sex to establish peer group status. Amir relates the fact that 82 percent of the all-black rapes were "planned" or "practically planned" to the greater chance of conscious intent by offenders in the second category.

Amir does not argue for a normative system of shared values, behaviors, and meanings specific to rape, but prefers to extend Wolfgang and Ferracuti's (1967) subculture of violence theory:

Rape is . . . only an epiphenomenon occurring under special circumstances. Members of these groups are constrained by their subculture to rape whenever the group demands. However, they are influenced by the group and accept, more readily than non-members, the idea of the offense and the justification of the act before and after its commission. (Amir, 1967, p. 70)

But just as Amir finds a significantly higher percentage of victim precipitation than in the national survey reported in Curtis (1974), so he culturally binds the victim to offender in a way that has been rejected in our more singular focus on the offender:

Studies of Negro delinquents indicate the lower-class origin of such girls and their intensive involvement in the life of the male-dominated peer group. It seems that the girls from these studies contribute to the dynamics of the male peer group, especially to its activities in the sexual realm. It was also found that in 58 percent the victims were not strangers to their assailants and in 25 percent they were actually neighbors or close friends. These results lead to the assumption that both victims and offenders are members of the same subculture. (Amir, 1967, p. 70)

If the cultural profiles of young black males and females are so similar, one must fault Amir for not working out why so many black females apparently must be forced to intercourse and why sizable numbers report to the predominantly white American police institution. The truth is that Amir gives only superficial consideration to the black studies and observation literature. As a result, his key assumption—that offenders and victims are members of the same culture—fails to recognize the possibility of a considerably lower black female than male attachment to violent contraculture, in spite of similar poverty subcultural attachments.

Rape by Blacks on Whites

Two of the more promising theoretical positions that help to understand rape by blacks on whites can be termed black politicalization and social interaction. Each can be linked to the broader framework here, of cultural response to structural inequalities.

Black Politicalization. Davis (1969) has presented a frustration-aggression theory based on rising and declining satisfactions over time. His ideas can be extended to suggest that black awareness, pride, and power have begun to reduce restraints against directly striking out at the frustrating objects.

What is the effect that black awareness has on young poor black males who already hold contracultural values? The typical poor street-corner male may or may not be as aware of and participate less in developing black identity than black college students and political activists, but Comer (1969) and others have maintained that a cognizance permeates to the ghetto's depths, especially among the young (Curtis, 1975). If this crucial assertion rings true, it is logical to expect that interracial homicide and assault is a natural way of expressing nascent black power and identity among certain frustrated young black males who may already share contracultural values and behavior.

These conjectures can be applied straightforwardly to rape. Black-white sexual attacks can be related to a new emerging sense of identity and confidence in the black community that originated in the civil rights and black power movements and has filtered down to the street-corner level. One result may be reduced inhibitions against attacking whites—whether or not the concept of frustration-aggression is attached to the framework.

Social Interaction. The second interpretation of black-white rape begins with the assertion that there is increasing social interaction between blacks and whites in the country, especially among the young and in more cosmopolitan cities or academic communities. This might be thought to indicate lowered racial interdicts by society because of the civil rights movement, more confidence by black men to seek out white women, more ability by black men to find white women because of greater education correlated with an absolute rise in income [however, the relative gap between black and white income has not narrowed (Curtis, 1975)], and finally the liberalization of white women. Reports of black-white rape then become interpretable as an inevitable, if undesirable, spinoff of social change, consistent with Durkheim's (1950) classic statement on the "normalcy" of crime.

The "liberalization of white women," a sweeping theme, is impossible to precisely define in contemporary America. For the moment, consider only young white women—students and peripheral nonstudents living in and around a liberal college community. These are the kind of women on which Nelson and Amir (1974) focus in their analysis of black-white hitchhike rape in Berkeley. The meaning of "liberalization" can be expected to vary widely from woman to woman. However, one fairly common component is likely to be a rejection of certain dominant cultural values and prejudices held by parents. For example, Nelson and Amir suggest rejection of distrust of strangers as well as racial, class, and ethnic prejudice. Another aspect of liberalization might be a more open and experimental sexual life-style—at least in comparison, say, to that held in the 1950s. The third and most pronounced element probably consists of a sensitivity to the exploitation of women and a rejection of certain traditional female roles.

Such liberalization of young white women can be thought to increase their ability and willingness to interact with black men. Just as some black males may react against black females and view white women as representing freedom from oppression, so certain white females may rebel against white males and perceive black men as symbols of liberation. In addition, it is possible that the sexual aspect of liberalization encourages her to experiment with the myth of black sexual superiority.

If this type of young white woman is then forced to intercourse in a social interaction—say on a date with a friend or after a meeting with an acquaintance—we have little information on how the various aspects of liberalization might influence her decision to contact the police. Perhaps she would acknowledge certain pitfalls in social and sexual experimentation as inevitable and not report. Perhaps she would be sensitive to the oppression of blacks and their treatment in the criminal justice system and not report. Or she might believe that the sex biases of the criminal justice system would exploit her even more. In contrast, a relatively older woman, also sensitive to the racial exploitation, might react differently from the college student. The older woman might not reject dominant cultural assumptions like distrust of strangers nor allow herself to fall into potentially compromising situations, such as hitchhiking.

There are few objective data that confirm the interactionist hypothesis (nor, for that matter, is there much empirical proof of the black politicalization argument). For example, in their examination of black-white rape in Oakland, Agopian, Chappell, and Geis (1974) found a relatively low incidence of multiple offenders and an overwhelming incidence of strangers. Commonly, initial contact was not in a social setting but at a public place; the victim, for example, was pulled into a car as she awaited public transportation or walked down the street after work. These and other data are interpreted as casting doubt on the social interaction position. This rejection would hold greater weight if the proportion of multiple offenders were greater in black-white encounters than in intraracial rapes, the proportion of outdoor initial contact locations were greater in black-white events, and the proportion of nonprimary group relationships were greater for such rapes. In fact, national survey findings are available that show this to be the case (Curtis, 1974). However, one can still argue that such crude police data are insensitive indicators of social interaction and that, at any rate, longitudinal data are the real need. In other words, the basic hypothesis requiring validation is that, over time, the black-white patterns have been and will continue to become more and more like the intraracial configurations.

Synthesis. Until adequate data become available, the wisest course seems to be joint recognition of black politicalization and social interaction. A small proportion of reported black-white rapes are interpretable as functions of close social interaction contexts, like dates or parties. The rest are probably more understandable in one of two ways. In each of these ways, a poor black street-corner male combines emphasis on sexual prowess and thrill seeking with some measure of politicalization, from blatant early Cleaver vintage to the less enraged version equating white women with freedom. Intent to rape is more apparent than in the social interaction setting.

What varies is the victim. In the first of the two patterns—the most frequent—the white victim plays no causal role. She is, for example, assaulted on her doorstep by a stranger or dragged into a car while waiting for a bus in a business district after work. In the second scenario, the woman's liberalization comes into play, and the subsequent offender is likely to capitalize on it. She makes herself accessible to varying degrees. However, in no context where the woman's actions are woven into the fabric of events need we automatically label her behavior as necessarily provoking (Curtis, 1974). It is insensitive to the unique behavioral dynamics of offender and victim to define a given situation, like a hitchhike, as precipitative by its structure per se. Although "victimology" is now a fashionable subject for scholarly inquiry, the motivational emphasis in black-white rape, as black-black rape, should remain on the offender, not the victim.

On White Male Chauvinism and Rape

American feminists tend to gloss over or be unclear about racial patterns in their discussions of sexual assault. For example, Griffin (1971) has concluded that forcible rape is essentially a product of white male chauvinism:

The same men and power structure who victimize women are engaged in the act of raping Viet Nam, raping Black people and the very earth we live upon. Rape is a classic act of domination where, in the words of Kate Millett, "the emotions of hatred, contempt, and the desire to break or violate personality" takes place.

As the symbolic expression of the white male hierarchy, rape is the quintessential act of our civilization, one which, Valerie Solanis warns, is in danger of "humping itself to death." (p. 35)

In building to this position, Griffin cites national survey findings (Curtis, 1974), observing that "90 percent of reported rape is intra- not inter-racial." Yet nowhere does she reveal that 60 of the 90 percent in the national survey involved black men raping black women. Black-white rape is said to be "outrageously exaggerated"—an observation with which we agree, although Griffin is apparently unaware that the reported rate of black-white encounters seems to be rising, at least in some places, and that it is already high in several cities (Curtis, 1974).[2]

Much of Griffin's focus is on the relationship dynamics between white men and white women. No thought is given to separate black-black patterns, cultural or otherwise, nor to how rape by black men, especially on black women, is "the symbolic expression of the white male hierarchy."

Whatever the reason, the failure of Griffin's otherwise insightful piece to follow through from white to black is unfortunate. For it is completely consistent with the thesis of this chapter to associate white male chauvinists with black male rapists. White males are the power brokers who have erected the racial and economic barriers forcing black adaptations and who have set the sexual exploitation theme in motion—without being able to similarly prevent blacks from expanding upon it.

Conclusion

Volatile enough when considered separately, race and sex are even more explosive when treated jointly. They needed to be juxtaposed here because of the disproportionate involvement of black offenders in forcible rape, according to both police statistics and victimization surveys.

The foregoing ideas are controversial. Blacks may resent the possible link between racial pride and black-on-white rape, but they should remember that it has already been made by other blacks, such as James Comer and Eldridge Cleaver. Feminists may perceive that the "liberalization" of white women has been set forth as a primary cause of rape, but the analysis only considers it to be a potential facilitation. And the white males in power have rarely accepted the hypothesized relationship between their actions and the reactions of blacks.

Action-oriented readers are reminded of the speculative and scholarly intent of this chapter. There is little theoretical understanding of rape. Discourse must begin with tentative thoughts. A framework for understanding some—not nearly all—of the behavioral variance has been offered. Culture has been suggested as a critical intervening variable between structural inequalities and outcomes of sexual assault. The next step is to build, through criticism, to a more refined conceptualization which integrates variables such as stimuli from white males, reinforcing black male sexual patterns, the verbal skill of the male, the ability of the female to control, the process of black politicalization, and the social interaction between victim and offender. This can lead to better data, the emergence of less preliminary hypotheses, their empirical testing, and eventually a workable theoretical foundation.

Notes

1. A discussion of the major related theoretical and research issues may be found in Curtis (1975).

2. However, Griffin's attention to white-on-black rape is well taken. This pattern is reported at very low levels, but the reasons why black women don't report can be easily documented. Hence, a substantial white-black percentage could be expected if all rapes were known (Curtis, 1974).

References

Agopian, M., Chappell, D., and Geis, G. Interracial forcible rape in a North American city. In I. Drapkin and E. Viano (Eds.), *Victimology*. Lexington, Mass.: Lexington Books, 1974, pp. 93-102.

Amir, M. Patterns in forcible rape. In M. Clinard and R. Quinney (Eds.), *Criminal Behavior Systems: A Typology*. New York: Holt, Rinehart, and Winston, 1967.

_____, *Patterns in Forcible Rape*. Chicago: University of Chicago Press, 1971.

Billingsley, A. *Black Families in White America*. Englewood Cliffs, N.J.: Prentice-Hall, 1968.

Blauner, P. Black culture: Lower class results or ethnic creation? In L. Rainwater (Ed.), *Soul*. Chicago: Aldine, 1970.

Blumenthal, M., Kahn, R., Andrews, F., and Head, K. *Justifying Violence: Attitudes of American Men*. Ann Arbor: Institute for Social Research, University of Michigan, 1972.

Clark, J., and Wenninger, E. Goal orientation and illegal behavior among juveniles. *Social Forces*, 1963, 42: 49-59.

Clark, K. *Dark Ghetto*. New York: Harper and Row, 1965.

Cloward, R., and Ohlin, L. *Delinquency and Opportunity*. Glencoe: The Free Press, 1960.

Cole, J. Culture: Negro, black and nigger. *The Black Scholar*, 1970, 1: 40-44.

Comer, J. The dynamics of black and white violence. In H. Graham and T. Gurr (Eds.), *Violence in America*. Task Force on Historical and Comparative Perspectives, National Commission on the Causes and Prevention of Violence. Washington, D.C.: Government Printing Office, 1969.

Curtis, L. *Criminal Violence: National Patterns and Behavior*. Lexington, Mass.: Lexington Books, 1974.

_____. *Violence, Rape, and Culture.* Lexington, Mass.: Lexington Books, 1975.

Davis, J. The J curve of rising and declining satisfaction as a cause of some great revolutions and a contained rebellion. In H. Graham and T. Gurr (Eds.), *Violence in America: Historical and Comparative Perspectives.* Task Force on Historical and Comparative Perspectives, National Commission on the Causes and Prevention of Violence, Washington, D.C.: Government Printing Office, 1969.

DuBois, W. *Souls of Black Folk.* New York: Fawcett World Library, 1968.

Durkheim, E. *Rules of Sociological Method.* (8th ed.) Glencoe: The Free Press, 1950.

Goode, W. Violence among intimates. In D. Mulvihill and M. Tumin with L. Curtis, *Crimes of Violence.* Task Force Report on Individual Acts of Violence. Washington, D.C.: Government Printing Office, 1969.

Greer, G. Seduction is a four letter word. *Playboy*, January 1973, 80.

Griffin, S. Rape, the all-American crime. *Ramparts*, 1971, 10: 26-35.

Gruen, W. Composition and some correlates of the American core culture. *Psychological Reports.* 1966, 18: 483-486.

Hannerz, U. The roots of black manhood. *Transaction*, 1969a, 6: 12-21.

_____. *Soulside: Inquiries into Ghetto Culture and Community.* New York: Columbia University Press, 1969b.

Hare, N., and Hare, J. Black women, 1970. *Transaction*, 1970, 8: 65-68.

Harmetz, A. Rape—an ugly movie trend. *New York Times*, Arts and Leisure Section, 30 September 1973, p. 1.

Hill, R. *Strengths of Black Families.* New York: Emerson Hall, 1972.

Keil, C. *Urban Blues.* Chicago: University of Chicago Press, 1966.

Kroeber, A., and Parsons, T. The concepts of culture and of social systems. *American Sociological Review*, 1958, 23: 582-583.

Ladner, J. *Tomorrow's Tomorrow: The Black Woman.* Garden City: Doubleday, 1971.

Liebow, E. *Tally's Corner.* Boston: Little, Brown and Company, 1967.

Nelson, S., and Amir, M. The hitch-hike victim of rape. In I. Drapkin and E. Viano (Eds.), *Victimology.* Lexington, Mass.: Lexington Books, 1974, pp. 47-65.

Rainwater, L. *Behind Ghetto Walls: Black Families in a Federal Slum.* Chicago: Aldine, 1970a.

_____ (Ed.). *Soul.* Chicago: Aldine, 1970b.

Rodman, H. The lower-class value stretch. *Social Forces.* 1963, 42: 205-215.

Schulz, D. *Coming Up Black: Patterns of Ghetto Socialization.* Englewood Cliffs, N.J.: Prentice-Hall, 1969.

Short, J., and Strodtbeck, F. *Group Processes and Gang Delinquency.* Chicago: University of Chicago Press, 1965.

Staples, R. Sexuality of black women. *Sexual Behavior*, 1972, 2: 4-15.

U.S. Bureau of the Census. *The Social and Economic Status of the Black Population in the United States*, 1974, Special Studies Series P-23, No. 54. Washington, D.C.: Government Printing Office, 1975.

Weis, K., and Borges, S. Victimology and rape: The case of the legitimate victim. *Issues in Criminology*, 1973, 8: 71-115.

Wolfgang, M., and Ferracuti, F. *The Subculture of Violence*. London: Social Science Paperbacks, 1967.

Yablonsky, L. *The Violent Gang*. New York: MacMillan, 1963.

Yinger, M. Contraculture and subculture. *American Sociological Review*, 1960, 25: 625-635.

12 The Social Definition of Rape[1]

Susan H. Klemmack and
David L. Klemmack

Much has been written about rape, rapists, and the consequences of rape for the victim, often with the implication that a tragic assault has occurred. Only infrequently is there a specification as to why rape is called a "fate worse than death." The legal definition of rape as sexual penetration of a woman without her consent outside the context of marriage provides only a beginning point. Subtle distinctions are frequently made, based on a web of concepts that involve appropriate role behavior for females and males.

Perhaps the definition of rape most extensively explored in current literature is that provided by the victim herself. The phenomenological studies of rape (for example, Amir, 1967; Giacinti, 1973), with their analyses of the social characteristics of the victim and the offender, the modus operandi, and the presumed context of the rape situation, are the best examples of this type of study. However, they suffer from the often-cited problem that the data come only from reported rapes. All situations in which the woman was unwilling to report the offense are excluded. Even more critically, the woman makes the first of many social definitions of rape. Having determined that she has been raped, she then makes the decision to report or not to report. As the case is processed through the legal system, others have the opportunity to validate or discredit her initial decision. With this further explication of the social definition of rape, the range of cases available for examination becomes increasingly limited in funnellike fashion. Since only the cases that have been validated by the initial phases of the legal system are available for study at later stages, a biased view of the nature of the rape situation is presented. Relatively little is known about those encounters that the victim defines as rape which never are entered in police records.

Behavior, as such, is neither deviant or nondeviant; deviance is a property conferred upon the behavior by individuals in a position to offer definitions (Erikson, 1965). Occasionally those who choose to define an act as deviant hold positions within the legal system and, as a consequence, are able to pose definitions which assume the force of law. However, the legal system, being a human creation, need not reflect the opinion of all or even the majority. As suggested by both attribution and labeling theory, characteristics of the victim, the offender, and the context within which their interaction occurs become

135

inextricably intertwined with definitions of deviance. In this chapter, both situational characteristics of the rape itself and selected attributes of the definers are explored in an attempt to explain what constitutes rape for whom.

Female/Male Relationships

Judgments about the behavior of victims and assailants in rape cases appear to be closely related to normative standards for appropriate sex roles. There is a basic dualism in views of female sexuality: on the one hand women are seen as sexually passive, uninterested in sex, and innocent (a view which Chafetz, 1974, terms the Virgin Mary image) and on the other is the equally prevalent view of women as seductive, flirtatious, coy, and somehow evil (wicked Eve tempting Adam). One would expect that people tend to consider the virtuous victim as less at fault (and hence more likely to be telling the truth about a rape) than her less respectable sister. This contention is supported by Hoffman and Dodd (1975), who found that college students were indeed more likely to attribute responsibility to the assailant who raped a virgin than to one who raped a divorcee. The subjects also attributed more responsibility to the assailant of a female physician than of a cocktail waitress.

The difficulty of isolating consensual attitudes on these matters is evidenced in the seemingly contradictory, but equally logical, finding that the victim of rape was considered to be more at fault if she were married or a virgin than if she were a divorcee (Jones and Aronson, 1973). Jones and Aronson explain this phenomenon in two ways: (1) people believe in a just world where people deserve what they get, and (2) the more respectable the victim, the greater the need to attribute fault to her actions since it is more difficult to attribute fault to her character.

Also, women are often seen as legitimate objects of sexual aggression. Rape can be viewed as the logical extension of a cultural perspective that defines men as possessors of women. The American dating system, in particular, places females in the position of sexual objects purchased by men. Women are groomed to compete for men who will shower them with attention and favors; men are socialized to expect sexual reward (or at least to try for that reward) for their attention to women. This perspective presents the woman as a legitimate object of victimization: if a man is unable to seduce a woman, and yet has provided her with certain attentions and gifts, then he has a right to expect sexual payment. Only the situation of rape by a total stranger escapes the influence of this reasoning. In any other case, if a woman knows her attacker even slightly, she is likely to be perceived as a legitimate victim of a justified aggressor. This view corresponds with that of Weis and Borges (1973), who contend that the less her experience corresponds to the myth of rape as a brutal attack by a stranger, the more difficult it becomes for others, and for the woman herself, to call the incident rape.

In another context, a close relationship is often seen as one in which rape could not occur. It is generally perceived that the woman in this case is likely to have encouraged sexual activity or that the man has difficulty interpreting her behavior as a refusal. Such an assumption is supported by Curtis' (1974) finding that frequency of victim-precipitated rape was higher when the assailant was a close friend or lover than when he was a relative, acquaintance, or stranger.[2]

These positions on male/female roles are summarized in Bohmer's (1974) discussion of judicial attitudes toward rape. The judges interviewed for the study appeared to divide rape cases into three types according to degree of credibility. First, there are those cases with "genuine victims," in which there is no problem identifying the circumstances as forcible rape. Most of these situations involve a brutal attack by a total stranger on an unsuspecting victim. The second situational type involves "consensual intercourse." The judges felt that the victim was "asking for it," such as in a pickup from a bar. The judges described the act in a variety of ways: "friendly rape," "felonious gallantry," and "assault with failure to please" (Bohmer, 1974, p. 305). In the third situation, termed "female vindictiveness," complainants were thought to be trying to "get even" with a man, for example an ex-husband or boyfriend.

Attacker Characteristics

The discussion above has focused on the victim in the rape situation. Fully as much information is available about the characteristics of the defendant as they affect determinations of verdict and sentence. Race is particularly related to the disposition of rape cases, notably in the Southern states. For capital cases, knowledge of whether a rape was intraracial or interracial substantially increased the accuracy in predicting sentences of life or death (Hagan, 1974). The evidence on socioeconomic status and age of the defendant is less clear, but there still appears to be a relationship between these variables and the definition of a crime as reflected in sentencing (Hagan, 1974).

On the basis of such information, one would expect people to differentially define rape depending on a complex relationship of factors involving characteristics of the victim, her attacker, and the circumstances surrounding the rape. In order to focus on the victim-assailant interaction and on the rape situation, items concerning characteristics of the victim or the assailant such as race, age, and chastity were purposely left ambiguous. Marital status and socioeconomic status were, at most, implied.

Definer Characteristics

The discussion has thus far concerned variables contributing to the differential definition of situations as incidents of rape. It is also possible that there are individuals who view all or most situations as rape and those who consider very few instances as such. One would anticipate that most women who consider themselves feminists would regard most occurrences of forced intercourse as rape. However, other than from occasional statements such as that of Lear (1972, p. 85), "many men think there is no such thing as rape—only forced seduction; many feminists do not believe in seduction—only disguised rape," little is known about social definitions of rape.

Social scientists investigating jury selection procedures have found a variety of sociodemographic variables related to individual definitions of crime (Schulman, Shaver, Colman, Emrich, and Christie, 1973; Adler, 1974). Nationality, race, sex, religion, and socioeconomic level of jurors all play a part in the determination of the verdicts. We would expect that similar characteristics differentiate those who define a variety of situations as rape from those who define few situations as rape.

This study explores the congruency between legal and social definitions of rape. At this point, our major question is simply whether normative standards are consistent with the legal definition. Next, we explore situational variability, attempting to isolate those factors that differentially influence the likelihood that any given situation will be labeled rape. The focus here is similar to that of attribution theory with the primary thrust being the identification of those elements that affect the definition of the situation.

In the second portion of the chapter we direct our attention to the respondents, posing the question of intersubject variability. We are particularly interested in the magnitude of consensuality between respondents' definitions. We are also interested in whether sociodemographic characteristics are related to a respondent's propensity to define situations as rape. Finally, we explore whether the definition of rape varies as a function of attitudes about women, family, and premarital sexual behavior.

Data Collection

The target population for this study included all females at least 18 years old who had completed eight or more years of school and were currently residing in Tuscaloosa, Alabama. A random sample of 400 dwelling units listed in the 1970 city directory was drawn. Fifty-seven units were eliminated either because no female was in residence or the unit could not be located. Of the 343 females contacted, complete information was obtained from 208, or 60.6 percent of the revised sample. Since the data were collected in conjunction with a larger methodological exercise involving a comparison of common survey research data gathering techniques, our information was based on a combination of interviews and questionnaires. These included 60 interviews (82 percent of 73 attempted), 58 hand-delivered questionnaires (79 percent of 73 attempted), 51 mailed questionnaires with telephone follow-ups (62 percent of 98 attempted), and 49 mailed questionnaires with mailed follow-ups (49 percent of 100 attempted).

Our modal respondent had completed high school (38 percent); 26 percent had less than a high school education, and 36 percent had some education beyond high school. She was likely to be middle-aged ($\overline{X}$ = 44 years, standard deviation = 18.50 years). Only 11 percent were age 21 or less, and 12 percent were over 65. A majority (60 percent) were married, and most (79 percent) had at least one child (median = 2.04). Finally, almost 44 percent of the respondents were currently working outside the home.

Respondents were presented with the following seven situations and were asked to evaluate the degree to which they believed that rape had occurred.

1. A woman is walking to her car in a parking lot after finishing work at 11 P.M. A man she does not know comes out of the shadows, beats her up, and drags her to a far corner of the parking lot. There he has sexual relations with her.
2. A woman meets a man in a bar and, after some conversation, agrees when he offers to take her home. He, rather than taking her to her apartment, takes her to a deserted road. Although she resists, he has sexual relations with her.
3. A woman has been dating the same man for three months. They are at the man's apartment where they are kissing and embracing. After some period of time, the woman states that she wants to stop. The man continues and after a struggle, he has sexual relations with her.
4. A woman living alone wakes up during the middle of the night to see a man she does not know entering her bedroom window. He pulls a knife and tells her to do as he says and he will not harm her. He approaches the bed and tells her not to resist. She doesn't and he has sexual relations with her.
5. A woman answers the doorbell to find a man who says he is a telephone repairman checking service in the area. She lets him in and he slaps her, forces her into the bedroom, and has sexual relations with her.
6. A woman's boss has made repeated advances to her and she has always said no. One night he asks her to work late and just before they are ready to leave, he forces her to have sexual relations with him.
7. A woman has been dating a respected bachelor. One night he makes advances to her, and she says no. He continues and has sexual relations with her. Afterward he apologizes, saying he didn't know what he was doing. As she is leaving, he tucks a $20 bill in her purse.

Since each situation involved a male having intercourse with a female without her consent outside the context of marriage, each represented, in a legal sense, a case of rape. Thus, the tendency of respondents to define the situations as nonrape reflected a discrepancy between legal code definitions and normative standards.

In addition to this index of the social definition of rape, we gathered information on the sociodemographic characteristics of the respondents, their attitudes toward family life, and their attitudes toward premarital sexual behavior. The following ten Likert-format items were used to measure role definitions within the family. Respondents were asked to report the degree to which they agree with each of these statements using the familiar "strongly agree" to "strongly disagree" continuum.

1. The wife should consider it her job to prepare the meals and keep the house clean.
2. In general, I belive that men are better suited to occupations that require a lot of education like doctor, professor, engineer.
3. Women should be able to have a career of their own in addition to the roles of housewife and mother.
4. I think the wife should assume primary responsibility for the care and upbringing of a couple's children.
5. I believe that men are innately more inclined to intellectualism than women.
6. A man has the right to be "head" of the household, and his wife has a duty to obey him.
7. A woman's place is in the home. The less time she spends outside the house, the better.
8. It is good that children fear their parents because without fear there is no respect.
9. Children are like little animals; one cannot trust them to behave unless they are strictly controlled.
10. All that a man should wish for in life is a secure job that is not very difficult but pays him enough money so that he can buy a house.

To obtain a measure of premarital sexual attitudes, we asked the respondents: for males and females separately, the degree to which they feel that kissing, petting, or full sexual relations were appropriate when individuals were engaged, in love, particularly affectionate, or not particularly affectionate. The sum of the scores for the 24 items resulting from specifying the sex of the individual, the type of behavior, and the degree of relationship represented the global measure of premarital sexual attitudes. Separate subscales were also obtained that measured differential norms for males and females.

Results

Examination of Table 12-1 suggests that normative standards as to what constitutes rape are fairly consistent with the legal code definition. Of the 1,419 responses to all situations, 54.3 percent (771) are consistent, indicating that rape has definitely occurred, and another 16.1 percent (288) are reasonably consis-

Table 12-1
Perception that Rape Has Occurred in Seven Selected Situations[a]

	Yes		Possibly		Uncertain		Probably Not		No	
	%[b]	(N)	%	(N)	%	(N)	%	(N)	%	(N)
Accosted in parking lot and beaten	91.8	(190)	3.4	(7)	3.8	(8)	0.0	(0)	1.0	(2)
Meeting in bar and taken to deserted road	40.5	(83)	27.8	(57)	9.3	(19)	12.2	(25)	10.2	(21)
Dating in man's apartment	18.8	(37)	20.8	(41)	15.7	(31)	23.4	(46)	21.3	(42)
Man entered through window with knife	80.3	(163)	9.4	(19)	3.9	(8)	3.0	(6)	3.4	(7)
Telephone repairman who slaps woman	78.2	(158)	13.9	(28)	4.0	(8)	1.5	(3)	2.5	(5)
Woman's boss after working late	48.8	(99)	19.7	(40)	12.8	(26)	11.3	(23)	7.4	(15)
Date with respected bachelor	20.3	(41)	17.8	(36)	17.3	(35)	19.3	(39)	25.2	(51)
Total	54.3	(771)	16.1	(228)	9.5	(135)	10.0	(142)	10.1	(143)

[a]The sum of N for each row is not always equal to 208 due to a failure of some respondents to answer some questions. Of a possible total of 1,456, 1,419 valid responses were obtained.
[b]Percentages are always based on the row total.

tent, indicating that rape has possibly occurred. At the same time, 20.1 percent (285) of the responses are inconsistent with the legal definition, with 10.0 percent (142) suggesting that rape has probably not occurred and 10.1 percent (143) indicating that rape has definitely not occurred.

Further examination of the table reveals substantial variation between situations in terms of the likelihood that a situation will be defined as rape. Although almost 92 percent (190) of the respondents reported that rape had occurred in situation 1 (the woman accosted in a parking lot at night), only 18.8 percent (37) believed that rape had occurred in situation 3 (the woman on a date in a man's apartment).

The most striking aspect of the data was that the likelihood that a given situation will be defined as rape varied inversely as a function of the degree of interpersonal relationship between attacker and victim. In the three situations where the assailant is a stranger to the victim (situations 1, 4, and 5), at least 90 percent of the respondents felt that rape had possibly occurred, and 75 percent or more were certain that rape had occurred. On the other hand, in the two situations where dating is involved (situations 3 and 7), approximately 40 percent of the respondents defined the situation as possible rape, and only 20 percent were certain that rape had occurred. Finally, in the two situations where the victim is acquainted with the attacker (situations 2 and 6), approximately 70 percent think that rape may have occurred, and between 40 and 50 percent are certain.

Turning attention to the respondents, there was substantial intersubject variability in definitions of rape. Only 7 percent (15) gave definitions congruent with the legal code definition in each of the seven situations, while 3 percent (6) failed to give any congruent responses.[3] The typical respondent defined almost four of the situations as constituting rape ($\overline{X}$ = 3.71, standard deviation = 1.75). Viewed from the negative side, 63 percent (131) of the respondents gave no perfectly incongruent responses where incongruency was interpreted that rape, contrary to the legal definition, did not occur. Another 7 percent (15) indicated that rape had not occurred in at least three of the situations. Finally, the mean score on the summated scale across situations was 14.31 (standard deviation = 5.10) implying that, on the average, respondents were at least uncertain as to whether rape had occurred in one or more situations.

Socioeconomic status appeared to be positively related to the respondent's disposition to define situations as rape (see Table 12-2). Further examination suggested that the relationship is relatively complex. The respondent's level of educational attainment was negatively related to the summated scale score, implying that those with more education were more likely to perceive that rape had occurred. Education did not have a statistically significant relationship with the number of definitions given by the respondent which were congruent with the legal code. Level of education was, however, inversely related to the number of incongruent definitions given, suggesting that while they were no more likely

Table 12-2

Correlation of Selected Sociodemographic Characteristics with the Likelihood that Situations Will Be Defined as Rape

	Rape Scale	Congruent Definitions	Incongruent Definitions
Respondent Background			
Age	-.02	-.00	-.02
Education	-.21*	-.08	-.13*
Length of Residence	.07	-.18*	-.01
Currently Employed	-.08	-.06	-.10
Occupational Status[a]	-.21*	-.19*	-.21*
Family Background			
Have Siblings	-.11	.06	-.06
Number–Older Brothers	.13*	-.15*	.10
Number–Younger Brothers	.08	-.12*	.02
Number–Older Sisters	.04	-.11	-.08
Number–Younger Sisters	.03	.03	.04
Father's Education	.11	-.10	.06
Mother's Education	.02	-.06	-.04
Current Family Status			
Husband's Age[b]	-.06	.06	.05
Husband's Education[b]	-.22*	.00	-.18*
Husband's Occupation[b]	-.03	.16*	-.09
Have Children	-.07	-.01	-.04
Number of Children	.14*	-.20*	.07

*Pearson product-moment correlation statistically significant at the .05 level using a two-tailed test.

[a]Based on the Duncan scale score (1961) for the 97 respondents who were employed and reported their occupation.

[b]Based on the 127 respondents who were currently married and provided data on their husbands.

than others to perceive that rape had occurred, those with higher education were less likely to indicate that rape had not occurred. Furthermore, for those who were married, a similar pattern emerged when the husband's education was used as the measure of status. For those women who were members of the labor force, occupational status was positively related to the propensity to give congruent definitions. Similarly, for those who were married, husband's occupational status was positively related to the number of congruent definitions given.

Attitudes toward a woman's role in general and within the context of family life were positively related to the propensity to give definitions congruent with the legal code, even after educational level, number of older brothers, and number of children were controlled. Those who adopted a more nontraditional outlook gave more congruent definitions than did those who were more traditional in their views. Definition of a larger number of situations as rape was significantly related to disagreement with the following statements: the wife should keep the house; men are better suited to professions than are women; children are little animals and must be strictly controlled; and security in a job is extremely important. However, the same does not hold for the number of incongruent definitions. Agreement with statements such as those presented above does not necessarily mean a respondent does not define situations as rape. Rather, she is more likely to give an answer reflecting a degree of uncertainty about definition. Only the items dealing with child rearing were significantly related. Those who adopted a more traditional approach reflecting a view of children as creatures in need of domination (items 8 and 9) were more likely to give incongruent definitions.[4]

Finally, attitudes toward premarital sexual behavior were also related to the number of congruent definitions given. Those who were more tolerant of sex before marriage were more likely to define situations as rape than those who were less tolerant. And, as in the case of the attitude toward women items, the relationship remained even after controls were introduced.

Discussion and Conclusions

Generally, our findings support the contention that a woman's perception of what constitutes rape is consistent with her positions on a variety of other related social issues. Women who are more tolerant of sex without marriage also subscribe to a definition of human sexuality that includes rape as simply forced, nonconsensual intercourse. Similarly, women who have fewer stereotypically traditional views of woman's role in contemporary society are more likely to operationally define rape at the level of forced intercourse.

If the results of this study can be taken as indicative, it would be extremely difficult to obtain a conviction in a rape case with prevailing social definitions of rape. Extrapolating from the results of definitions of all situations (which, as previously noted, all fit the legal definition of rape), from a randomly selected, female jury, there would be 8 to 9 votes to convict, 2 to 3 for nonconviction, and one undecided.[5] The only apparent opportunity to obtain conviction is the case in which the complainant is raped by a stranger. If any relationship is known to exist between the victim and the accused, no matter how casual, the proportion of those who consider the event rape drops to less than 50 percent.

The prosecutor who is interested in obtaining a conviction should search for educated women who express tolerance toward premarital sexual activities and who have adopted a nontraditional orientation toward the role of women in the family. Ideally, they would work outside the home in high-prestige occupations.

If married, their husbands would have at least a high school education and would work in high-status occupations. Preferably, the women would have no male siblings; they would have no children or, at best, very few.

Turning to the types of situations that members of our samples were willing to define as rape, the perceived relationship between victim and attacker deserves some discussion. Respondents are willing to acknowledge a situation as rape, providing that there were fairly evident indications that the victim had no control over the event. The cases involving a stranger (the parking lot, the bedroom, and the repairman) were judged to be rape by at least 75 percent of the respondents. These instances correspond to the cultural myth that the typical rape situation involves a stranger leaping out of the shadows in a dark alley. When the situation is not congruent with this stereotype, the respondent is forced to look for interpretations other than rape, often reflecting the view that the woman is in some way to blame. Either she promoted the sexual activity and received what she deserved, or she was stupid/gullible and received her just reward. Both explanations place the responsibility on the victim.

The perception of woman as seductress, discussed earlier in the chapter, again is apparent as an interpretation of the findings. When she is raped, a woman is seen as, and often thinks of herself as, the provocateur, who unleashed an uncontrollable male urge or gave the wrong impression about her sexual availability. She thus deserved the sexual consequences. She is additionally faulted, in that she should have, in some way, been able to avoid the assault. Women are taught from childhood that since they are defenseless females, it is their responsibility to avoid dangerous and compromising situations. When she is raped, a woman feels victimized and, instead of blaming the attacker, all too often blames herself for her apparent lack of judgment.

Support for such views is clear in the results presented here. Of the respondents 92 percent term the assault on a woman by a stranger in the parking lot as rape. However, fewer (78 percent) are willing to label the assault by the telephone repairman as rape. One explanation for this difference is the implication that the woman should not have let him into the house. Similarly, in two other cases, although there was generally less agreement that rape had occurred, the woman assaulted by her boss could be judged to have less control over the situation than the woman in the bar. Consistent with our interpretation, the former situation was more often considered rape by the sample (49 versus 40 percent indicating that rape had definitely occurred in the two situations respectively).

The fact that women receive subtle social cues from a male-oriented culture that a raped woman is considered a responsible rather than an innocent victim is also reflected in our results. We found that the degree to which respondents were raised in a situation where males were present, particularly with (presumably influential) older brothers, the more responsibility they were willing to ascribe to the victim, as judged by type of situation defined as rape. At the same time, when there is some mitigating factor, such as a higher educational level, the effects of socialization become less relevant.

In sum, current normative definitions of rape are inconsistent, both internally and in relation to legal codes. Either society must change legal definitions to conform to perceptions, or people must be reeducated about the situation, a change that involves altering long-standing concepts about male-female interaction. In part, with the advent of the women's movement and growing awareness and discussion of male-female roles, this process has begun, but only along certain dimensions. Particularly needed are changes in attitudes about appropriate sexual roles. Men must come to view women less as objects that can be purchased or must be won, and women must stop competing for men's attentions, as if a male is a prize to be collected. Women must also change their views on femininity and aggression and see themselves as capable of defending against attack, rather than as creatures who must be, even in dangerous situations, understanding, submissive, and nonaggressive.

Destroying the myths about sexuality could remove at least part of the ambiguities surrounding rape. Without a basis for rationalization and justification, rape could be redefined in the context of a violent attack on an individual.

Notes

1. We would like to acknowledge the aid of the Survey Research class, Spring 1975, for their work in data collection as well as graduate students in sociology for their aid in interviewing. This project was partially funded by a grant from the University of Alabama.

2. Victim-precipitated rape is defined as an episode ending in forced intercourse when a female first agreed to sexual relations, or clearly invited them verbally and through gestures, but then retracted before the act (Curtis, 1974, p. 600). Percentages of rapes that are encouraged by the victim range from Amir's 19 percent (Amir, 1967) to a low of 2 to 4 percent found in data collected during 1967 in a study by the National Commission on the Causes and Prevention of Violence (Curtis, 1974).

3. A response congruent with the legal code is one in which the respondent answered with certainty that a situation represented rape. Similarly, an incongruent response was a "certain no" that a situation did not represent rape. Both "possibly" and "probably not" responses were excluded from this count.

4. See the section on data collection for the full wording of the items on attitudes toward family.

5. We cannot discuss any implication for a male or mixed jury. Because of methodological considerations for other aspects of the study, an a priori decision was made to limit the survey to an all-female sample. In future research sex should be included as a potentially relevant variable related to the social perceptions of rape.

References

Adler, F. Empathy as a factor in determining jury verdicts. *Criminology*, 1974, 12: 127-128.

Amir, M. Victim-precipitated forcible rape. *Journal of Criminal Law, Criminology, and Police Science*, 1967, 58: 493-502.

Bohmer, C. Judicial attitudes toward rape victims. *Judicature*, 1974, 57: 303-307.

Chafetz, J. *Masculine/feminine or human?* Itasca, Ill.: F.E. Peacock, 1974.

Cunningham, C. The Gainesville Eight trial. *Criminal Law Bulletin*, 1975, 10: 215-227.

Curtis, L. Victim precipitation and violent crime. *Social Problems*, 1974, 21: 594-595.

Duncan, O. A socioeconomic index for all occupations. In Albert J. Reiss (Ed.), *Occupations and Social Status*. New York: The Free Press, 1961, pp. 109-138.

Erikson, K. *Wayward Puritans*. New York: John Wiley & Sons, Inc., 1965.

Giacinti, T. "Forcible Rape: The Offender and His Victim." Unpublished master's thesis, Southern Illinois University, Carbondale, Illinois, 1973.

Hagan, J. Extra-legal attributes and criminal sentencing: An assessment of a sociological viewpoint. *Law and Society Review*, 1974, 8: 357-383.

Hoffman, S., and Dodd, T. "Effects of Various Victim Characteristics on Attribution of Responsibility to an Accused Rapist. Paper presented at the twenty-first annual meeting of the Southeastern Psychological Association, 1975.

Jones, C., and Aronson, E. Attribution of fault to a rape victim as a function of respectability of the victim. *Journal of Personality and Social Psychology*, 1973, 26: 415-419.

Lear, M. What can you say about laws that tell a man: "If you rob a woman you might as well rape her too—the rape is free." *Redbook*, 1972, 83-87, 137.

Schulman, J., Shaver, P., Colman, R., Emrich, B., and Christie, R. Recipe for a jury. *Psychology Today*, 1973, 6: 37ff.

Weis, K., and Borges, S. Victimology and rape: The case of the legitimate victim. *Issues in Criminology*, 1973, 8: 71-115.

13 Justice after Rape: Legal Reform in Michigan

"Missoula Rape Poem"

*There is no difference between being raped
and being pushed down a flight of cement steps
except that the wounds also bleed inside.*

*There is no difference between being raped
and being run over by a truck
except that afterward men ask if you enjoyed it.*

*There is no difference between being raped
and losing a hand in a mowing machine
except that doctors don't want to get involved,
the police wear a knowing smirk,
and in small towns you become a veteran whore.*

*There is no difference between being raped
and going head first through a windshield
except that afterward you are afraid
not of cars
but half the human race.*

Marge Piercy[1]

Michigan's Matrix Approach

On August 12, 1974, the governor of Michigan signed into law a bill titled "Criminal Sexual Conduct." A wrenching change from the old state law, it represented the first comprehensive attempt by a state to break away from century-old myths and legal traditions surrounding the crime of rape. The new statute had barely made the distance to the governor's desk, passing its final hurdle in the legislature at 5:30 A.M., July 13, near the end of the last marathon session. Had it not been for a small, sleepless group of dedicated feminists, lobbying all that night, this experimental new law might still be in committee. Instead, the new law went into effect April 1, 1975, and the real work of reform had just begun.

149

Since the passage of the new Michigan statute, many antirape movement activists have hailed it as a model law; some judges and lawyers have called it an abomination. While our Michigan reformers must have done something right to so upset the traditionalists, I would nevertheless caution the enthusiasts against the belief that an untested law can be a model law. Its carefully chosen words may say what many of us want a fair law to say. But we do not yet know if in practice it will help to right what is so desperately wrong. More than a legal reform, the Michigan law is an experiment in which we hope to learn how a major revision in the criminal code can deter, control, publicize, and *equalize the treatment* of a very destructive set of acts against human beings. In the light of Michigan's experiment, it becomes critical that other states' law reforms become laboratories, not exercises in duplicating a model.

Except for those very innovative, committed lawyers and law students who worked for almost a year on the reform, Michigan's lawyers were a largely defense-oriented interest group. Sitting in control of the legislative committees which oversee the criminal code, they did not welcome change which would enhance the status of the crime victim—much less the woman crime victim. This reform threatened not only their "machismo," but also their professional pocketbooks. One can see that the law was too important to be left entirely to lawyers!

A group of nonlawyer women initiated the reform project with a meeting in June 1973. Participants forming the Michigan Women's Task Force on Rape were activists and rape victim counselors frustrated by seeing their sisters revictimized by the criminal justice system. The participants perceived a covert violence in the system's careless and degrading treatment of rape victims, even as they tried to use the system to affirm their democratic rights to equal protection of the law, to life, and to liberty. It appeared as if "carnal knowledge"—that legally defined, narrow band out of the wide spectrum we call rape—had in reality become decriminalized. Subjected to low-priority status by skeptical police investigators, to indifference or mockery by prosecutors, and to judicial interpretations ranging from incompetent to obscenely chauvinist, rape had become a "gift." Offenders were unlikely to be subjected to prosecution, let alone conviction. They were more likely to be penalized, if at all, for an accompanying minor crime such as petty larceny.

Some statistics from the city of Detroit, which annually contributes the largest share of Michigan's violence, give an idea of how decriminalized these acts of genital violence had become. In 1973 Detroit police counted 1,647 reports of forcible and statutory rape. In addition, there were 505 reports of attempted rapes. For brevity, let us track only what happened to the completed sexual assaults.

A mere 10 percent of the reported cases resulted in a warrant for the arrest of an offender. Of the 163 defendants actually charged with forcible or statutory rape, 89 had been convicted by a plea or verdict as of mid-1974. These convictions amounted to only 5 percent of the crimes originally reported, and a mere half of those charged. In the entire state, moreover, only 66 men went to prison on a charge of carnal knowledge.

Protesting the de facto legalization of rape, antirape activists had found responsibility passed from one part of the system to another. The all-purpose nonresponse was: "It's the law." Knowing well that the "law" was merely the cover for 117 years of travestied justice, the task force determined that it was a visible place to start the process of change.

After outlining unexpurgated goals for a reform statute, the group approached several legal minds for expert help. Virginia Nordby, then a part-time instructor and the only woman on the faculty of the University of Michigan Law School, stepped forward with enthusiasm and resources. She had time, feminist students, and the rare skill of drafting legal language, having rewritten California's entire educational code. Nordby quickly organized the key legal questions into research projects carried out by law students, some of whom became highly involved in lobbying with the task force. Based on their research papers,[2] the task force had a preliminary statute drafted in December 1973. With the acquisition of its first legislative sponsor in February 1974, the draft became a bill. Its contents, which will be summarized later in this chapter, are explored in detail in Nordby's position paper written for the legislature, *Legal Effects of Proposed Rape Reform Bills.*

The Potential of Law Reform

There are three key functions of law reform in contributing to the elimination of rape: (1) exerting control on the decisionmakers at various levels in the criminal justice system; (2) recriminalizing rape and other forms of genital violence by extending equal protection to excluded groups, and by normalizing requirements for evidence, bringing the legal standards for rape cases in line with those used in other violent crimes; and (3) increasing the value of the law itself in deterring actual criminality.

Why a law reform should attempt to exert control over the very institutions which enforce it becomes most clear when we see law enforcement from the victim's point of view. To know the criminal justice system in this way is to understand with the cold slap of certainty that we in the United States do not have a system of justice which promotes lawful order, let alone a system which protects the people's democratic rights.

A rape victim comes to know the system's worst side, learning that to be a woman and a victim of an assault misperceived as mainly "sexual" is to be one of the criminal justice system's third-class citizens (that's next after impoverished or minority defendants, its second-class citizens). White males, whether defendants or decisionmakers, are first-class members. The rape victim often finds herself the target not only of institutional impersonality, but also of the sum total of male fear, sexual fantasy, and hostility toward her class—that is, women. It is this system which processes the rape victim. The attack on her body does not become an attack on her formal rights until she exposes herself to an experience in this male-controlled maze of institutions and procedures.

Who are the decisionmakers in this system? At one level, they are the elected representatives who make new laws and keep breathing approval on the old ones; at another level, the system is the state courts, where the laws seem to acquire a life of their own, metastasizing with every quaint judicial interpretation. The system is also the standing army of social order, the police, fighting a war against crime that seemingly cannot be won and whose usual victor is boredom or corruption. It's the lawyers, prosecutors and defense attorneys, the hired debaters. Their job is to persuade a dozen "random" people (so often elderly and poorly educated) that a many-sided situation was really all one side. It's the local judges who are supposed to strive to balance community safety against individual freedom; they also strive to stay awake in court.

What links all these decisionmakers is not a concern for the welfare of any particular victim, but a mandate to exert social control. The vast proportion of their time and resources focuses on that individual—call him "suspect," "accused," "alleged rapist," "offender," "assailant," or just "brute"—whose apparent lawbreaking has plunged the system into another round of paper flow.

What can law reform do to transform a system which gives the letter of the law its true spirit? And just as important, what can it not do? Here are some guesses. Bear in mind that it may be five or ten years before we know; our own jury is still out.

Controlling the Decision-making Part
of the Criminal Justice System

First, we can improve the precision of the law as a control on the law enforcers; we can make a clear statement about which behaviors we citizens consider wrong and criminal. To accomplish this we must be very certain about which acts we want to criminalize and just as certain about which behaviors we consider acceptable or insignificant. We must above all distinguish between sexual union and coercive genital contact.

This is not an easy task. To broaden the legal definition of genitally assaultive acts offers us great gain, such as the inclusion of a complex sequence wherein an adult is forced by the presence of a gang to perform a oral-anal connection on another victim. The risk, however, is that we catch by definitional accident such innocent acts as a parent's taking a child's temperature by rectal thermometer.

As soon as we move from the narrow rape standard—"carnal knowledge" in technical terms—we are forced to delineate our own values on a great range of coercive human behavior. That is the price we pay for removing these minute definitional decisions from the discretion of police, prosecutors, and judges.

In the Michigan effort we chose to organize acts of genital violence in a matrix of degrees. Under the old code there existed a confusing overlap among laws on gross indecency, carnal knowledge, sodomy, and indecent liberties. There were serious omissions from all of them. Under the new statute, degrees of the crime articulate the seriousness of the offense, determined not just by whether there was penetration of the victim's body, but also by the lethality and amount of coercion used, the infliction of personal injury, and the age and incapacitation of the victim.

The new scheme permits a closer tailoring of the charge and associated prison sentence with the actual seriousness of the specific deed. Coercion and penetration resulting in physical injury or extreme psychological damage constitutes first-degree "criminal sexual conduct." Penetration where the force used includes a dangerous weapon or a gang is first degree regardless of injury. The potential for death substitutes for injury in such a charge. In the case of a victim under 13 years of age, the injury is presumed, as is force.

The degree matrix removes some of the extreme disparity between sanctions for penetrative and molestative acts, recognizing their essential similarity as part of a coercive, violent sequence. Thus, some acts which would previously have been charged only as assault and battery misdemeanors (90 days in jail or less) or gross indecencies (5 years or less) are now candidates for 15-year-maximum sentences. The degree structure has recriminalized the coercive penetration of a victim which results in no personal injury. Such cases, which were often not recognized as crimes due to the absence of physical trauma such as bruises, are now third-degree "CSC," with a maximum penalty of 15 years in prison.

The new, more precise definitions have already shown their effects on law enforcers. Even from remote areas of the state we have reports from women who were told by police that the case would not previously have been investigated, but that with the new law, "we'll have to take it." In Detroit, police have by their own assertion been following up on a greater proportion of "bad" cases—usually cases where the victim was not injured, or knew the assailant, or did not strenuously resist. The introduction of the new code provided a catalyst for retraining of investigators, and the quality of police offense reports has improved. The overall result: more cases are getting into the criminal justice system, and more arrest warrants are being requested.

The new definitions have allowed prosecutors to advance more charges in each case presented by police, and to charge crimes where bizarre, previously nonproscribed forms of coercion are used. Under the old law, a prosecutor almost never recommended a warrant against the assailant who raped a prostitute, or against the rapist whose gun remained holstered. Yet not long after the new law went into effect, a prosecutor charged two armed police officers with multiple counts of first-degree criminal sexual conduct against several individual streetwalkers. The officers had never "used" the guns, yet the new law recognizes the deadly threat inherent in the mere presence of a dangerous weapon.

By removing some of the judge's frequently abused latitude to interpret the law, the reform aims to control decisions by judges as well. The old one-paragraph statute was so vague and incomplete that Michigan judges filled the gaps with a century of misogynist case law, adding inequities, burdens of proof, and plain insult. The following example of judicial thinking comes from a case in which a gang had attacked a single subteen female, and two of the gang had already testified that the main defendant struck the victim repeatedly.

... Every woman, no matter how far she may have stepped aside from virtue, has a right to return to that path, and if she desires to follow in the path of rectitude, to be protected by the law. (*People v. Crego*, 70 Mich. 319, 38 N.W. 281, 1888)

What the new statute cannot do, however, is guarantee that these decision-makers will understand the law or apply it competently. An investigation that produces facts not organized to fit the elements of the crime, or a warrant on which the charges are confused, will produce only a dismissed case.

The reform will not ensure that jurors will understand the law. And a confused jury won't convict. Nevertheless, jurors have often had to wade through complex questions of law, and the jury system appears to survive. Our hope is that a new set of jury instructions and adequate homework by judges will ease the problems of complexity.

Reconfirming and Protecting Democratic Rights

A second major function of law reform is confirming and protecting democratic rights. Michigan's old statute, mouldering under the garbage of case law, exhibited all the inequitites of the sexist and hypocritically moralistic social order which shaped it. Applied only to the female victim of genital violence, the old law required proofs demanded of no other victim of a crime. A rape victim had to prove—beyond a reasonable doubt—that her mind was unconsenting, that she resisted to the utmost strength of her "nonetheless delicate feminine" muscles, without relenting for a single moment, and that her chastity, although severely "compromised" by the incident, persisted unblemished for all time.

Yet how is it possible to objectively prove "nonconsent"? For absurd parallels, try to prove to another person that you did *not* just have an apple for lunch. Try to prove that you did *not* just intend to share your money with the thief who stole your wallet. Prove even now that you are *not* relishing the idea of experiencing a violent attack on and in your body. Proof of a subjective state of mind, or of the absence of a state of mind, is almost impossible. The failure to prove that the act was "against her will," which has so often excused an offender from conviction for rape, has resulted from the impossibility of this burden of proof. Moreover, the requirement reinforced the tendency of a sexist court to focus on the behavior of the woman victim rather than the male offender.

All this was justified by the assumption of a male legal community that "consent"—a vague term having little to do with the fully reciprocal participation most people regard as necessary for healthy sexual union—was mutually exclusive with the use of force. Force, however, was defined only in its most blatant, overt form; its presence was further defined by the victim's resistance to it. This circular illogic (since resistance equals force, then lack of resistance equals lack of force) added to the injustice of trial-by-psychologizing-the-victim.

There have been many cases where the victim has been threatened with a gun, beaten up, kidnapped or forcibly confined, forced to watch while her companion was beaten up, or in some other way intimidated prior to the actual penetration, such that she became passive when the "carnal knowledge" finally took place. What became of the requirement to prove resistance in such situations? The case of *People v. Phillips*, in 1971, enunciated a refinement of the earlier, inflexible resistance standard.

We think it is well and properly settled that the terms "by force" do not necessarily imply the positive exertion of actual physical force in the act of compelling submission of the female to the sexual connection, but that force or violence threatened as the result of noncompliance, and for the purpose of preventing resistance, or extorting consent, if it be such as to create a real apprehension of dangerous consequences or great bodily harm, or such as in any manner to *overpower the mind of the victim* so that she dare not resist, is, and upon all sound principles, must be, regarded, for this purpose, as in all respects equivalent to, force actually exerted for the same purpose. (385 Mich. 30, 187 N.W. 2d 211, 1971, emphasis added)

What sort of acts were enough to "overpower the mind of the victim?" Appellate decisions suggested that the threat of a dangerous operation in the future might not be enough, but having been raped immediately before by two of the defendant's companions probably was enough. Being threatened with a gun was enough. The judges' statements seemed to say that the requirement of resistance was met if the victim was in abject fear of her life.

By requiring her to resist to the utmost until the act was completed, or until her mind was overcome by abject fear of her life, the old law situation required of a rape victim a level of resistance demanded of no other victim of violence. It denied her the opportunity to rationally assess her danger and to choose the safest course of action. It even forced her to ignore the advice of police and self-defense experts to appear to comply, or to calmly try to distract the assailant.

The new Michigan statute deals with these complex issues in several ways.

First, the burden or proof of nonconsent has been removed from the prosecution. Consent might still be an affirmative defense, as in any criminal case (a defendant charged with theft asserts, "they gave me that TV!"), but the burden of the proof that the victim invited the act is very much on the defendant, assuming that the prosecution has met its own statutory burdens: force, the nature of the act, the identity of the offender, personal injury where relevant, age of victim where relevant.

Second, resistance is specifically not required under the new law. Instead, force and coercion are extensively defined. The statute lists coercive situations in which the element of force will be presumed to exist. These include the potentially fatal instance where the actor is armed with a dangerous weapon, or where the actor threatens the victim with violence or retaliation, and cases where the actor confines, kidnaps, robs, or otherwise assaults the victim. The reform law lists situations where no showing of force will be required. These include instances where the victim is physically helpless, mentally defective (and the actor has reason to believe this), mentally incapacitated as a result of actions by the offender, or taken by concealment or surprise.

In the traditional "forcible rape" case, the new law redefines force as overcoming the victim through the actual application of physical force, physical violence, or superior physical strength. The new statute makes sexual penetration a crime when the actor engages in the medical treatment or examination of the victim in a manner or for purposes which are not medically recognized as ethical or acceptable. Finally, the reform recognizes as force threats of violence to persons other than the victim. Thus the statute incorporates the wiser and more humane rules enunciated by Michigan's appellate courts over the years.

In extending the protection of democratic rights, the aim was to include under full protection of the law three entire classes of people who had effectively been declared unworthy of that protection. One group was men assaulted in some form other than "sodomy." The new law is gender-neutral, applying to victims and actors of both genders. A second group was persons sexually attacked by a spouse during a hostile divorce. The reform, reflecting the legislature's refusal to protect all persons regardless of marital status, protects a person from assault by the spouse when one partner has filed for divorce and they are living apart.[3] The third, and largest, unprotected group were those who had ever engaged in sexual relations in any unchaste or unconventional manner, or had a reputation for same. Under the old law, victims could be questioned publicly about their prior sexual conduct with anyone. Defendants could bring in witnesses who claimed that they too had sexually engaged with the "unchaste" victim. Such testimony was not, however, considered relevant in any other criminal proceedings.

Traditionally, the victim's prior sex life was held to have some bearing on two issues in a rape trial: the victim's consent, and the victim's credibility.

From the earliest cases, the victim's prior reputation for chastity was thought relevant to whether she consented. The victim could be asked on cross-examination about specific instances of sexual behavior, although other evidence of specific instances could not be brought in to contradict her testimony. In the 1970s it is hard for women to accept the burden of a judgment made by male jurists 50 or 100 years ago. Certainly today no woman would agree that there is any logical relationship between her having consented to sexual relationships with one man in the past and her likelihood of consenting to another man in the future. Even the judicial presumption that a virgin will fight harder against a rapist than a sexually experienced woman would not find general support today. Therefore, the new law eliminates evidence of prior sexual activity with persons other than the actor, in light of its irrelevance, its highly prejudicial and inflammatory effect on the jury, and in light of the fact that permitting such evidence was one of the principal factors inhibiting the persistence of a victim through the entire prosecution.

If such evidence is not admissible on the issue of "consent," it ought not be admissible to impeach the victim's credibility. In this area the trial judge was formerly given unfettered discretion. Not only was the victim's reputation for "truth and veracity" considered important—as in any criminal proceeding—but "reputation for chastity" was somehow also deemed relevant to veracity. The appellate decisions made it clear, however, that the trial judge did not unduly prejudice the defendant's case by excluding evidence of the victim's prior sexual activity. The new Michigan law, therefore, similarly does not interfere with the defendants' rights, but merely assures that highly inflammatory and arguably irrelevant matters will not be injected.

The reform does, of course, take away from defendants in rape cases the opportunity, unique to rape cases, to escape punishment by smearing the victim's reputation and by making her personal life the key and deciding issue in the case. The new law does not deny to criminal sexual conduct defendants any opportunity now accorded persons charged with other crimes. They still have all the traditional safeguards against false charges on which the law rightly relies—screening by police investigation, prosecutorial discretion in the interest of justice, the "reasonable doubt" standard of proof, the ability of the jury to evaluate credibility, and the power to the trial judge to set aside the verdict of an obviously biased jury.

Arriving at this all-important exclusion of evidence was a difficult legislative feat. Even though it had been a fundamental premise of the old law that every person had a right to decline sexual activity, and that every victim was intended to be protected, many legislators did not agree. Some argued that prostitutes should be "fair game," and outside the scope of the law's protection. Some offered amendments similar to a provision of the Model Penal Code which would give rape defendants an absolute defense if the victim was "sexually promiscuous." One state senator even stated, "I am opposed to protecting the victims of rapists." Fortunately, no such ideas had ever formally been part of Michigan law, and the majority of the 95 percent male legislature voted to affirm the state's democratic traditions.

Increasing Deterrence of the Crime

Finally, law reform has a third function in eliminating rape—deterring the criminal. The face of the statute has only a small role in direct deterrence, in that some offenders—especially repeat offenders with criminal records—do know the law and what they can do without being prosecuted. Most offenders are probably not aware of the law itself, but are indirectly influenced by their perception of the certainty of apprehension and conviction for a crime. Recent research suggests that the severity of punishment for an offense is not an effective deterrent; rather, the key to deterrence is *certainty* of punishment. The new Michigan statute on criminal sexual conduct specifically responds to this finding by imposing a mandatory minimum prison sentence of 5 years on an actor convicted of a second or subsequent criminal sexual offense.

Conclusions

Passage of the comprehensive Michigan law, along with the success of reforms in Iowa and California, has triggered similar legislative efforts in a score of other states. Drafted and lobbied by coalitions of feminist and women's organizations, new laws have been enacted in Colorado, Nebraska, Texas, and New Mexico. Aware of both the potentials and limitations of law reform, feminists have increasingly involved themselves in criminal justice planning, police-community relations, and training for police, prosecutors, and judges. In Michigan, for instance, women organized a regional training conference on the new law, produced a mobile video-tape training package, and printed special multicopy medical report forms keyed to a detailed medical protocol/guide for use statewide.

The promise of law reform to end a crime crisis hinges on its being part of a planned, total social intervention. That intervention has been most effectively initiated by the very citizens whose direct interest as potential victims gives them a stake in making reform work.

Summary of Changes in the Michigan Law
Public Act 266 "Criminal Sexual Conduct"

	The Old Law: "Carnal Knowledge," "Rape"	The New Law: "Criminal Sexual Conduct," "CSC"
Degrees of the Offense	The statute defines a single offense, which requires that there has been sexual penetration, however slight.	Four degrees of sexual assault are defined, the seriousness of a given offense depending on the presence or absence of a deadly weapon,

Summary of Changes in the Michigan Law (cont.)

	The Old Law: "Carnal Knowledge," "Rape"	The New Law: "Criminal Sexual Conduct," "CSC"
		whether the victim suffers serious injury, and whether there is sexual penetration as opposed to sexual contact.
Sentencing	A convicted offender may be sentenced to imprisonment for life or any term of years.	Sentences range from 6 months to life maximum, depending on the degree of the sexual assault.
Consent	The woman is required to prove that she did not at any time consent to sexual intercourse—she must resist to the utmost to the end. Thus even in cases where the victim submitted when threatened with serious injury, she may be unable to prove that she did not consent.	Nonconsent of the victim need not be proved by the prosecution, although consent may be raised as an affirmative defense in certain situations.
Use of Force	The law requires that the rape be accomplished by force.	Not only the use of actual force, but the threat of force and other forms of coercion (such as threat of kidnapping) may be sufficient to support a finding of sexual assault. The victim need not resist.
Corroboration	Michigan courts do not require corroboration of the victim's testimony.	The proposed law statutorily recognizes that corroboration is not required. A jury can find that there has been a sexual assault based on the testimony of the victim alone, where the jurors are convinced beyond a reasonable doubt that the victim is telling the truth.
Statutory Rape	The previous age of statutory rape is under 16—if a man is found to have had sexual intercourse with a girl under 16, he has committed the crime of rape regardless of whether she consented.	Sexual assault in the first or second degree is committed where the victim is under 13, or where the victim is under 16 and the actor is a member of the same household. The offense of third-degree sexual assault is committed when the victim is under 16.
Chastity of the Victim	Evidence of the victim's prior consensual sexual activities with third parties is admitted at the discretion of the trial court. Some courts admit the evidence as relevant to the issue of consent; others permit it only to impeach the victim's credibility.	Evidence of the victim's sexual activities with persons other than the actor is not admissible. This provision reflects a policy decision that the highly prejudicial nature of such evidence far outweighs its probative value. An individual's chastity is not deemed relevant to the question of whether he or she has been sexually assaulted or is worthy of belief.

Notes

1. This is excerpted from the full poem of the same title, with permission of the author.

2. Of particular relevance and assistance were the papers by Barb MacQueen, "Evidence in Rape Cases"; Joyce Bihari, "Consent"; and Elaine Milliken, "Force and Resistance."

3. The 1975 Colorado sex law reform states that forcible rape can occur when the spouses are simply living apart.

14 Changing Perspectives in Sex Crimes Investigations

Mary L. Keefe and
Henry T. O'Reilly

The New York City Model

Until fairly recently, the topic of forcible rape has been the subject of great controversy, greeted variously with embarrassment, horror, suspicion, or indifference. However, in the past three years there has been a growing awareness of the severity of the problem. Serious efforts have been made to deal with the problem. Police agencies throughout the country have been particularly active in this area.

In response to a 37 percent increase in the crime of forcible rape in 1972 over 1971 in New York City, the Sex Crimes Analysis Unit was formed as a unit of the Chief of Detectives' Office. Commanded by a female lieutenant and staffed by female investigators, the unit collected and analyzed data relative to rape first degree, sodomy first degree, sexual abuse first degree, and attempts to commit these crimes, and provided support and assistance to rape victims who might more readily relate to a female officer.

Provisions were made that copies of reports of all forcible sex crimes which were committed in the city would be forwarded to this unit for recording and analysis. Due to the large volume of such crimes, male investigators continued to conduct most of the sex crimes investigations. However, in cases where the victim indicated a preference for a female investigator, or where the male investigator felt that the victim would be more at ease with a female investigator, a member of this unit became involved in the investigation. At no time, however, was an entire investigation assigned to members of the unit; nor did such members at any time make arrests for sex crimes.

In September 1973, a pilot project was undertaken in the Bronx. A sex crimes investigation unit was set up that was completely responsible for the investigation of sex crimes, from the initial phone call to the police through the final adjudication in court. This was a major departure from the assistance and support role in New York City. The unit was staffed by one lieutenant, two sergeants, and thirteen male detectives. The pilot was viewed as so successful that later in the year it was implemented citywide. This receptivity has led New York City to make the largest commitment of personnel and resources to sex crimes investigations of any city in the United States.

161

The duties of the unit's members were, then, to assist field investigators and to maintain records of sex crimes. Officers assigned to sex crimes investigations possessed a wealth of experience and investigative talent, but few had any formal training in the area of sex crimes investigations. The task of training these investigators was delegated to the Sex Crimes Analysis Unit.

The New York City Police Department has grown increasingly aware of the need for specialized attitudinal training for sex crimes investigators. Victimology studies and interviewing experience suggest that sex crime victims are unique among victims of crimes. Crime victimization places any individual in a state of crisis. In addition to the usual stresses accompanying this state, the sex crimes victim must cope with feelings of shame, embarrassment, and guilt because of the stigma which society imposes. The burden of these mental pressures can be overwhelming; and the presence of a sympathetic, understanding, supportive, authority figure, such as the investigating detective, is of great value to the future psychological well-being of the victim. Conversely, poor attitudes, insensitive questioning, and unsympathetic bearing can have serious negative effects on the victim.

Sex Crimes Training: Constructive Attitudes and Helping Skills

A training program was formulated for sex crimes investigators. Teaching investigation techniques was relatively simple and mechanical. Such topics as evidence gathering and processing in sex crimes, search of the crime scene, and conducting lineups were incorporated into the curriculum and were readily assimilated by sex crimes investigators. However, the challenge of bringing about attitudinal changes posed some problems. How would the personnel react to such training? A truly professional police officer is either consciously or instinctively aware of and attentive to the feelings of the complainants. Would the inclusion of this material be misconstrued by the officers to mean that they were not sufficiently sensitive to sex crimes victims? The decision was to avoid any soul-searching "group therapy" approach.

Crisis Intervention Techniques

The initial training effort consisted of presentations by two psychologists with expertise in the field of victimology and crisis intervention. The session was attended by approximately 50 sex crimes investigators and supervisors. The first speaker was extremely knowledgeable, but his presentation was somewhat stilted and formalistic. He discussed concepts which assumed prior knowledge of psychological theory on the part of the police officers.

The second speaker had previously taught family crisis intervention in the Police Academy. This speaker was able to convey concepts in a clear, practical manner. He discussed crisis theory and reactions to stress and vividly described the emotional turmoil suffered by sex crimes victims. Police are immediately available and are authority figures; thus they can be of great assistance in reducing stress if they are gentle and understanding. He related a case history displaying correct application of crisis intervention techniques and provided a list of practical means by which the theory could be applied. Briefly summarized, the following are the guidelines he suggested:

1. Avoid any suggestion of force. The rapist was forceful and aggressive. If you hope to gain the victim's confidence, your behavior must not be so overzealous as to cause you to be perceived by her as an aggressive person.
2. Be nonjudgmental and patient. Put the victim at ease and create an atmosphere which will allow her to discuss the incident willingly and naturally. This may take longer than direct questioning would, but the quality of information will be superior.
3. Use a gentle approach. Despite your own feelings of discomfort or embarrassment, encourage the victim to talk about the crime, to "ventilate."
4. Conduct questioning at an appropriate location. Generally, the victim's home is the best place, since this adds to the victim's sense of safety and security and since complainants seldom feel at ease in a police station. When in doubt, ask the victim, "Where would you feel most comfortable talking about this?"
5. It may become necessary for the investigator to deal with the victim's family, since they, too, are in a state of crisis at this time. Be equally tactful and supportive in dealing with them.
6. See the victim privately, away from other family members. If necessary, interview other family members. Assure all concerned that the victim is blameless and should not feel shame or guilt. Let them know that the victim acted correctly in submitting, for she is still alive. Enlist the family as helpers in the investigative process. Have them listen to her story and report any new information to you. This will serve two purposes: (1) the victim may easily ventilate, and (2) some of the family's feelings of helplessness are alleviated.
7. A victim coming to the station house alone to report a sex crime may want and need support in dealing with her family. Ask if she wants to be taken home and have the officer explain the situation to the family. Establish an immediate, confidential, close relationship with the victim and her family. Make the family aware of the significance of the crime to the victim so that they will not repress her from telling the story or pass judgment upon her. Help them to relate to the victim with the same compassion and understanding which you have shown to her and to them.
8. In later interviews, explain court procedures to her and remain physically close to her in court. She needs your support in these strange surroundings.

Refer her to appropriate women's organizations or counseling services if she needs such support.

9. If a victim specifically and spontaneously requests a female officer, one should be provided for her. However, there are advantages to having a sensitive male with sex crime victims; an understanding, supportive male officer may help to show the victim that not all men are aggressive and harmful. Such an attitude may ease her job of relating to the other men in her life. More important than the sex of the investigator is individual officer's crisis intervention and investigative competence.

In conclusion, the psychologist pointed out that an understanding of crisis intervention techniques by an investigating officer can be immeasurably helpful to the psychological well-being of the victim. It also will aid the officer in identifying and apprehending the sex crime offender and in the preparation of a solid court case. This lecture content has since been made available in the police professional literature (Bard and Ellison, 1974).

The response to this lecture was overwhelming. The audience enthusiastically accepted the presentation. For the first time, the officers became truly aware of the importance of their actions and attitudes towards the sex crime victim. Prior to this presentation, complaints of insensitivity on the part of investigating officers were frequently received in the Sex Crimes Analysis Unit. These complaints came from various women's groups who had spoken to victims, as well as from individual victims who would call the unit directly. Almost immediately, the complaints decreased after this presentation. Such complaints have become rare and usually involve the uniform force. Investigation into complaints commonly reflects a misunderstanding on the part of the victim rather than any conscious negative behavior by the officers. It became evident that the techniques advocated were of great value to sex crimes investigators, simply because they worked! The number of successful investigations and arrests increased dramatically, due in great measure to increased complainant cooperation.

Since members of the uniform force were usually the first to respond to the scene of sex crimes, it was necessary to disseminate this information throughout the department. It would not be practical for the Sex Crimes Unit to personally train the 23,000 male and female police officers assigned to patrol duties. As an alternative, personnel involved in the training of uniformed officers were invited to the seminars. A Sex Crimes Investigation Training Folder was compiled and distributed to those in attendance. Area and precinct training officers, as well as newly assigned sex crimes investigators, participated in the seminars.

Psychologists and other experts from the academic and medical fields were warmly received. Insights into the mentality of the rapist presented by one psychologist were of great value in that the actions and statements of the offender during the commission of his crime may enable the officer to compile a tentative "personality portrait" of the rapist (Selkin, 1975). This will provide some direction in the efforts to identify and apprehend the criminal. It should be noted that this speaker's manner of presentation was also low key and practical. Training officers who attended that seminar left with a wealth of knowledge which they have since incorporated into their training curricula.

A chapter on sex crimes investigations was prepared by the unit and has been added to the recruit training manual. A movie script has been submitted for the shooting of a training film. This film will depict two uniformed officers responding to a sex crime scene and conducting a proper investigation. It will illustrate proper evidence gathering techniques and proper attitudes toward victims.

Psychological Intervention Techniques

Another project undertaken was a Psychological Intervention Techniques Workshop, which was held from 9 A.M. to 12 noon on six consecutive Fridays. The meetings were spaced over a six-week period to allow time for absorption of the material presented, practical application of the theories discussed, and feedback from the group. The course was conducted by two psychiatric nurses from the New York City Health and Hospitals Corporation, with the two supervisors of the Sex Crimes Analysis Unit directing and coordinating the workshop. The role of the supervisors was to integrate the theories presented by the nurses with practical police work. Participating in the workshop were training officers from detective and uniform commands, as well as sex crimes investigators from each Sex Crimes Squad. The investigators were selected on the basis of their ability to relate the knowledge gained to other members of their squads via in-service training programs conducted in-house by each squad commander.

The workshop primarily dealt with anxiety of the victims and with techniques by which police officers might reduce anxiety and depression and help victims to adjust and resume their normal life-style. Interviewing techniques were discussed, and officers engaged in role-playing situations. Female officers played the parts of rape victims, and volunteer teams of investigators conducted interviews of these "victims." Their techniques were critiqued by the group; constructive criticism and interchange of viewpoints occurred. Varied interview situations were portrayed, and unsettling influences were thrust into the settings. An angry father ordered the officers out of his house and said he would handle the matter himself. A nagging mother accused her daughter of provoking the rape by wearing short skirts. Investigators were made to cope with a broad spectrum of interviewing problems. Strong points were praised, weaknesses were tactfully noted and corrected, and alternative techniques were discussed.

One major point was that all police officers have had to cope with persons in states of anxiety in their personal and professional lives. They have instinctively used intuitive techniques of "calming down" persons who are upset. It was shown that the same language, manner, and attitudes which officers utilized in reducing anxiety in injured persons at the scene of an automobile accident, or while conducting interviews of robbery and assault victims, may be utilized in dealing with victims of sex crimes.

During the course, officers frequently related instances in which they had applied the techniques to their complainants and were amazed by the positive results. One detective sergeant reported that he had to deal with a family situation involving accusatory parents under circumstances which were virtually identical to those depicted in one of the role-playing scenes. He employed the tactics which the group had decided would be best in such cases (isolating the parents from the victim, explaining her need for understanding, and urging them to avoid recriminations). He had succeeded in bringing about attitudinal changes in the parents and in so doing, he had won the confidence, gratitude, and cooperation of the victim. The theories had proved applicable in field situations, and the sergeant's success served to motivate the group and to make participating officers more receptive to the program. The enthusiasm of the participants and the readily observable results of the workshop demonstrated the value of such training.

The Sex Crimes Analysis Unit conducts quarterly seminars, as well as one-day sex crimes workshops as the needs of the service dictate. Based on past experiences, crisis intervention and anxiety reduction techniques continue to constitute a major part of the curricula of all the sex crimes training endeavors.

Conclusions

The success of this program is reflected by the numerous letters of commendation received extolling the sympathetic, professional work of sex crimes investigators throughout the city. Statistics for 1974 reflected a citywide increase of 26 percent in the number of arrests for forcible rape over a comparable period in 1973. The number of reported rapes was up 8 percent as compared to 1973. It is felt that the increase in arrests was due in great measure to the improved quality of investigations being performed and that such better-quality investigations were due in large measure to a freer flow of information between victims and investigators. Detectives have grown more aware of the needs of victims. Their daily contacts with victims expressed this new climate of consideration and sensitivity.

Sex crimes are notoriously underreported, due in great measure to feelings on the part of victims that nothing can be done in such cases and that they will be treated poorly by the police (Amir, 1971). The stereotype of the hard-nosed, callous detective has been perpetuated by several recent television shows dealing with the crime of rape, which depicted the detectives as crude and insensitive. In efforts to refute this stereotype, members of the unit had appeared frequently on major television and radio news and discussion shows. Numerous articles relative to the unit have appeared in the metropolitan area press and in newspaper and magazine articles throughout the country.

The unit maintains an outreach van which is driven to various communities and parked in heavily trafficked areas. Staffed by members of the Sex Crimes Analysis Unit and by volunteers from women's groups, the unit provides lectures, graphic displays, a slide show, and printed material to the public. It appears that this public exposure, which invariably includes discussion of the Crisis Intervention Training Program, has been instrumental in the increased number of reported rapes. This, hopefully, reflects increased public confidence, rather than an increase in the incidence of sex crimes.

The Sex Crimes Analysis Unit strongly advocates that other law enforcement agencies incorporate crisis intervention techniques into their training curricula. In summation, we have made the following recommendations:

1. Personnel assigned to devise such training programs should consult with sociologists and psychologists with expertise in this area and receive formal training in crisis intervention techniques.
2. Lecturers who will be presenting this material to police officers should be police-oriented, down-to-earth types to whom officers will relate, as opposed to formal, hyperintellectual types.
3. All theoretical data should be expressed in a manner which is readily transferable and applicable to the practical, day-to-day police function.
4. Role-playing, which will enable officers to elicit their own feelings, to develop empathy for victims and their families, and to act out interview situations covering a broad spectrum of possible difficulties, should be encouraged.
5. The support of the press and media should be enlisted to increase public awareness and to instill confidence in the public that the police agency is concerned with the plight of sex crimes victims and is making efforts to create a psychologically healthy investigative climate.

The end results of such training will be the development of skillful, professional, humane sex crimes investigators and, consequently, better-quality investigations and improved case clearance.

The New York City Police Department has participated in a concerted effort toward a single goal—the best possible attention to the needs of sex crimes victims. Rape and other violent sex crimes are a frightening reality of our society. It is incumbent upon that society to utilize fully the resources of its helping professions to humanely and capably assist victims of these crimes through the critical aftermath of sexual violation.

References

Amir, M. *Patterns in Forcible Rape.* Chicago: University of Chicago Press, 1971.

Bard, M., and Ellison, K. Crisis intervention and investigation of forcible rape. *Police Chief*, 1974, 41(5): 63-73.

Selkin, J. Rape. *Psychology Today*, 1975, 8(8): 71-76.

15

Rape Reduction: A Citywide Program

David I. Sheppard, Thomas Giacinti,
and Claus Tjaden

The city of Denver has one of the highest incidences per capita of reported rape in the nation, and the rate is increasing. During 1973, 461 rapes were reported to the Denver City Police Department. This represents an incidence rate of approximately 180 per 100,000 females, a figure well above the national average of 47 per 100,000 females and well above the 100 per 100,000 figure reported for major cities in the United States. The incidence of rape in Denver increased by 25 percent in 1973 over 1972, and has increased by 160 percent over the past six years.

Character of the Problem

The crime of rape is a difficult problem for law enforcement agencies which requires special law enforcement countermeasures. The character of the rape problem can be examined under five major headings of concern for law enforcement agencies.

The first major aspect of the problem is the impact of the crime on the victim. The effect of rape on the victim is usually profound, often leaving deep, long-term psychological effects. Many victims must cope with feelings of fear, vulnerability, guilt, and loss of control in their lives. In rape cases, victims also face possible stigma and alienation from friends, relatives, and fellow workers. Many citizens do not realize the grave character of rape. This misguided attitude adversely affects the treatment extended to rape victims by institutions, particularly the criminal justice system.

Stemming partly from this neglect is the second area of concern—getting the victim to report and to report promptly. The National Victimization Survey (1967) indicated that the volume of actual rapes may be several times the reported incidence. Part of this difficulty lies basically outside the control of law enforcement agencies and relates to the trauma experienced by victims and the cooperation extended by other institutions such as hospitals. Part of the problem also lies with the practice and procedures of the law enforcement agencies. Law enforcement agencies can do more to facilitate reporting.

The third area of concern is rape investigation which requires special attention to technical detail, such as the identification of semen, hair combings, and other physical evidence. Since rapes often occur with no witnesses, the main evidence supporting the charge of rape and identifying the assailant is the physical evidence collected by law enforcement and hospital personnel. Improvement in rape investigation techniques should lead to more efficient disposition of rape cases.

Arraignments are notoriously low in rape cases. During the two-year period 1971-1972, for example, only 41 cases of the 950 forcible rape cases reported to the Denver police were brought to trial. Even when rapes are reported and suspects are arrested, there is a low probability that the accused will be convicted. This "filtering system" confirms the victim's feeling of futility in pursuing the criminal justice process.

Rape prevention is the fifth area of difficulty. The paucity of knowledge concerning the dynamics of rape compounds the general problem associated with all crime prevention strategies.

Analysis of Rape in Denver

The Denver Anti-Crime Council, under the sponsorship of the Law Enforcement Assistance Administration and with the permission of the Denver Police Department, developed a two-year data baseline on the crime of forcible rape. The period of time covered by the study was July 1, 1970 to June 30, 1972. All available police records for the 965 rape offenses during this time period were examined and entered on a 44-item code sheet. Information which was entered included data on the victim, the crime setting, the offender, and the criminal justice system's response to the offense. The information was processed to determine the patterns of variables associated with the offense. There were 602 forcible rapes, 170 assaults to rape, and 128 attempts to rape during the two-year baseline period. For the purposes of this analysis, the latter two groups of offenses were considered aborted or unsuccessful rapes, although they are in themselves significant crimes. In addition, there were 50 statutory rapes reported during the two-year period. The exact classification of offense was not distinguishable in 15 cases. Data from the 50 statutory cases were excluded.

Analysis of the data from the 915 cases of reported rape indicated that the majority (60 percent) of rape offenses occurred around the downtown city center area and northeast Denver—two areas of the city containing a high concentration of single women. Of the rape victims 66 percent were single; 53 percent were between the ages of 16 and 34. Approximately one-quarter of the victims were accosted while walking in a commercial or residential area. The largest single group of victims (41 percent) was attacked in their own residences. In 67 percent of the cases the victim and offender were strangers. This represents a significantly higher percentage of stranger-to-stranger rape than reported in studies of other cities. In 24 percent of the cases where the victim and offender were strangers, the victim was interacting with the offender in response to his request for assistance at her residence or on the street. In 20 percent of stranger-to-stranger cases, the rape occurred in connection with a residential burglary.

Of the 915 rape offenses reported during the two-year period, 16 percent were cleared by the arrest of a suspect(s). In addition, the police reported 24 percent of the cases "exceptionally cleared." This means that investigators followed all steps which normally would clear the offense by arrest, yet for some reason they were unsuccessful. Of the rapes 49 percent were inactive or not cleared. These cases were classified inactive or not cleared due to lack of suspect identification (68 percent), lack of information (10 percent), or lack of victim cooperation (17.7 percent). Of the 88 cases (9.6 percent) declared unfounded, in only 30 instances did the complainant confess to falsifying the charge. Fifty-one percent were declared unfounded due to corpus delecti; 18 percent were unfounded due to refusal to prosecute by the victim.

Police charges were filed or juvenile action was taken in 150 of the rape cases. The district attorney subsequently filed charges in 126 cases, and 46 cases eventually went through the criminal justice process. There were no data on actual convictions. Gaps between the number of cases in which charges were filed and the number proceeding through the courts probably can be attributed to plea negotiation, conviction for another offense, etc. Due to the low percentage of arrests and even lower percentage of convictions, it is difficult to make generalizations about offender, victim, and situational variables.

For the 915 cases there were 1,247 assailants; 371 suspects were arrested. Of those arrested 81 percent were 16 to 39 years old. Thirty-eight percent of the arrested suspects had no prior record by the Denver Police or the FBI. The most prevalent offense (30 percent) for those with prior records was drunkenness. Twenty-two percent did have prior arrests for sexual assaults. Of the suspects arrested, 40 percent were known to the victim prior to the attack; overall, only 32.9 percent of the offenses involved persons known to each other. Thus there was a slightly greater chance of arrest if a prior victim-offender relationship existed. The reverse was true, however, when it came to the district attorney's willingness to prosecute. The district attorney refused to prosecute 40 cases. Thirty of these cases involved a prior victim-offender relationship.

Rape Analysis Conclusions

The findings of the Denver Rape Study were used to identify content areas for the rape reduction phase. Information on victim characteristics and locations of highest frequency was used to encourage the reporting of rapes. The data indicate that a woman was most susceptible to the offense while performing routine activities in her home, walking outdoors, or hitchhiking a ride as a passenger. Each of these likely target areas suggested different approaches to rape prevention.

Two-thirds of the women who reported rape in Denver were attacked by strangers. Those women who reported that they were assaulted by someone they knew were usually socially interacting with their attacker before the crime. This may suggest that these offenses are not easily prevented and that a greater reduction would be effected in directing efforts at the stranger-to-stranger offense.

Over 50 percent of the victims had some forewarning of the impending rape, but were restricted in their avenues of resistance because of the threat of the use of a weapon by their offenders. In 50.4 percent of the cases, the victim reported attempting resistance to the attack. The most frequent type of resistance used was physical or verbal resistance. Of the 319 cases in which the attack was interrupted or aborted, 24 percent resulted from flight, 18 percent from physical resistance, 26 percent from verbal resistance, and 27 percent from interruption by police or another person. Many of the women who did resist their attackers were successful in their attempts; still, some suffered injuries in the process. The data indicate that if a woman decided not to resist, she reduced the likelihood of injury and also reduced the likelihood of warding off the attack. If she chose to resist, the victim increased her chances of successfully aborting the attack, but also increased the likelihood of injury.

The Denver rapist was predominantly a lone offender and, as such, was difficult to stop. When the rapist attacked a woman in her residence, he most often broke in, entered through a window left open, or convinced his victim that his entrance to her residence was necessary to conduct some transaction. Prevention of these types of entry required community education in home security and potential intrusions.

The data indicate that the victims of rape are the most influential factor in the successful processing of the rape case. They usually are the only witness who can identify the offender and who can directly affect the prosecution of the case. Our attempt to aid the criminal justice processing function by utilizing the victims of the offense, either to educate other potential victims or in an advocacy effort to ensure successful case processing, was central to this rape reduction effort.

Denver's Rape Reduction Program

Following completion of the analysis of rape in Denver, the Anti-Crime Council staff began designing strategies to achieve a reduction of rape. Program design, discussion of alternative strategies, and support of operating agencies were sought initially through a rape reduction workshop.

Four major topics were discussed at this workshop: victim support, police investigation and training, prosecution, and offender evaluation and treatment. These projects were subsequently funded by the Denver Anti-Crime Council as a citywide effort to reduce the incidence of forcible rape. The program components of the rape reduction effort were developed and implemented from the analysis of rape data and workshop discussions and recommendations.

Supplementary Victim Support

A supplementary victim support program evolved under the auspices of Denver General Hospital. The victim support program involves the follow-up of victims to determine the physical and psychological problems resulting from the rape.

Victim research, the first step, is currently being conducted by Drs. James T. Selkin and Carolyn Hursch of the Center for the Study of Violence. They are interviewing rape victims and rape resisters to determine approaches by the rapist, responses of the victim, and personality of the victim, and to compare differences between women who successfully resist attack and those who do not.

Preliminary data indicated that rape victims were confronted with a weapon more often than rape resisters. The victim was approached by the assailant(s) with a weapon in 52 percent of rape cases and in 41 percent of attempted rapes. There was no significant difference in age and experience of rape resisters and rape victims.

Data on the California Personality Inventory did evidence a difference in personality variables. Resisters had significantly higher dominance, sociability, social presence, and achievement via conformance scores than victims. Victims had higher communality scores. The Cornell Medical Index evidenced no significant differences between victims and resisters. In the long run it may be possible to identify behavioral complexes having a high probability of eliciting the crimes of rape. The study will provide further information about the range and intensity of services needed by the victim.

A community-based victim support service was developed and implemented by the Denver Anti-Crime Council, through funding to the Southeast Denver Neighborhood Services Bureau. This agency has the dual responsibility of working with the juvenile population in the area and aiding the victims and potential victims of violent crimes. The bureau provides direct counseling and referral services to crime victims. Rape victims contact the bureau directly or are referred by the police. Bureau counselors assume an advocacy and supportive role with rape victims, encouraging them to report the attack and to follow through with prosecution.

Police

Progress in the implementation of the working recommendations in law enforcement was represented by 50 new patrol officers who were added to the department and two female investigators who were added to the sex crimes unit. The role of the police in rape cases is important. Police are usually the first to arrive at the scene of the incident; they search for the assailant; and they investigate the case and collect evidence for prosecution. Thus, police should have special training to cope with the victim and the situation and to collect evidence. In addition, an in-service training program was implemented to provide all officers in the department with information related to rape prevention and apprehension techniques. The addition of new patrol officers allowed rotation of persons through the in-service training program and specialization within each unit. That is, some officers in the sex crimes unit specialized in rape investigation.

Prosecution

The Rape Reduction Program within the district attorney's office also focused on increased personnel and specialization. Prosecuting attorneys, as a rule, do not have time to offer support to the victim or to thoroughly investigate the crime of the defendant. Denver developed a program with five new special investigators to fill the gaps existing in the prosecutor's office. These trial preparation specialists were assigned to a district court, where each was involved in investigation and trial preparation of those cases involving violent crimes. Also, a priority case assignment was instituted with the office of the district attorney. Under this system, violent stranger-to-stranger crimes were given priority for prosecution.

Offender Evaluation and Treatment

An offender diagnostic and evaluation program was developed. The evaluation process was modeled after those used at the state institution for defective delinquents in Patuxent, Maryland and at the state hospital in Bridgewater, Massachusetts. The beginning of treating and rehabilitating rapists is to separate, through evaluation and testing, those men who are termed "predators." In all likelihood they cannot be changed or helped by any rehabilitative process. The failure of corrections in dealing with rapists lies in the fact that no attempt is made to separate those who cannot be helped from those who can. If hardened, dangerous offenders can be imprisoned for as long as the law allows, then the rest of the convicted rapists can be treated in a community-based setting, possibly with great recidivism reduction.

Under the Denver plan, as part of the presentence investigation, rapists are tested at a diagnostic center. This program classifies the different types of rapists in terms of their psychological development and their prognoses under several different types of treatment modalities. Eventually guidelines will be provided for the most effective disposition of each type of sex offender.

Public Information and Education

A public information program on rape was part of an overall crime information program conducted by the Denver Anti-Crime Council. The public information program relating to rape addressed two audiences—the public, in general, and women, in particular.

The portion of this program directed to the general public focused on increasing awareness and understanding of the special problems of rape victims, addressing rape as a violent crime, and identifying the psychological effects of rape on the victim. A local television station produced and aired a documentary on this subject.

The segment of the public information program directed at females involved two elements—prevention and postcrime. High-attack geographical areas were identified through the rape analysis, and this information was incorporated in the education program. Methods of preventing a rape attack were described, concentrating on self-protection, especially in the home. The postcrime education effort focused on the importance of reporting the crime promptly and cooperating with law enforcement agencies.

Conclusion

The Denver experience shows that planning for rape reduction is not an easy process. Rape is an emotional issue, and it is difficult to analyze the problem objectively. No program, however well planned and executed, will ever satisfy the police, prosecutors, judges, jurors, doctors, victims, and offenders.

Each city must study its own rape patterns and methods of detection, apprehension, and prosecution to determine where improvements can and should be made. The controversial aspects of rape investigation and prosecution should not deter efforts to plan and implement rape reduction programs. The careful gathering of knowledge is the major first step. Then each city must make a locally tailored, explicit commitment of funds, personnel, and programs to reduce the crime of forcible rape.

Index

Index

Abel, G., viii, ix, 99-115
Accessory to sex, 24
Acquiescence, verbal response of, 77, 82, 84, 85
Against Rape, 50, 76
Agopian, M., 10, 129
Alford, H., 104
"Alledged sexual assault," 55
Ambivalent refusal, verbal response of, 77, 82, 84, 85
American College of Obstetricians and Gynecologists, protocol of, 55
Amir, M., 66, 92, 125, 127-128, 129, 135, 146, 166
Ampicillin, 57
Andrews, F., 119
Annihilation, fear of, 45-46
Anthropological theory, of behavior, 121
Aphanasis, 45-46
Aqueous Bezanthine Penicillin G, 57
Aronson, E., 136
Assailants, characteristics of, 171, 172; perspectives on, 5-7. *See also* rapists
"Assault with failure to please," 137
Atascadero State Hospital, 104, 110
Attitude-value measurement instruments, 118
Attribution of blame, models for, 1-2
Attribution of responsibility, 136, 145
Attribution theory, 135, 138
Aversive therapy, 95

Bard, M., 164
Barlow, D., 105, 107, 109
Becker, J., ix, 99-115
Behavior therapy, 95
BenDor, J., viii, ix, 149-160
Bergin, A., 100
Berkeley, 129
Bernard, J., 49
Biderman, A., 65-66
Bihari, J., 160
Billingsley, A., 124
Black-black rape, cultural interpretation of, 123-128
Black females, sexual values and behaviors of, 124

Black politicalization, 128, 129, 130, 131
Black poverty subculture, 118-119, 120, 121, 126
Black power, 128
Black studies literature, 118, 123, 127
Blacks, interpretation of rape and, 123-130
Blanchard, E., ix, 99-115
Blume in Love, 124
Blumenthal, M., 119
Body weakness, verbal response of, 77, 84, 85
Bohmer, C., 137
Boozer, G., 104
Borges, J., 125, 126, 136
Boston, 17, 23, 61; City Hospital, 23, 24
Bridgewater, Massachusetts, 174
Bristow, A., 105
Brodsky, C., vii, 35-51
Brodsky, S., viii, ix, x, 1-7, 75-90
Burden of proof, 154-155
Burgess, A., viii, 23-33, 44

California, 21n; law reform in, 158
California Psychological Inventory, 76, 173
Callahan, E., 109
Capital punishment, 10
"Carnal Knowledge," 16, 124, 150, 152, 153, 155, 158-159
Case histories, of rape in work settings, 37-43
"A Case of Rape," 72
Case reports, 100, 102, 103, 104, 105, 108, 109
Castration, 106, 107, 108
Cautela, J., 109
Center for the Study of Violence, Denver, 173
Chafetz, J., 136
"Character disorder," 16
Chappell, D., viii, 9-22, 129
Chauvinism, white male, 130-131
Civil rights movement, 128
Clark, K., 123, 124
Clark, W., 16

Cleaver, E., 9, 130, 131
A Clockwork Orange, 95, 124
Cloward, R., 121
Cohen, B., 10
Colorado, law reform in, 158, 160
Comer, J., 128, 131
"Compensation neurosis," 36
Consciousness-raising, 69
"Consensual intercourse", 137
Consent, requirements of, 155, 156, 157, 159, 160
Contraculture, 118, 119, 120, 125, 126. *See also* violent contraculture
Controlled group outcome, 101, 108, 110
Controlled, single-case experimental design, 100, 105, 107, 108, 109, 110
Coping skills, 25, 27, 28, 30, 31, 32
Cornell Medical Index, 173
Corroboration, requirements of, 21n, 159
Counseling, 24, 30-32, 46-49, 58
Credibility of victim, determination of, 137, 156, 157, 159
Crime and delinquency, studies of, 119
Criminal justice system, controlling decision-making part of, 151-154; filteration process of, 5, 63, 170; racial biases of, 129; response of, viii, ix, 9-22, 150, 151, 153, 169, 170, 172; sex biases of, 129
"Criminal Sexual Conduct" statute, Michigan, 149, 150, 155, 157, 158-159
"Criminal Sexual Psychopath," 1
Crisis Intervention Program, Jackson Memorial Hospital, 53, 55, 58, 167
Crisis intervention techniques, 162-165, 167
Cultural interpretation of rape and race, 117-134
Cultural levels, index of, 120
Cultural transmission, 121
Curtis, L., viii, xi, 61-68, 117-134, 137, 146
Cyproterone acetate, 108

Dade County, Florida, 53, 57, 59
Dating, American system of, 136
Daum, S., 35

Davis, J., 128
Defective delinquents, 174
Definition, legal, of forcible rape, 15-18, 65, 71, 135, 138, 139, 140, 142, 146, 149-160
Degrees of offense, 6, 153, 158
Democratic rights, reconfirming and protecting, 151, 154-158
Demonstrative expression, in speech and action, 118
Denmark, Herstedvester, 108
Denver, 75, 76, 169, 170, 172, 174, 175; Denver Anti-Crime Council, 170, 173, 175; Denver City Police Department, 169, 170, 171; Denver General Hospital, 173; Denver Rape Reduction Program, 172
DES (diethylstilbesterol), 57
Determinism, 118, 121
Deterrence, by the potential victim, 75-90; from rapists' perspectives, 79-80, 85-87; role of legislative reform, 151, 158
Detroit, 150, 153
Deviancy, 135-136
Disability benefits, 35, 36, 37, 44
District of Columbia, 21n
Dodd, T., 136
Dominant culture, 118, 119, 120, 121, 122, 124, 129
Drugs, use of, in castration, 108
Durkheim, E., 128

Economic attainment, 122
Eisler, R., 104
Ellison, K., 164
Emergency room, 53, 54, 55, 58
Employment, disruption in, 28-30, 32, 37-40, 44, 47
Ennis, P., 63, 64
Erikson, K., 135
"Evidence in Rape Cases," 160
External influence or distraction, verbal response of, 77, 81, 84, 85

Family therapy, 95
"Fate worse than death," 135
F.B.I., 17, 18, 53, 171; Uniform Crime Reports, 61, 62
Feldman-Summers, S., 76
"Felonious gallantry," 137

Female sexuality, views of, 136
"Female vindictiveness," 137
Feminism, influence of, 70, 130-131,
  138, 149, 151, 158. *See also*
  Women's movement
Feminist writings on rape, criticism of,
  64
Ferracuti, F., 118, 127
Fielding, H., 75
Finger, J., 32
Flanagan, B., 107
"Floating team concept," of treat-
  ment, 54
Force, requirements of, 155, 156, 159
"Force and Resistance", 160
Forebearance, identification with, 118
"Friendly rape," 137
Frustration-aggression therapy, 128
Furman v. Georgia, 10

Geis, G., 10, 17, 129
"Genuine victims," 137
Ghetto, 123-125, 128; literature, 119
Giacinti, ix, 75, 135, 169-175
Goode, W., 125, 126
Greer, G., 70, 124
Griffin, S., 130, 131, 132
Group rape, 126, 129
Gruen, W., 118
Gynecologic examination, 55. *See also*
  victims, medical treatment of

Hagan, J., 137
Hamburg, B., 32
"The Handbook of Hymen," 61
Hannerz, U., 117, 124
Hare, J., 124
Hare, N., 124
Harrassment, sexual, 49-51
Head, K., 119
Heide, W., 7
Hersen, M., 104
Herstedvester, 108
Heterosexual fear and avoidance, 106
Heterosexual phobia, 107
Heterosocial skills scale, 105
Heterosocial skills training, with
  psychiatric patients, 104
Hicks, D., viii, ix, 53-59
Hill, R., 124
History of the Criminal Law of Eng-

land (Stephen), 9
Hitchhike rape, 129, 130
Hoffman, S., 136
Holmstrom, L., viii, 23-33, 44
Homemaking, disruption in, 27, 31
Hotline telephone counseling, 53, 55,
  70
Humor, in discussion of rape, vii
Hursch, C., 76, 173

Incest, 18, 19
Incidence. *See* statistics
Indecency, gross, 153
Indecent liberties, 153
Independent adjustment, concepts of,
  121
Interactionist hypothesis, 129. *See
  also* social interaction
Interpersonal liaison, verbal response
  of, 77, 80, 81, 84, 85
Interracial rape, 9, 10, 62, 117, 128-
  130
Intraracial rape, 117, 123-128
Iowa, law reform in, 158

Jackson Memorial Hospital, 53
Jonathon Wild, 75
Jones, C., 136
Judicial attitudes toward rape, 137
Jurors, attitudes of, 20-21
Jury decisions, 154
Jury selection, 138, 144
Just-world hypothesis, 1, 136

Kahn, R., 119
Keefe, M., viii, ix, 161-168
Keiser, L., 45
Kinsey, A., 66
Klemmack, D., viii, ix, 135-147
Klemmack, S., viii, ix, x, 135-147
Korzybski, A., 3
Kroeber, A., 117

Labeling theory, 135
Ladner, J., 121, 124
Largen, M., viii, ix, 69-73
Law Enforcement Assistance Adminis-
  tration (LEAA), 63, 170; Census
  survey, 63-64; Pilot survey, 22n
Laws, D., 107
Lear, M., 64, 138

"Leering-smirking syndrome," vii
Legal Effects of Proposed Rape Reform Bills, 151
Legislative digest, of rape statutes, 15
Legislative reform, ix, 3, 10, 12, 13, 16, 71; functions of, 151-158; criminal justice system, control of, 151-154; democratic rights, reconfirming and protecting, 151, 154-158; deterrence, increasing, 151, 158; in Michigan, 149-160
Leitenberg, H., 109
Liberalization of white women, 128-130, 131
Liebrow, E., 121, 124
Life cycle, task disruption at varying stages of, 23-33
"Little rapes," 50-51. *See also* teasing, sexual
Los Angeles, police records, 17, 61, 63

MacDonald, J., 75, 77, 104
Machismo, undercutting motives of, 3
MacQueen, B., 160
Male/female roles, 137, 146
Male image, compensatory distortion of, 123
Marshall, W., 16, 107
Masculinity, expression of, 122, 123, 124
Mathias, C., 72
"M. E. case," 55
Medea, A., 50, 64, 76
Media, response of, x, 21, 70, 71, 167, 175
Medical evidence, collection of, 57
Medical history, contents of, 56, 57
Medical personnel, training of, 53-54
Medical treatment, physician and nurse procedures, 54-58
Medroxyprogesterone, 108
Mentally Disordered Sex Offender Act, Florida, 79
Michigan law reform, ix, 6, 71, 149-160
Michigan Women's Task Force on Rape, 150, 151
Miller, P., 104
Millet, K., 9, 130
Milliken, E., 160
"Minimal dating," among college

males, 104
"Missoula Rape Poem," 149
Model Penal Code, 21n, 157
Modus operandi, 135
Monahan, J., 2
Moral appeal, verbal response of, 77, 83, 84, 85
"Morning-after-pill," 57
Muggings, compensation neurosis in, 36
Muggings, at work, reactions to rape compared with, 45-46
My Secret Life, 124
Myths, dispelling of, x, 6, 72, 149

National Center for the Prevention and Control of Rape, 72
National Commission on the Causes and Prevention of Violence, 146
National Crime Panel Study, 63, 64, 65
National Health Survey of U. S., 65
National Institute of Law Enforcement and Criminal Justice, 11
National Institute of Mental Health, 72
National Legal Data Center, 15, 21n
National Organization for Women (NOW), 6, 70, 72
National Task Force on Rape, NOW, 70
National Victimization Study, 22n, 169
National Violence Commission Study, 62, 66
Nebraska, law reform in, 158
Nelson, S., 129
New Jersey Treatment Center, 104
New Mexico, law reform in, 158
New York City Health and Hospitals Corporation, 165
New York (City), Sex Crimes Investigations Unit, ix, 161-168
New York Radical Feminists, 69
Nordby, V., 151
"Normalcy" of crime, 128

Oakland, 129
Offender, evaluation and treatment, 173. *See also* rapists, treatment of
O. Henry, 61

Ohlin, L., 121
O'Reilly, H., ix, 161-168
Owens, M., 7

Pacht, A., viii, ix, 91-97
Parenting, disruption in, 27, 31
Parsons, T., 117
Participant observation literature, 118, 119, 123, 127
Patuxent, Maryland, 174
Pedophiliacs, 106, 107, 109
Peters, J., 95
Phenomenological studies, of rape, 135
Philadelphia, 125, 127
Philadelphia Police Department, 92
Physical prowess and toughness, emphasis on, 119, 122, 123
Piercy, M., 149
Planned rapes, in all-black context, 127
Platt, C., ix, 53-59
Ploscowe, M., 16-17
Police, response of, ix, 17, 59, 161-169, 173-174; statistics, 117, 131, 135, 170; training of, 13, 14, 161-169
Postrape symptoms and reactions, 44-45, 46
"Predators," 174
Pregnancy, prevention of, 57, 58
Premarital sexual attitudes, 124-125, 140, 144
Prevention, deterrence by the potential victim, 75-90; methods of, ix, 1-2, 3, 6, 49-51, 172; perspectives on, 1-5, 6; unconventional proposals for, 2-5, 7
Prior sexual conduct, of victim, 156, 157, 159
Probobenemid, 57
Prostitution, 157
Psychological intervention techniques, 165-166
Psychotherapy, treatment for offenders, 6
Psychotherapy evaluation, process of, 99-101
Public education, 6, 13, 14, 71-72, 89

Race, as factor in increasing rape statistics, 12
Race and rape, cultural interpretation of, ix, 117-134
Race, relation with disposition in rape cases, 137
Racial discrimination, by police, 62, 63, 129
Racism, institutional, 121, 122
Radical-economic constraints, 121
Radical proposals, for rape prevention, 2-5, 7
Rainwater, L., 123, 124, 125
Rape crisis center, 15, 20, 64, 69, 70, 73
Rape laws, inequities in, 71
Rape: Offenders and Their Victims, 75
Rape Prevention and Control Act, 72
Rape reduction, 169-175
"Rape: Research, Action, Prevention," vii, viii, x, 7, 78
Rape Research Group, The University of Alabama, vii, x
Rape resisters, characteristics of, 173
"Rape Squad," 72
Rape trauma, 24, 26, 27, 32, 44
Rape Treatment Center, Jackson Memorial Hospital, 53
Rapists, categories of, 5, 76, 88, 127; characteristics of, 79-80, 91-93, 137; disposition of, 171; "personality portrait" of, 165; race of, 9, 92, 117-134; research on treatment of, 91-97, 99-115; sexual arousal of, 105-106; treatment of, ix, 1, 3, 6, 91-97, 99-115
Reality details, in counseling, 30, 31
Recidivism, 99, 109-110, 174
Records, medical, 55, 56, 57
Records, police, 17, 61-63
Reporting, by victims, 3, 12, 18, 135, 169
Resistance, requirements of, 155, 159; methods of, 172
Resister, of rape, 76
Respectability of victim, 136
"Reverse records check," 65
Roberts, L., 94
Rodman, H., 119

Roether, H., 95
Role definitions within family, measure of, 140, 143, 144, 146
Role-playing, 77, 165, 166, 167
Rules of evidence, the need for change of, 71
Ryan, W., 1

"Safe ground," 43, 44
San Jose, California, 65
Save the Tiger, 124
Schafer, S., 17
School performance, disruption in: child and adolescent, 26, 32; adult, 30, 31
Schulz, D., 124
Seattle, Washington, 14-15; Rape Reduction Project, 15; Sexual Assault Center, 15; Rape Relief, 15
"Secondary rape," by justice agencies, 3
Seduction, 136, 138
Self defense, methods of, 2, 70, 75
Self-punitiveness, verbal response of, 77, 83, 85
Selkin, J., 76, 88, 165, 173
Sentencing, 6, 13, 159
Serber, M., 95
Sex Crimes Analysis Unit, NYC, ix, 161-167
Sex crimes investigations, 13, 53, 169-170; changing perspectives in, 161-168; training in, 19, 162-168
Sex Crimes Law, Wisconsin (1951), 93, 94
Sex education, as a treatment for sexual aggressives, 104
Sex role expectations, 2, 125, 129, 135, 136, 143, 146
Sexism, societal, inherent in rape, 69, 72
Sex-stress situation, 24, 25
Sexual aggression, women as legitimate objects of, 136
Sexual aggressives, treatment of, 101-109; aversion therapy in, 108; behavioral modification in, 101, 103, 106, 108; confrontation methods in, 102-103; covert sensitization, 109; decreasing sexual arousal to rape, 107; electrical aversion, 109; ethics in, 96, 108, 109; fading, 106, 107; group therapy in, 101, 102, 107-108, 110; heterosocial-heterosexual skills training in, 103-105; increasing arousal to adult females, 105-107; individual therapy, 107-108; masturbatory conditioning, 106-107; milieu therapy in, 101, 110; pastoral counseling in, 101, 102; psychoanalytically oriented psychotherapy in, 101, 103, 107; sexual counseling, 104. *See also* rapists, treatment of
Sexual Battery Law, of Florida, 59
Sexual behavior and mores, 12, 16, 131
Sexual exploitation, by males, 122, 123, 124, 127, 129
Sexual prowess and exploitation, emphasis on, 119, 122, 123, 125, 126, 130, 131
Sexual psychopath statute, Alabama, 94
Sexual relations, disruption in, 38, 39, 40, 41, 45, 48
Sexual teasing, 1
Sexual values and behaviors, in ghetto-slum, 123-125
Shrewdness and manipulativeness, emphasis on, 119
Sheppard, D., viii, 169-175
"Sick society," 2
Siegel, L., 17
Silverman, M., 32
Situational characteristics, of rape, 136
Social change, justification of violence for, 119
Social characteristics, of victim and offender, 135
Social definition, of rape, ix, 135-147
Social distance, between victim and offender, 125-128
Social interaction, 128-130, 131
Social skills training, 95, 103, 104, 105
Social system, reaction of, 31-32
Social values and mores, changing of, 2, 12, 16, 117, 118, 119, 122, 131
Society, reeducation of, 72

Sodomy, 18, 19, 153, 156, 161
Solanis, V., 130
Soul on Ice, 9
Southeast Denver Neighborhood Services Bureau, 173
Speak Out On Rape, New York Radical Feminists, 69
Spectinomycin, 57
Sperling, S., 49
Staples, R., 123, 124, 125
Statistics, 10, 12, 18, 61-68, 169
Statutory rape, 18, 159
Stellman, J., 35
Stephen, J., 9, 21
Stranger rapes, 65, 126, 129, 142, 144, 170-171
Straw Dogs, 124
Strupp, H., 100
Stumbo, B., 21
Stürup, G., 95, 108
Subculture, 118-119, 120, 121, 122, 125, 126, 127. *See also* black poverty subculture
Svalastoga, K., 16
Systematic desensitization, 95

Task performance, effect of rape on, 23-33; child, 25-26; adult, 26-30
Teasing, sexual, 49-51
Testimony, of physicians, 55
Tetracycline, 57
Texas, law reform in, 158
Thompson, K., 50, 64, 76
Thrill seeking and change, emphasis on, 119, 130
Tigan, 57
Tjaden, C., ix, 75, 169-175
Tragedy, identification with, 118
Training film, in sex crimes investigations, 165
Trauma, sexual diagnostic categories of, 24-25
Traumatic neurosis, 36, 42, 47
Tuscaloosa, Alabama, 138

Uniform Crime Reports, 61, 62
University of Alabama, vii, x, 7, 146
University of Michigan Law School, 151
U.S. Bureau of the Census, 63-64, 117

U.S. Congress, 72
U.S. Supreme Court, 10

Value space, multidimensional, 119-121
Value stretch, lower-class, 119
Venereal disease, prevention of, 56, 57, 58
Verbal attack, 77, 83, 84, 85, 86
Verbal responses, in prevention by victim, 75-90; effectiveness of, 78-80; matching, with type of assailant, 88-89; taxonomy of, 77
Victim Counseling Program, Boston City Hospital, 23
Victimization, ix, 5, 21-22n, 61-68, 117, 131; women as legitimate object of, 136
Victim-offender relationship, 66-67, 125-128, 142, 145, 170, 172
Victimology, the study of, 67, 130, 162. *See also* victim precipitation
Victim precipitation, 66, 67, 125, 127, 137, 146
Victims, changing status of, 18-20; acquiescence 75, 80, 87; adult, 23, 24, 26-30; child, 23, 24, 25-26, 32; fighting, 75, 76, 87; flight, 75, 76, 87; impact of rape on, 6, 23-33, 46-47, 169; prior sexual behavior of, 156, 157, 159; research on, 23-33, 75-90, 135-147, 173; responses to prevent rape, avoidance, 75; screaming, 75, 89; task disruption in, 23-33; verbal refusal, 75, 77, 80, 87
Victims, treatment of, viii, ix, 23-60, 69-73; criminal justice, 13, 19, 150; medical, 12, 19, 53-59; psychological, viii, 10, 12, 13, 14, 173. *See also* Brodsky, C.; Burgess, A.; Holmstrom, L.
Victim Witness Assistance Commission, 20
Videotapes, heterosocial-heterosexual skills training, 105; of verbal response categories for prevention, 77-78
Viet Nam, 130
Violence, 4, 76, 118, 119, 120, 121, 122, 123, 127; theoretical literature on, 119

Violence Research Unit, Colorado Division of Psychiatric Services, 76
Violent contraculture, ix, 118, 119, 120, 121, 122-123, 126, 128
Virgin Mary image, 136
Virginity, verbal response of, 77, 82, 84, 85

Weapon, use of, 76, 155, 156, 158, 173
Weis, K., 36, 125, 126
Whorf, B., 3
Williams, S., 107
Wisconsin, 91, 92, 93
Wisconsin Sex Crimes Treatment Center, 94

Wolfgang, M., 10, 118, 127
Wolpe, J., 95
Women Against Rape (WAR), 69
Women, changing status and role of, 9, 18-20
Women's movement, role of, ix, 9, 12, 21, 69, 71-72, 146
Women, professional role of, in criminal justice system, 19, 20
Work is Dangerous to Your Health, (Stellman and Daum), 35
Work, rape at, 35-51
Workers' compensation, 35

Yinger, M., 117-118, 119

List of Contributors

Gene G. Abel, Department of Psychiatry, The University of Tennessee Center for Health Sciences and Tennessee Psychiatric Hospital and Institute, Memphis, Tennessee.

Judith V. Becker, Department of Psychiatry, The University of Tennessee Center for Health Sciences and Tennessee Psychiatric Hospital and Institute, Memphis, Tennessee.

Jan BenDor, Michigan Women's Task Force on Rape, Ypsilanti, Michigan.

Edward B. Blanchard, Department of Psychiatry, The University of Tennessee Center for Health Sciences and Tennessee Psychiatric Hospital and Institute, Memphis, Tennessee.

Carroll M. Brodsky, Professor of Psychiatry, University of California Medical Center, San Francisco, California.

Ann Wolbert Burgess, Associate Professor, Community Health Nursing, Boston College, Chestnut Hill, Massachusetts.

Duncan Chappell, Director, Law and Justice Study Center, Battelle Memorial Institute, Seattle, Washington.

Lynn A. Curtis, Research Associate, Bureau of Social Science Research, Washington, D.C.

Thomas Giacinti, Denver Anti-Crime Council, Denver, Colorado.

Dorothy J. Hicks, Director, The Rape Treatment Center, Jackson Memorial Hospital, Miami, Florida and Associate Professor, Department of Obstetrics and Gynecology, University of Miami School of Medicine.

Lynda Lytle Holmstrom, Associate Professor, Department of Sociology, Boston College, Chestnut Hill, Massachusetts.

Mary L. Keefe, Commanding Officer, Sex Crimes Analysis Unit, New York Police Department, New York City, New York.

David L. Klemmack, Associate Professor, Department of Sociology, the University of Alabama, Tuscaloosa, Alabama.

Susan H. Klemmack, Coordinator, Rape Research Group, The University of Alabama, Tuscaloosa, Alabama.

Mary Ann Largen, Coordinator, National Task Force on Rape, National Organization for Women, Chicago, Illinois.

Henry T. O'Reilly, Sex Crimes Analysis Unit, New York Police Department, New York City, New York.

Asher R. Pacht, Chief, Bureau of Clinical Services, Wisconsin Division of Corrections, Madison, Wisconsin.

Charlotte R. Platt, Director of Nursing Services, Emergency Room, Jackson Memorial Hospital, Miami, Florida.

David I. Sheppard, Director, Denver Anti-Crime Council, Denver, Colorado.

Claus Tjaden, Denver Anti-Crime Council, Denver, Colorado.

About the Editors

Marcia J. Walker served as Coordinator of the Rape Research Group at the University of Alabama from May 1974 to April 1975. She compiled and edited *Toward the Prevention of Rape—An Annotated Bibliography* and *Rape—Research, Action, Prevention: Proceedings of the Sixth Alabama Symposium on Justice and the Behavioral Sciences*. Ms. Walker graduated Phi Beta Kappa from the University of Alabama in May 1974 with the B.S. degree in psychology. She is presently a Criminal Justice Counselor at the Rape Crisis Center, Grady Memorial Hospital, Atlanta, Georgia.

Stanley L. Brodsky received the B.A. from the University of New Hampshire and the M.A. and Ph.D. degrees in psychology from the University of Florida. He completed a clinical psychology internship at Walter Reed General Hospital, and has served as chief of the Psychology Division at the United States Disciplinary Barracks, Fort Leavenworth, Kansas. Mr. Brodsky has taught at Southern Illinois University, and is now an associate professor in the Department of Psychology, The University of Alabama, Tuscaloosa, Alabama.

Mr. Brodsky has been co-editor of *The Military Prison: Theory, Research, and Programs* (Southern Illinois University Press, 1970), and *Psychology 2001: An Anthology of Psychology in Speculative Fiction*, which is in press. He previously authored *Psychologists in the Criminal Justice System* (University of Illinois Press, 1973) and *Families and Friends of Men in Prison* (Lexington Books, D.C. Heath and Company, 1975), and is editor of the journal *Criminal Justice and Behavior* and a member of the editorial board of *Criminology: An Interdisciplinary Journal* and the *American Journal of Community Psychology*.

Related Lexington Books

Chappell, Duncan, Monahan, John, *Violence and Criminal Justice*, 176 pp., 1975
Curtis, Lynn A., *Violence, Race and Culture*, 128 pp., 1975
Drapkin, Israel, Viano, Emilio, *Victimology: A New Focus, Volume V, Exploiters and Exploited*, 240 pp., 1975